Modern Architecture Through Case Studies 1945-1990

Peter Blundell Jones and Eamonn Canniffe

AMSTERDAM • BOSTON • HEIDELBERG • LONDON • NEW YORK • OXFORD
PARIS • SAN DIEGO • SAN FRANCISCO • SINGAPORE • SYDNEY • TOKYO

Architectural Press is an imprint of Elsevier

Architectural Press is an imprint of Elsevier
Linacre House, Jordan Hill, Oxford OX2 8DP, UK
30 Corporate Drive, Suite 400, Burlington, MA 01803, USA

First edition 2007

ISBN–13: 978-0-7506-6374-8
ISBN–10: 0-7506-6374-X

British Library Cataloguing in Publication Data
A catalogue record for this book is available from the British Library

Library of Congress Cataloging-in-Publication Data
A catalog record for this book is available from the Library of Congress

For information on all Architectural Press publications
visit our web site at books.elsevier.com

Printed and bound in Italy

07 08 09 10 11   10 9 8 7 6 5 4 3 2 1

Working together to grow
libraries in developing countries

www.elsevier.com | www.bookaid.org | www.sabre.org

ELSEVIER   BOOK AID International   Sabre Foundation

Contents

Acknowledgements

The extension of the case studies method into a second book has brought it into my own lifetime, involving several architects whom I met personally and whose works I have written up in architectural journals. At the start of the project Aldo Van Eyck, Ralph Erskine, Peter Smithson and Giancarlo De Carlo were still alive, and one rather took their great paternal presences for granted, but now that they are gone the chapters about them inevitably take on the character of an obituary. I hope we have caught something of their personalities and registered the importance of Team Ten in discovering and defining problems wrought by the modernist revolution, even if they did not always manage to provide adequate solutions. The chapter on the Leicester Engineering building gave me an excuse to renew contact with James Gowan, my former teacher at the Architectural Association, and it was a pleasure to encounter once again his acerbic wit and analytical understanding. Günter Behnisch was always generous with time and support, but primary contact with his office came via Christian Kandzia, who provided copious material and allowed free use of his Munich photographs. Helmut Striffler was equally generous and cooperative over the material for the Dachau chapter, and made the connections with his photographer Robert Häusser. Lucien Kroll, long a personal friend, has provided material and commentary. I should also thank Giorgio Marini of the Castelvecchio Museum Verona, the RIBA Picture Library, the Amsterdam City Archive, Lenita Gärde of the Swedish Museum of Architecture, Studio De Carlo, Martin Charles, Arkitektenbureau van Eyck, Karljosef Schattner, Venturi and Scott Brown, the Eiermann Archive in Karlsruhe, Peter Bareham, and the Diozesanbauamt Eichstätt. The book could not have happened without the help of the University of Sheffield, and I thank my fellow professors Jeremy Till and Roger Plank for permitting me the time to do it. David Wild has once again made a special collage for the cover which perfectly expresses our blend of respect and good-humoured scepticism.

Peter Blundell Jones

My contributions to this book originated in the opportunity offered in 1991 by Professor Roger Stonehouse to teach a course in twentieth century architectural history to third year undergraduates at Manchester University School of Architecture. The period covered in that course began in 1917 and included the pioneering works of modern architecture, but the emphasis was on the consequences of those early examples for more recent work, both in terms of the widespread application of modern movement principles as a new tradition, and in reaction to their negative effects, a duality which is also the broad theme of this book. The case studies selected, originally organised as a set of comparative lectures, were intended to help students in understanding the contemporary context of architectural design choices, and that continues to be the aim. In preparing that material I was supported by two eminent architectural historians, John H.G. Archer and Frank Salmon, who provided inspiration for this enthusiast's foray into their professional territory. Following my appointment at Sheffield University the material was extended and developed in courses there, and I would like to pay particular tribute to the hundreds of students at both universities who studied the buildings concerned through the construction of critical models. The results of their hard work were very revealing to me, and in supporting that time consuming but worthwhile endeavour I am indebted to the forbearance of Satwinder Samra, and also to Peter Lathey for his photographic record of the models. Both of us are deeply indebted to him also for scanning and processing of photographic material.

Eamonn Canniffe

Introduction

This book is a sequel to Peter Blundell Jones's *Modern Architecture Through Case Studies*.[1] That book was inspired by two things: first the value of the architectural Case Study in allowing some depth and getting closer to the architectural work; second the conviction that 'modernism' as a campaign to join or as a straw man to hate could no longer be considered a unified 'project'. The author's own experience as unraveller of an 'alternative' or organic tradition prepared the way for this,[2] but the idea broadened when it became apparent that the Weissenhofsiedlung, supposed birthplace of modernism, and the subject of the first chapter in that volume, could reasonably be construed as sixteen different architectures, some departing in totally opposed directions. The experiment of the book soon proved that the four thousand word essay was adequate to describe a building and set it against its ideological background, and that it was possible to fit about eighteen of these into a normal sized monograph. The rule was quickly made not to allow more than one chapter per architect, correcting the usual bias towards a mere handful of heroes and giving hitherto lesser figures an equal voice. The choice of works and the decision to run them chronologically produced an unfolding narrative which moved sometimes in unexpected directions, yielding frutiful contrasts.

Once the book was published, reviewers debated the selection, but they also suggested that the process could go further. An obvious next stage was to deal with the post-war generation of architects, to explore the developing modernism of the 1950s and 1960s followed by the postmodern reaction of the 1970s and 1980s. Eamonn Canniffe and I, having developed material independently as colleagues teaching some of the same courses at Sheffield, decided to share the chapters and to develop the book together as a dialogue. At first we made lists of architects under headings such as 'Team Ten', 'technological optimism' and 'patterns of context', but this seemed forced, for several broke the bounds of their categories and the overall chronology made little sense. Returning to a strict chronological sequence highlighted the co-existence of opposed tendencies and pulled a new thread through the period, again with unexpected results. The essays are signed to make it clear who is the primary author in each case, for we hold different ideological positions, would not have included the same examples if working alone, and do not always agree in our judgements, but we have in the process of writing and laying out the book criticised, and in places contributed to, each other's chapters.

The first three chapters, concerning buildings conceived in the 1940s and 1950s, belong to high modernism, the period when the Modern Movement as conceived in the late 1920s became the dominant architectural ideology worldwide. It was driven by the new technical and constructive possibilities, the notion that form should follow function, and the abstract compositional language of modern painting. The earliest work considered, the **Eames House** of 1945-49 built while Europe was still on its knees, does not escape the after-effect of war production in the United States. Made of industrially produced components, it pioneered the view of architecture as a standard but flexible kit of parts, gaining its form from the discipline of assembly, while its contents celebrated the arrival of the consumer society which the exclusivity of pre-war modernism had failed to achieve.

In the absence of the great master Ludwig Mies van der Rohe, who had gone to the United States, Egon Eiermann became the most important German architect in the Miesian direction of the 1950s and 1960s, and his **German Pavilion at the Brussels Exhibition** designed with Sep Ruf in 1957-58 shows this tendency at its ideal extreme. The neat geometric discipline of square on square allied the perfectly detailed rationality of steel construction to prevalent beliefs in the aesthetics of pure geometrical composition. Clever layering of steel and glass exaggerated the buildings' lightness and transparency to evoke a feeling of freedom and generosity, and they were set off object-like against the green background of the park. As with the Eames House, such self-contained perfection surrounded by a *cordon sanitaire* of open space was the architectural ideal of the time, reflecting the widespread choice to start afresh in a new and modern manner on the outskirts of towns, working tidily and entirely within one's own terms. Eiermann and Ruf's Pavilion also lent itself exceptionally well to reproduction in black and white photographs, the record through which we are obliged to view the demolished Pavilion today.

Along with both previous examples, Aldo van Eyck's **Orphanage in Amsterdam** of 1954-59 reflects the assumption that the future of construction lay in mass production, for he designed it on a square grid with precast concrete components and small concrete domes. The choice of a rather small, low basic cell reflected the scale of the child, however, and van Eyck assembled the cells in groups to articulate the territories of the different 'families'. This social articulation, along with the making of courtyards as outdoor rooms and a great sensitivity about thresholds, reflected a new interest in anthropology which van Eyck brought to architectural discourse. He spread his ideas through Team Ten, the international group which grew out of the famous CIAM (International Congresses of Modern Architecture), and which produced some of the earliest and most penetrating critiques of the post-war modernist orthodoxy.[3] It was van Eyck who contested the very title of modernism's bible, Sigfried Giedion's *Space Time and Architecture* with the remark: *'Whatever time and space mean, place and occasion mean more.'*[4] Like other Team Ten members, he cared about the city and the integration of new buildings within it, but typically for its time, the orphanage was built in glorious isolation on the outskirts of Amsterdam, becoming a city in itself. This recalls another of van Eyck's dicta, derived from Leon Battista Alberti's Ninth Book:[5] *'A big house is a small city and a small city is a big house.'*[6]

During the 1950s and early 1960s, architecture was dominated by the Utopian and utilitarian idea that technical and economic circumstances would force submission to the discipline of mass production, therefore to rectilinearity, modules and repetitive components. This notion was so strong that the alternative view represented by the organic tradition hardly received any attention. The work of Hans Scharoun for example (Blundell Jones 2002 Ch. 13), which was widely seen as antithetical to that of Eiermann, was often condemned as anachronistic and 'personal', despite the functional logic of its social articulation, and despite the fact that it could be built for competitive prices.[7] But one kind of job had to break with the module and accept such irregularity: integration into an old setting. At a time when the hearts were being torn out of cities across Europe, Gottfried Böhm's **Bensberg Town Hall** of 1962-71 was an astonishing exception. Instead of building anew on the outskirts, the town decided to rescue the remains of its old castle which had almost disappeared, re-marking the centre. Böhm won the competition with a design skilfully mixing new and old, even daring to add a useless new tower to express the entrance and to balance a skyline of towers. This was a work about the importance of place and memory, of preserving streets and squares, of accepting the layering of history.

These issues were also being discussed by Team Ten, and it is the chief distinction of the Smithsons' most famous work, the **Economist Building** of 1960-64, to have redefined the nature of its urban setting. Due to the replication of its motifs in less talented hands, the shift in consciousness that this represented is now hard to see, but in a world where architects conceived buildings as free-standing objects, and clients sought to realise the rentable value of the last centimetre of a site, it was an extraordinary idea to create a public space and to extend the pedestrian network in a more enclosed manner than the standard Miesian plaza adjacent to an office tower, a building type that was actively destroying traditional urban space.[8] It would have been yet more revolutionary had it been extended across the city as the Smithsons intended. The built volume was articulated into three blocks of varying size and presence, using the same vocabulary in a kind of theme and variations, but managing the changes of scale and level most artfully.

The Smithsons had opened their career with a work in homage to Mies, and the treatment of the Economist towers again reflected their debt to this master, but they were also much beholden to Le Corbusier, who as Peter Smithson once remarked: *'seemed to have had all one's best ideas already'.*[9] The influence of these two great masters was so dominant in post-war British architecture that it came as a complete shock when two young architects turned to completely different sources. With **Leicester University Engineering Building** of 1959-64, James Stirling and James Gowan mixed ideas from Russian Constructivism and Dutch De Stijl with lessons from our nineteenth-century industrial inheritance of warehouses, factories and kilns. They also revived an aspect of early functionalism by aggressively articulating the programme, and invented a new vocabulary of red brick and patent glazing. Site and orientation provoked a break away from the right angle to 45°, most memorably in the northlight roof that was set diagonally, and the whole building lent itself to presentation through axonometric projection, almost suggesting a kind of abstract and anti-gravitational thinking. It was the most original British work since the war and laid the foundation for Stirling's international career. His Staatsgalerie, Stuttgart, of 1981-84, designed in partnership with Michael Wilford, was so important an example of postmodernism and so influential that but for our rule of one building per architect, it would have deserved a chapter to itself. To bring it into the discussion it is included as a postscript to the Leicester chapter.

There was more readiness in Germany to plan buildings in an irregular manner because of the continuing presence of the organic tradition, not only in Scharoun and Häring but also in Böhm as seen above, and in many more, but one building of the 1960s presented the extreme case of avoiding the right angle in plan. Helmut Striffler won the competition for the **Protestant Memorial Chapel at Dachau** concentration camp (1964-67) with a design intended to negate the merciless axial order of the camp. Poetically, it provided 'a protective furrow' for the outcast, a place of refuge from the surrounding horrors. The question of memory was at its most acute and painful, and had already produced twenty years of difficult debate. With his downward entrance and bleak concrete structure, Striffler struck just the right note, showing that architecture had lost none of its memorial power.

As the chapel was being buillt, Germany was preparing to play host to the world at the 1972 **Munich Olympics**, and needed to display the redeemed character of the Federal Republic as opposed to the pomp of the Third Reich seen at the Berlin Olympics in 1936. The competition of 1968 proposed an 'Olympics in the green' built at the edge of Munich, and established a firm that was to lead German architecture in the 1980s and 1990s: Günter Behnisch and Partners. They proposed an enormous artificial landscape which would absorb the great stadia in the sides of hills like unrhetorical classical amphitheatres. For the stadia that needed roofs they proposed hanging cable nets at unprecedented dimensions, built with the help of lightweight structures pioneer Frei Otto. This

extraordinary free-form project marked a radical change in direction for Behnisch. In the early 1960s his firm had been at the forefront with prefabricated concrete, disciplined, repetitive and rectangular, but after 1965 they reacted strongly in the opposite direction, advocating a *Situationsarchitektur* that attended to place and circumstance. They went on to produce work of increasing complexity and irregularity, and Behnisch became the principal German inheritor of the organic tradition.

In contrast with this great task pushing technology to the limits, a small Italian job equally significant for world architecture was quietly developing in a piecemeal fashion. Carlo Scarpa had started his reinterpretation of the **Castelvecchio in Verona** in 1958, but it was not substantially finished until 1974, two years after the German Olympics. Scarpa's buildings were modest in scale and he was famous for his mastery of detail, which turned attention back to craftsmanship, trying to reinterpret it for the machine age. But his greatest contribution was in the question of new and old, of entering a dialogue with a historic setting. In this he shared interests with Gottfried Böhm (mentioned above) and Giancarlo De Carlo (to be discussed below), but he worked more delicately. The old castle at Verona was converted into a museum, and Scarpa designed the setting for each work, the reinterpretation of each window, every transition of the floor and ceiling. The new parts are finely wrought and reinterpret the way that paintings or sculptures are framed, but the old parts are exposed and edited, thrown into sharp relief through surgical demolition.

In his intense concentration on what might be called chamber works, Scarpa was rather apolitical, while Lucien Kroll is by contrast the most politically engaged of architects. His **Maison Médicale** and residences at the University of Louvain, outside Brussels, of 1969-74, were a direct outcome of the student revolts of 1968. Beginning his career within the fold of conventional modernism, Kroll had become increasingly critical of the kind of architecture that had arisen for mass housing, driven entirely by production processes and relentlessly repetitive. Lining people up in identical houses was like forcing them to wear uniform: they had become standardised human beings devoid of individuality. The way out of this was to allow them to participate in the formation of their own dwellings, replacing enforced uniformity with a natural diversity. The university had built a brutal new hospital and was about to apply the same techniques to its student residences when the students rebelled. A compromise was reached by hiring Kroll as architect, introduced by the students because of his interest in participation. Taking into account their needs and wishes, he made a radical experiment in self-generating architecture whose anarchic image flashed across the world. Its lasting significance lay in the way it shifted attention from the finished architectural object to the process, thereby challenging the architect's aesthetic rights.

Ralph Erskine was another pioneer of participation and a member of Team Ten. Born and trained in England, he went to live in Sweden at the end of the 1930s where he stayed, imbibing the subtle organic work of masters like Gunnar Asplund and Alvar Aalto, and designing housing for the Swedish welfare state. By the beginning of the 1970s he had become one of the leading architects in Sweden, and was beginning to get jobs in Britain. **Byker Housing in Newcastle** 1970-74 (first phase) was a special case because the old slum possessed a legendary community spirit which the council wanted to preserve during rebuilding. Erskine went out of his way to consult the inhabitants. In an old shop on site he set up an office where local people could drop in to consult the architects, demolition was delayed to allow people to move from old to new in groups, and neighbourly relations were preserved. Shops and community facilities were included, and much of the housing took the form of terraces with back yards, but the development became famous for the Byker Wall, a linear block originally intended to screen off an intended motorway, but also effective as a climatic barrier – a major Erskine interest. By exploiting the landscape and developing simple house types through seemingly endless variations, Erskine created a homely environment that has survived despite a collapse of faith in social housing in Britain. In thirty years the community has changed, but the community spirit which he strove to protect lives on.

There could hardly be a greater contrast between the socialist Erskine and the technocrat Norman Foster, or between social housing and a wealthy company pursuing its image in a new heaquarters, but both came to fruition in England at the same time. **Willis Faber & Dumas** 1971-75 was an insurance company moving out of London to Ipswich. They managed to buy a whole irregular urban block for their new offices, and included a swimming pool on the ground floor and a canteen on the roof. The deep open plan, regular column grid and sophisticated flexible servicing system were typical of the kind of minimal post-Miesian architecture that Foster pursued as a matter of course, developing and perfecting his system of components. But rather than building square and leaving the fringes of the site vacant as most Miesians would have done, he decided to fill the site to its very edge and accept the curving perimeter. In dealing with the variety of conditions met in creating a continuous glass skin, he initiated frameless glazing, which has since become commonplace. Foster's main innovations have all been of this kind, involving insight into the way technical developments can engender dramatic changes in architectural concept.

If by this date even the technologically radical Foster was registering the need for a building to engage with its site, Team Ten's complaints about the destructive effects of modern building on the traditional city and the divisiveness of zoning were beginning to hit home. The leading figure in this revision, for whom the compulsory 'reading of the territory' became a watchword, was the Italian Giancarlo De Carlo. In the 1950s he had been commissioned to develop a master-plan for the ailing Renaissance town of Urbino, and to plan for the building of a new university there. He added new colleges on the outskirts of the town but decided to place faculties within the old fabric. His **Magistero** (Faculty of Education) of 1968-76 was built within the walls of an old convent, completely reinterpreting the enclosed space with the addition of a circular court and a great divisible amphitheatre. Conceived when most architects' perception was geared to the building as a sculptural whole, this inside-out scheme was a complete surprise, as was its dependency on establishing a dialogue between old and new.

The founding project of Renzo Piano and Richard Rogers, **Centre Pompidou** in Paris of 1969-77, could hardly have been more different. This cultural centre pushed to an extreme the idea of architecture as a kit of parts, making no concessions whatever to the memories of the site or to the nature of its contents. It could hardly respond directly to them, because the guiding idea was the most dramatic kind of flexibility and convertibility, allowing for cultural phenomena to grow and change. In practice, though, the insititution has been relatively static, and the range of flexibility proposed did not anticipate the changes that needed to be made. Rather than celebrating process and change as intended, the building ended up monumentalising its own structure and services, but it achieved social success for the street life of its attendant urban square and the escalator view of the roofs of Paris.

Piano and Rogers, Giancarlo de Carlo and Aldo Rossi all had much to say about the nature of cities, as 'the urban' became a dominant topic of discussion among architects in the late 1960s and early 1970s, but while Pompidou celebrated the liberating effects of new technologies, De Carlo and Rossi were more concerned with dealing with the past, with urban memory. While De Carlo developed his ideas and methods empirically in the specific context of Urbino, Rossi, architect of the **New Cemetery of San Cataldo, Modena** 1971-1990, theorised more abstractly and generally towards a new rationalism, especially through his 1966 book *The Architecture of the City*. He noted the persistence of form in cities despite complete changes of purpose, and proposed a fundamental vocabulary of archetypes based on simple geometric solids. Because of its inherent monumentality and intended transcendence, this worked particularly well as an architecture of death, but Rossi's buildings and projects were more persuasive as images than in reality. His work was influential worldwide for about a decade, partly for a poetic sensibility that needed no explanation, partly for the popularity of traditional roofs and windows that he reintroduced without apparent anachronism.

Peter Eisenman, based in New York, represents another kind of postmodernism later redefined as deconstructivism. He began his career with a reaction against modernist functionalism, pursuing instead the notion that architecture is an abstract form language independent of use and construction. After making sophisticated 'readings' of early modernists, especially Terragni,[10] he reapplied the formal system he had defined in small works of his own, mainly houses. The **Wexner Center**, Columbus, Ohio, of 1983-89 proved a breakthrough, not only because of its size and public purpose, but because the formal interaction was driven by elements found in the site, enriching the potential meaning of the building through local and contextual references. The supporting theory and footnotes are voluminous, which underlines Eisenman's role as a leading reflective practitioner in US East-coast architectural discourse, and in the international exchange of architecture primarily experienced through print.

Also dedicated to the function of education, the intimate work of Karljosef Schattner shows quite another kind of contextualism, and at the opposite end of the scale. Employed for thirty years as Diocesan architect in the tiny German town of Eichstätt, he was a local architect engaged in small high-quality jobs, and his fame in Germany grew in the 1980s not through theory but through the sheer quality of built work. Starting as a rather fastidious modernist with a great sensitivity for materials, he came under the influence of Carlo Scarpa, and started to experiment with the same kind of contrasts and layerings. The **Waisenhaus** in Eichstätt rebuilt in 1985-88 is a historical curiosity. It started life as two Renaissance houses, was converted into an eighteenth-century orphanage behind a new facade, and after being narrowly saved from demolition by Schattner, was finally reconverted into two university departments. All three layers are exposed and contrasted in his conversion, resulting in a fascinating building which makes the passage of history almost tangible. At a time when too many old buildings are hastily swept away or converted out of all recognition, and when all cities are becoming alike, Schattner provides a rich example of how to preserve the urban and personal memories that constitute genius loci by sensitively combining new and old.

Some people would rather have no 'new' at all, and part of the conservative reaction to Modernism in Britain was a movement declaring itself *Real Architecture*, which in the 1980s produced a rash of shamelessly anachronistic work.[11] This tendency was encouraged by Prince Charles, whose foray into architecture began with a condemnation of the first proposal for extending the National Gallery in London, the **Sainsbury Wing** eventually built in 1986-91. A competition held in 1982, won by a relatively modernist scheme from Ahrends, Burton and Koralek, was about to go ahead when it was condemned by the Prince as '*a carbuncle on the face of a well-loved friend*'. The ensuing consternation led to a second international competition in 1986 with an evident anti-modern bias, in which a whole series of hitherto modernist architects tried to design a nineteenth-century building with a stone facade.[12] Robert Venturi and Denise Scott Brown won partly for their skilful response to the awkward site, but mainly because an ironic and stagey treatment proved in the end the only convincing way of marrying the demanding modern conditions of use to galleries and facades that played with historical dress. Completed at the beginning of the 1990s, this building brought to a close the reactive period known as postmodernism, and it was fitting that the last word should be given to those who had provided the first in the 1960s, for Venturi had produced the ground-breaking book *Complexity and Contradiction in Architecture* (1966), that more than any other launched postmodernism, making explicit demands for a kind of mannerism in reaction to modernist premises. Together with Steven Izenour, Venturi and Scott Brown had also written *Learning from Las Vegas* (1972) which first legitimised kitsch in architectural debates.

Venturi and Scott Brown, together with the Smithsons and Eamses, fulfil one other change to the architectural profession during the period: the acknowledged presence of women as equals in creating buildings. Although all three were or are in professional partnerships with their husbands, the acknowledgement of their names and roles marks a steady transition from the first modernist generation, in which women were almost absent, to today's condition in which women can be solo architectural stars heading international practices.

PBJ/EC January 2007

Notes

1. Blundell Jones 2002.

2. Blundell Jones 1978, 1995, 1999.

3. The best general source on Team Ten including period documents is Risselada and van den Heuvel 2005.

4. *'The Medicine of Reciprocity'*, first published in Forum, 1961, and much reproduced.

5. Alberti 1986 (original 1485).

6. Also in *'The Medicine of Reciprocity'*, see note 4 above.

7. Scharoun's Romeo and Juliet housing project in Stuttgart of 1954-57 was a successful speculation sold to owner-occupiers and brought further commissions. His Berlin Philharmonie was completed in 1963 at the lowest cost per seat for comparable buildings in Europe at the time. See Blundell Jones 1995.

8. Mies's Seagram Building, New York 1957 was the trend-setting example.

9. Banham 1966, p. 86.

10. Starting in a thesis at Cambridge, finally published as Eisenman 2003.

11. *Real Architecture* was the title of an exhibition including work by John Simpson, Robert Adam, Demetri Porphyrios and Quinlan Terry held at the Building Centre, London, in 1988. The eponymous catalogue was edited by Alan Powers.

12. See *'Two views on Venturi'* by Peter Blundell Jones, *Architects' Journal*, 13 May 1987, pp. 22-26.

Chapter 1. Charles and Ray Eames: Eames House, Pacific Palisades, 1945-49

Following the defeat of Germany and Japan in 1945, the victorious liberal democracies looked to the United States for direction. Politically, American leadership affected the world through the power confrontation with the Soviet Union and the economic assistance provided by the Marshall Plan. Culturally, the presence of American troops augmented the influence already established through films and music, converting the economic power of the previously isolationist superpower into a tangible Utopia of opportunity. In architecture there was a willingness to dispense with traditional European historic styles for public projects because of their association with failed totalitarian regimes. The role of architects as transformers of the social scene was disseminated from academic centres by European exiles like Mies and Gropius, whose pioneering pre-war work was exposed to a larger audience.[1] Not only was the built environment transformed: the change also affected the public image of the architect. The partnership of Charles and Ray Eames departed from conventional practice by representing an alternative vision. Instead of the typical faceless male administrator, or the romantic figure of the lonely genius glamorously exemplified by Gary Cooper as Howard Roark in *The Fountainhead*,[2] the Eameses presented themselves as a married couple happily at play in their work. Typically portrayed in good humoured engagement with design, film work and exhibition creation, they seemed to dedicate their entire *oeuvre* to open communication, the explicit nature of the form providing a self-conscious context for the implicit nature of the content. Unlike their slightly younger British contemporaries the Smithsons (see Chapter 5), they did not appear to take themselves too seriously, but their products grew formally and technically from a painstaking development process which they were happy to share through constant documentation.[3] Their image of sunny optimism epitomised the material comfort of Eisenhower's America, but beneath it lay the dark shadow of the couple's earlier experiences during the Great Depression, Roosevelt's New Deal, and the Second World War.

Charles Eames was born in 1907 in St Louis and began training there as an architect at Washington University, but did not complete the course. A European tour in 1929 exposed him directly to the work of early modernists. Architectural practice during the Depression era, when he and his partners completed a few conventional houses and a church, was followed by projects for the federal government through the Works Progress Administration.[4] The church (St Mary's Catholic Church in Helena, Arkansas, 1936) came to the attention of Eliel Saarinen, who appointed him to a fellowship at Cranbrook Academy. There he encountered Ray Kaiser, born in Sacramento in 1912, a young artist studying crafts, and, following his divorce from his first wife, they were married in 1941. The couple moved immediately to Los Angeles, where Charles

1. Eames House: The multicoloured facade.

2. The world-famous Eames chair and ottoman designed for Herman Miller in 1956.
3. (opposite) Contemporary publication.

was employed by Metro-Goldwyn-Mayer as a set designer, while Ray worked on furniture designs from home, the pair living and working in Richard Neutra's Strathmore apartment building. America entered the Second World War at the end of that year, and Californian firms became involved in the war effort, taking the lead in aircraft production. The Eameses and their friend John Entenza set up a company which was commissioned by the US Navy to produce plywood splints for injured service personnel. This gave them privileged access to new technologies during a period of material shortages and encouraged them in their experiments with furniture design. A late and indirect product was the plywood shell of the lounge chair and ottoman, the so-called Eames chair of 1956. Plywood was strong, innovative, but eminently functional, and its inherent suitability for folded sheet forms presented new aesthetic possibilities which Ray was particularly adept at exploiting. This new material remained, along with fibreglass and aluminium, at the intersection of the Eameses' different design and material interests.[5]

The Case Study houses
As the war progressed, American and exiled creative minds turned to the world to come once peace was restored. Architects were concerned to create a new public language of representation, as exemplified by the new monumentality of Josep

Lluis Sert, Fernand Léger and Sigfried Giedion.[6] There was also a keen concern to improve domestic conditions for returning service personnel and their families, which led to the Case Study Houses Program developed by the magazine *California Arts & Architecture* (later *Arts & Architecture*). Under the editorship of the Eameses' commercial partner John Entenza, this magazine identified the aesthetic of modernity with the political agenda of the Allied Powers, and intended to make a practical demonstration of how modern techniques might be applied to the looming housing question. In 1943 Entenza organised a competition *Designs for Post-War Living* which was published in the magazine the following year with a contribution by Charles Eames entitled '*What is a House?*' In January 1945, with victory in sight, an answer to that question was sought with the Case Study Houses Program. *Arts & Architecture* announced that it would sponsor the acquisition of suitable sites for individual dwellings, designs by eight Southern Californian architects, and the subsequent construction, publishing the results to further the cultural and social aims of new ways of living.[7]

Commercial alliances with manufacturers, and exhibition of the houses prior to occupation (350,000 visits were recorded), placed this project somewhat ambiguously within the tradition of European modernist housing exhibitions like the Weissenhofsiedlung at Stuttgart of 1927 (Blundell Jones 2002, Ch. 1). However, unlike that precedent, which implied a transformed urban landscape, the Case Study houses were individual family dwellings rather than examples of collective prototypes. This fact alone indicates the adaptation of the broadly socialist modernist agenda to the more individualistic American society, obscuring some of its original ideological intentions. Although initially timber construction was expected, the development of steel frames allowed ever more dramatic proposals to be realised.

The architects involved included Craig Ellwood, A. Quincy Jones, Pierre Koenig and Rafael Soriano, but the Eames house stood out as the most influential. Charles Eames did in fact design two houses on adjacent sites at Pacific Palisades: Case Study House 8, known as the Eames House and attributed to Charles and Ray Eames; and House 9, built for the bachelor Entenza, which was attributed to Charles Eames and Eero Saarinen. Set in contrast by their proximity, the two houses demonstrated different attitudes and formal choices, the

LIFE IN A CHINESE KITE

Standard industrial products assembled in a spacious wonderland

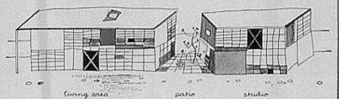

living area　　　　patio　　　　studio

Diagram by Eames shows flexibility of frame, many ways of rearranging facade of patterns

The sparkling construction shown on these pages happens to be the place where one of America's foremost young designers and his wife are having the time of their lives. More important, it is also one of the most advanced house structures built in this country to date.

So far as Charles Eames is concerned, there is no reason why a house should not be:

▸ Spacious—space being the greatest luxury there is;

▸ A sophisticated industrial product;

▸ And as light and airy as a suspension bridge—as skeletal as an airplane fuselage.

Having got this straight in his own mind, Eames asked himself these questions: How cheap is space? How industrial is our building industry? How light is steel?

LOCATION: Santa Monica, Calif.
CHARLES EAMES, Designer*
LAMPORT, CAFER, SALZMAN, INC., General Contractor

Two-story living room (opposite) faces south-west. Eames-designed step-ladder at left is useful in opening projecting sash, climbing up to bedroom gallery in rear.

Porch at southwest end of building (left) is partly enclosed by 8 ft. retaining wall. Latter is 200 ft. long, accounted for large chunk of building budget.

*Designed and built for the Case Study House program of the magazine Arts & Architecture.
Photos pp. 90-99 (except top p. 94) Julius Shulman.

4. (left) Vogue model photographed in the house in 1954.

5. (above) Bridge-like early version of the house designed by Charles Eames and Eero Saarinen.

6. (opposite) Ground and first-floor plans of the Eames House, folowing the graphic conventions of the contemporary publication.

7. (below opposite) One of the original perspectives showing the kitchen and a feminine figure.

Eameses creating a family home and workplace as opposed to Entenza's individual retreat, an open framework contrasted with an enclosed shell. The Eameses' home proved the most enduring because of their long occupancy, and because of the house's use as a vehicle for their developing design ideas. The cooling of friendship between the Eameses and Entenza, the sale of his house in the mid-1950s, and subsequent alterations, left the field free for admirers of the work of the Eameses to devote undiluted attention to their dwelling.

The Eames aesthetic

In the history of domestic modernism the Eames house stands apart. Not since the work of Adolf Loos had there been such a direct separation between the visual and technical language of the exterior and that of the contents. But if the Viennese master presented this separation in the ironic terms of *fin-de-siècle* polemic, his Californian successors preferred a less confrontational and apparently more casual patois.[8] As if in some frightful case of overcompensation, the spare frame of the exterior, where economy is definitely the key, conceals an interior world of magpie acquisitiveness and eclecticism. The Eameses' passion for collecting, and for displaying their collection in different ways within their personal realm, did much to remove any harshness from the presentation of their architectural vision. But quite apart from the building's occupation by its architects, the mechanical logic of the exterior could not be allowed to dictate the interior for one very clear reason. The kind of interior presented by Ludwig Mies van der Rohe with the Farnsworth House (1946-50), essentially for the appreciation of the professional connoisseur, would have been too uncommercial. Such austerity might suit the office or showroom, but for the domestic market it was too uncomfortable except for a few wealthy intellectual aficionados.

Despite its later reputation as a model for casual but luxurious individual houses, the Eames House involved a design strategy that could almost be described as self-denial. The simplicity of the frame reflected Charles Eames's intention on grounds of economy to enclose the maximum volume within the least surface. The relation to the dramatic site was similarly reticent, simply standing the steel frame alongside the existing

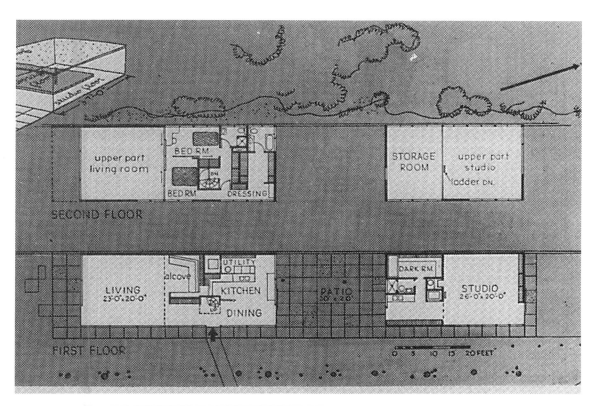

SECOND FLOOR

upper part
living room

BED RM

BED RM   DRESSING

STORAGE
ROOM

upper part
studio

ladder DN.

FIRST FLOOR

LIVING
23'-0'×20'-0'

alcove

UTILITY

KITCHEN

DINING

PATIO
20'×20'

DARK RM

STUDIO
26'-0'×20'-0'

0 5 10 15 20 FEET

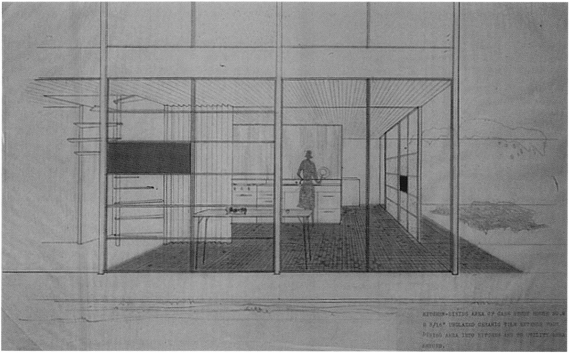

natural meadow against a change in gradient. This contrasted with the modernist motif of integrating a house into the landscape, as forcefully expressed in American domestic architecture by Charles Eames's early architectural hero, Frank Lloyd Wright (Blundell Jones 2002, Ch. 12). Instead one is presented with what could be seen as a defining Eames motif, especially in their film and exhibition work: the laconic juxtaposition of two independent elements, which encourages the observer to make the connection. An early project for both houses, as published in *Arts & Architecture* in December 1945, juxtaposed the square of the Entenza House against an L-shaped version of the Eames House which had a separate studio. Its principal domestic volume cantilevered out over an existing meadow (fig. 5), set perpendicular to the existing embankment on the site. An entry driveway ran beneath the house, relating it to modernist villa prototypes like the Villa Savoye (Blundell Jones 2002, Ch. 7). The steel frame, which Eames designed in conjunction with structural engineer Edgardo Contini but rearranged after delivery to the site, demonstrated a significant concept in the ideology of the Case Study Houses Program. Mass production and rapid assembly had greatly improved during the Second World War, particularly in the construction of aircraft. In the new era of peace, the architectural community sought to revive the 'swords into ploughshares' strategy that had followed the First World War.[9] There was again a desperate need for housing, but there was also a hope that industrialised building could re-employ those who had produced armaments. In Britain the Hertfordshire Schools programme followed the social agenda of Attlee's Labour government, its architectural modesty suiting the self-image of the declining imperial power.[10] In the triumphant and expanding United States, the same attitude could be presented and appreciated in a more alluring light, with the concomitant problem that the image was mistaken for the substance.[11]

The early project for House 8 in the form of a bridge bore an undeniable similarity to a sketch by Mies, whose work Charles Eames had observed at an exhibition at the Museum of Modern Art in New York, although according to Ray Eames this could not have been until November 1947.[12] A second project moved away from Miesian precedent by rotating the volume of the living space through 90° in relation to the separate studio, so that it was parallel to the fall on the site, replacing the intended cantilever with a single storey retaining wall. The prefabricated parts, 4 inch (100 mm) H columns and 12 inch (300 mm) deep open-web trusses were then rearranged on the site to make the new configuration, as published in *Arts & Architecture* in May 1949.

The physical and aesthetic motif of the frame, sometimes compared with a box kite,[13] controls the separate volumes of the house, studio and the patio between them. The ensemble was now modestly placed against the embankment, sitting on a concrete retaining wall on one side, and screened on the other by a row of eucalyptus trees, which obscured the house's impact. The patio was intended to be the focus of the most densely occupied parts of the solid volumes. The kitchen/dining room and bath/bedrooms in the house volume, and service areas such as storage and darkroom in the studio volume, were stacked next to it, while the double height volumes for living and studio were placed at the extremities. This produced an alternating rhythm of open and closed spaces, the central one open to sky and landscape. The alternation of spaces continued with the positioning of the main entrance between dining and living areas, directly opposite the open spiral stair to the bedrooms. The south-facing end bay was left open, the roof decking extended to provide a sheltered terrace with views of the ocean.

A primary module of 7 feet 6 inches (2.28 metres) controlled the length of the whole ensemble: eight bays for the house including the open end one, five for the studio, and four for the patio. Crosswise, the square drawn paving at half module and tripartite division of the end glazing suggest three bays of the same module, but closer inspection reveals two bays of 7 feet 6 and a narrower one of around 6 feet 3 for the doors, adding up to a whole width around 20 feet, marked on some drawings as 20 feet 4: it is not altogether clear how they dealt with thicknesses. The overall length of the house was recorded as 51 feet and of the studio as 37 feet, and both were 17 feet high. Accepting a width of 20 feet, number combinations suggest that a subtle proportional matrix underscored the matter-of-fact economic industrial construction (e.g. 51=17 x 3, and 37= 20 + 17).[14]

The frame was bolted directly onto the concrete slab, although each volume was distinguished by a different floor surface: a tiled floor in the living-room, brick paviours in the patio, and parquet in the studio. The back wall of the double height living-room facing the embankment was timber-panelled,

8. Studio with simple steel structure, minimal staircase and Eames-designed furniture.

with a seating area located under the bedroom balcony. Privacy for sleeping was supplied by sliding screens fitted onto the solid surface of the balcony front, which keyed into the module of glazed and opaque panels in the principal facade. The sense of open and closed volumes is enhanced by a contrast of transparent and opaque panels in the elevations. The glazed areas, sometimes with large sheets of glass but mostly divided horizontally in six panels on each level, create dematerialising reflections externally, and frame views of the landscape internally. Such visual

9. View of the house from across the meadow with the line of eucalyptus trees in front.
10. (opposite) House and studio facades with Mondrian-like composition.

effects develop the contrast between the house and its setting in a modest and subtle manner, without the need for major external works. Some aesthetic indebtedness to the sliding screens of the Japanese house has been suggested, reflecting a long history of relations between the United States and Japan which bore obvious fruit in the work of Frank Lloyd Wright and Greene and Greene.[15] However, this connection was hardly likely to be trumpeted in a proposal for ex-servicemen returning after a bitterly fought war in the Pacific, and after wartime internment of Japanese Americans. The architects were reticent, preferring a non-controversial no-nonsense emphasis on economy of means. The 'Japanese' effect was particularly evident in black and white photographs of the house, but in actuality colour was preferred, especially with solid panels painted in strong primary colours. This aspect brought quite different associations with European modernism of the previous two or three decades, especially Dutch De Stijl. Ray Eames had met Piet Mondrian while part of the American Abstract Artists movement in New York before her marriage, and some similarity with his paintings can be recognised in the house's juxtapositions of frame and colour, but the spatial attitude is different. As demonstrated in Rietveld's Red-Blue Chair and Schröder House, a dynamic attitude to previously closed forms was central to De Stijl. In contrast, a degree of stasis characterised the Eames aesthetic, dominated by

the rigid nature of the frame and the permanence of the coloured panels. Although there had been an intention to change them from time to time, the original colour scheme was maintained intact. Changefulness was achieved instead through daily and seasonal rhythms.

Unlike some of the later Case Study houses, the spatial experience of the interior was not one of expansiveness. The openness of the double height space encouraged instead a sense of visual and material complexity, as the space and its surfaces were filled from the start with an eclectic range of artefacts and furniture, a decision at odds with the designed uniformity of earlier modernist houses. Nor was the austere high-mindedness of the European avant-garde reflected in the ludic promotion of the Eames House to its commercial audience. Besides publishing the house in *Architectural Forum* in September 1950 under the headline '*Life in a Chinese Kite'*, the Eameses reproduced the house's language of frame and panel in storage units which they designed for the Hermann Miller company between 1950 and 1952, enabling any home owner to share in the Eames experience at an affordable rate. The house also featured as the backdrop of a fashion shoot for *Vogue* in April 1954, and in 1951 the Eames Studio produced 'The Toy', a set of brightly coloured triangular panels which could be assembled to create tetrahedral structures and children's play spaces. A smaller version was

11. End of the house, which sits on a retaining wall to left.
12. (opposite) The architects taking pride in the frame of their burgeoning house.

produced in 1952. In 1959, small-scale repro-ductions of the Eames House were sold as the Revell Company's Toy House at three-quarter inch to the foot scale (1:16), furnished with model Eames furniture.

Experience of the house as built was communicated to a wider public unable to visit it through the film *House: After Five Years of Living,* a ten-minute short consisting of still images of house and contents in saturated colour. This was the classic format of the Eames films, akin to a controlled slideshow (in this instance with a score by the film composer Elmer Bernstein) which allowed concentration on the abstract compositional values of light and shade, colour, modern machined elements and folk art. This formal method underscored the importance of the house's frame in organising disparate elements into a coherent whole.

An apolitical stance?
The Eameses claimed, like other modernist protagonists, to have preserved a professional detachment from politics, and that the personal genius demonstrated in their films at the American National Exhibition in Moscow of 1959, for example, was without 'official' approval.[16] This suggests the naivety of the closeted designer pursuing a personal vision irrespective of what might be inferred by others. The same supposed detachment accompanied the critical reception of abstract expressionism, which was portrayed both as quintessentially American and as apolitical: as evidence of individual genius which American society prized. But despite its apparent self-sufficiency, the Eames House cannot be removed from its political context. Conceived as a prototype for a new way of dwelling, it became instead, through propagation of its image, a subtle tool of the Cold War period. The laudatory nature of the Eameses' benign view of Americana led from a

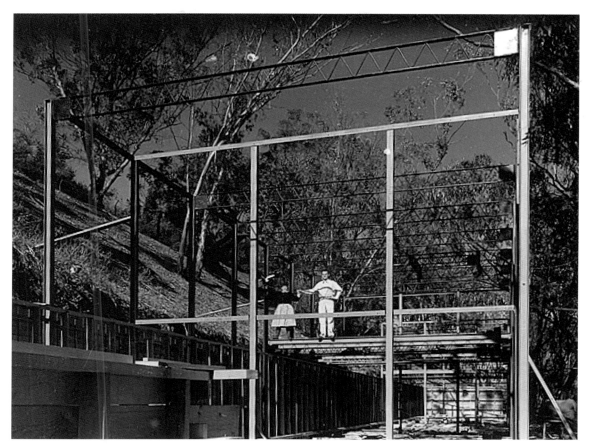

contract with the military during the Second World War through government commissions like the film and exhibition work in Moscow of 1959 (the scene of the 'kitchen debate' between Nikita Khrushchev and Richard Nixon) to the official commission for the American Bicentennial exhibition in 1976. Following their deaths, their archive was deposited with the Library of Congress. Their vision of America, with its seamless interaction between the corporate and the personal, became a signal of the good life. Its popular acceptance as the epitome of domesticity was an achievement to which European modernists had only aspired.

The self-referential nature of the Eameses' work, the documentation of the process of creation shown as a playful activity, the juxtaposition of the technologically complex with the disarmingly simple, lent a charming face to modern design as a relief from architectural high seriousness. Here was a cheering individuality, a can-do modernism, in contrast with the increasingly bureaucratised state modernism promoted in Europe, its monotone homogeneity emerging from a ruined urban landscape.

The unsatisfactory nature of the present and the baggage of the past could be jettisoned in favour of the promised Californian future. The Eameses' vision chimed with the spread of American popular culture through film, music and eventually television, and their own films and colour-saturated palette provided some of the period's definitive images. What could never satisfactorily be squared was the lack of applicability of the Eames model to a wider community, one unable to share their exquisite taste or visual skills. The Eameses declared that the frame of their house had effectively disappeared, but repeated at larger scale by other designers that frame asserted a new architectural dominance in coming decades, becoming a necessary armature for proposals by high-tech architects, like Renzo Piano and Richard Rogers' Centre Pompidou (Chapter 14).

As a late expression of New Deal optimism, that tonic for the Great Depression promised by the Roosevelt Administration between 1933 and 1941, the Eames House presented an image of how industrial technologies could be applied to housing, but the political context determined its fate. In contrast with Europe, the economic system of the United States required ideas to be adopted by the market to reach beyond the lifestyles of the elite. Mass production and fast erection techniques came to dominate the American housing market, but in the form of timber framing and aluminium siding, with an aesthetic based firmly on traditional models. The Eameses' radical furniture was both commercially successful and appealed to the artistic avant-garde, but the market for their architecture was much more limited, with only two projects seriously attempted, and only one realised. The Hermann Miller Showroom, constructed at the same time as the Case Study Houses, was a more widely accessible demonstration of the Eameses' talents and tied their furniture production to the company. But the failure to build the house designed for the film director Billy Wilder, as an extension of ideas expressed in their own house, marked the end of this branch of their work.

It took appreciation of the house by other architects to nurture the spread of its ideas, especially high-tech architects. In their projects the concept of frame as neutral support for changing functions developed beyond the domestic scale to become the *parti* for a large public institution. But the Eames House also produced its own progeny within the domestic sphere. For example, the house of architects Michael and Patty Hopkins in London, completed in 1984, adapted the prototype to a gloomier climate, retaining the principles of exposed frame and simplicity of form. Sleeker in its finish than the original, thanks largely to developments in glass technology, the Hopkins House owes much to the Eameses' feeling for space if not to their passion for clutter.[17] In both cases an apparent modesty, and the owners' apparent comfort, conceals radical ideas about living essential to the decades when they were conceived. Quite apart from any increased convenience, they represented a radical alternative to the historicist aesthetic which still dominates the Anglo-American suburban housing market today.

The enduring legacy of the Eameses lay not just in the house but in the way they presented it. The milieu they developed for themselves combined the technical specification of industrial production with the craft values and simplicity of folk art. The organic forms of their furniture resulted from an inventive approach to the use of new materials. The rigorous matching of colours through pursuing modernist colour theory produced a collage of fragments from many sources, with an apparent randomness which belied the orthodox modernist starting point. The ambiguous appeal of this combination laid the foundation for the Eameses' success as designers of a particular lifestyle.

EC

Notes

1. This phenomenon revolved around three main centres: Cambridge, Massachusetts, Chicago and New York. Walter Gropius arrived at Harvard as Chairman of the Architecture Department in 1937 following a brief sojourn in Britain, remaining influential in that school until his death, and as late as the early 1980s the Graduate School of Design observed his birthday. Marcel Breuer joined him there, and Gropius's direct influence was supplemented by the appointment of Josep Lluis Sert, a Catalan exile from Franco's Spain, as Dean in 1953. Ludwig Mies van der Rohe's influence was exerted from Chicago. In 1938 the Museum of Modern Art in New York exhibited the work of the Bauhaus between 1919 and 1928.
2. The 1948 film was adapted from Ayn Rand's eponymous novel of 1943. See Colin McArtur, *'Chinese Boxes and Russian Dolls: tracking the elusive cinematic city'* in Clarke 1997, pp.19-45. For examples of the representation of the faceless administrator see John R. Gold and Stephen V. Ward, *'Of Plans and Planners: documentary film and the challenge of the urban future, 1935-52'* in the same collection pp. 59-82.
3. The most thorough collection is that assembled in Neuhart, Neuhart and Eames 1989.
4. See Kirkham 1998.
5. See Joseph Giovannini *'The Office of Charles Eames and Ray Kaiser'* in Albrecht 1997, pp. 44-77.
6. Josep Sert, Fernand Léger, and Sigfried Giedion, (1943) *'Nine Points on Monumentality'* in Costa and Hartray 1997, pp. 14-17.
7. See Kirkham 1998, p. 103, also Smith 1998.
8. In particular see the chapter *'Interior'* in Colomina 1994, pp. 233-281.
9. With the exile of many of its leaders, the political significance of the integrated model of Bauhaus design had been apparent before the Second World War. See Alexander Dorner *'The Background of the Bauhaus'* in Bayer L, Gropius and Gropius 1938, pp. 9-13.
10. See Saint 1987.
11. See Beatriz Colomina *'Introduction'* in Colomina, Brennan and Kim 2004, pp. 10-21.
12. Neuhart, Neuhart and Eames 1989 p. 107.
13. Tamar Zinguer *'Toy'* in Colomina, Brennan and Kim 2004, pp. 143-167.
14. Proportion was a contemporary theme best exemplified by Le Corbusier's *Le Modulor*, but also present in the work of Mies van der Rohe.
15. See among others Blundell Jones 2002, p.178.
16. See Helene Lipstadt, *'"Natural Overlap" Charles and Ray Eames and the Federal Government'* in Albrecht 1997, pp. 150-177.
17. Davies 1993, pp. 11-12.

Chapter 2. Egon Eiermann and Sep Ruf; German Pavilion at Brussels World Expo, 1958

Egon Eiermann is not well known in the English-speaking world and has not been given much space in our histories.[1] Nonetheless, for German historians writing in the 1960s and 1970s he was one of the leading figures of the post-war scene. In an interview of 1977, Günter Behnisch referred to him as *a very good architect... THE German architect of the last twenty years'*.[2] Critic and historian Wolfgang Pehnt consistently saw him as the opposite number to Hans Scharoun, claiming as early as 1963:

In this middle generation, which was young in the twenties and occupies chairs at the colleges and academies, Egon Eiermann and Hans Scharoun represent extreme positions: Eiermann who is concerned with the lucidity and perspicuous arrangement of the formal image and with elegance of design; Scharoun who works on each assignment as though the planning problem that it exemplifies had never occurred before. [3]

Normally the architect cited in this opposition – as in Blundell Jones 2002 – is Ludwig Mies van der Rohe,[4] and Eiermann certainly has much in common with the better known Mies, including his reductionism, perfectionism, and obsession with detail. Caught in the shadow of this greater master, Eiermann has received less international attention than he deserved,[5] but he was certainly no Mies clone, and he introduced major innovations of his own. Even so, he was close enough in spirit to Mies to suffer the same scorn when the Miesians fell from grace, when the promise of elegant simplicity that they pursued with such rigour and commitment was revealed to leave so many things wanting. To treat Eiermann merely as a lesser Mies is also to deny that, born eighteen years later, he belonged to a later generation, and that his mature work arose not like Mies's in the Weimar Republic before Hitler, but in the recovery period of the German Federal Republic following Hitler's downfall. Beginning in the *Stunde null* (zero hour) of bombed ruins in 1945, it came to symbolise the German *Wirtschaftswunder* (economic miracle) of the 1960s.

Egon Eiermann was born in 1904 near Berlin, the son of a railway engineer from whom he claimed to have inherited his precision in thinking and design.[6] He studied architecture under Hans Poelzig at the Technische Hochschule in Berlin, along with the historian Julius Posener, Walter Segal, and Helmut Hentrich among others.[7] Although Poelzig is usually categorised as an expressionist, his work was varied, complex and builderly, and he was an extraordinarily wise and liberal teacher, encouraging each student to find his or her own way and hotly forbidding imitation of his own work.[8] As Julius Posener described:

We learned from him to encounter each project afresh, as though we had never solved one before... We learned to doubt every presumption, every routine, every method that tends to take over. We learned to suspect forms established too early, and to clear from

1. German Pavilion at Brussels 1958, corner of one of the two-storey pavilions suspended above the carpet of lawn.

our work those notorious short-circuits that one too easily excuses as artistic or creative. [9]

Eiermann did not say much about having learned from Poelzig, and when asked about it remarked that *'a genius has no pupils'*, but Posener thought there had been a crucial influence, citing Eiermann's statement *'learning to build means learning to think'*.[10] That Eiermann was active and articulate among the student group is shown by his organising a weekly discussion circle on architecture that continued until 1933.[11]

Eiermann's first building was industrial, a type of job that would recur throughout his career, and which seemed to suit him doubly: positively in its demand for objective efficiency, and negatively in the lack of pressure for rhetoric – at least rhetoric of the kind that modernists wanted to avoid. It was a small extension for the Berlin electricity works, with a flat roof and horizontal emphasis. The construction of steel frame with brick infill in Prussian bond[12] was strongly expressed, precise and simple. From 1930 until 1936 Eiermann worked in partnership with Fritz Jaenecke, and they started off well by gaining places in two oversubscribed design competitions for small mass-produced houses, carefully planned, geometrically precise, and obedient to the discipline of construction.[13] By 1933 they had built the single-storey Hesse house in a Berlin suburb which was praised by the editor of *Bauwelt*. He excused the flat-roof – by the time it had been built, the Nazis were in power – on the basis of economy. There followed a series of family houses with the compulsory pitched roofs and rectangular wings in exposed brickwork, which by concentrating on simple forms and directly expressed materials ran the gauntlet of Nazi building

control without succumbing to folksy rusticity.[14] Some had gardens by Herta Hammerbacher, one of the leading modernist landscape designers who also worked with Scharoun, and Eiermann conducted bold experiments with transparency and spatial transitions that anticipate his later work. His way of getting his work past unsympathetic and philistine planners by making it deadpan and straightforwardly constructive contrasts intriguingly with the game-like tactics of Scharoun, who accepted a more overtly vernacular shell, even verging on caricature, so that he could develop his unprecedented spatial pyrotechnics within.[15]

Retreat into 'objectivity'

It seems that Eiermann, like Mies, did his best to stay out of politics, but he retained his stubborn integrity and could be outspoken. He employed a Jewish secretary until publicly denounced in the Nazi newspaper *Stürmer*, for example, and in 1935 he launched a risky and scathing critique in *Bauwelt* about the competition for a theatre in Dessau in which he had taken part, lambasting other entrants for borrowing past styles, and for seeking monumental effects while ignoring technical imperatives.[16] Psychological pressure on the non-conforming gradually increased, and Eiermann's partner Jaenecke emigrated to Sweden in 1936. It was in the following year, 1937, that Eiermann compromised himself by designing the hall for an exhibition of Nazi propaganda,[17] and perhaps he needed to prove his credentials with the party, but otherwise he seems to have kept clear of official projects, working directly for the regime only towards the middle of the war, when he planned an airfield and a temporary hospital.[18] His refuge was industrial work: under the assumption that it

was merely technical, and that technical efficiency was a good thing, this was the only area of building free from stylistic interference.[19] Once the war had started, his work included both a propellor factory and a shipyard, so it cannot be regarded as free from Nazi ambitions, but it allowed some sense of detachment. Astonishingly, Eiermann was able to design three factory buildings in the heart of Nazi Germany between 1938 and 1940 so uncompromisingly modernist in spirit and appearance that they could be ten years earlier or ten years later.[20] The architecture seems so complete in itself, so strict and elegant in following faithfully its own rules, that it could override the changing politics and social mores to become timeless.[21] But this comforting view is not beyond challenge: some might argue that industry with its amoral pursuit of technique and economy is already inherently fascistic, while others would claim that in denying their social context buildings are necessarily autistic. We shall reconsider these arguments later.

After the war the industrial work continued and remained an essential part of Eiermann's office workload. The handkerchief factory at Blumberg of 1949-51 gained international recognition and set the tone for other industrial projects: a big efficient hall with very wide spans and a couple of lower buildings for the entry and boiler house. The whole made a well-composed and carefully scaled ensemble, nicely proportioned and immaculately detailed. By careful treatment of edges, Eiermann managed to make that most banal of materials – corrugated asbestos-cement sheet – look delicate and elegant. Besides its factories, Eiermann's office built offices, department stores and many other buildings, all carried out with consummate efficiency and generally counted among the best of

2. (opposite left) Extension to electricity works, Berlin-Steglitz 1928-1930.
3. (opposite right) Hesse House, Berlin-Lankwitz 1931-1933.
4. (below left) Steingroever House, Berlin-Grunewald 1937.

5. (above) Degea factory Berlin-Wedding 1938.
6. (below) Handkerchief factory Blumberg, 1949-51.
7. (bottom) Steingroever House plan.

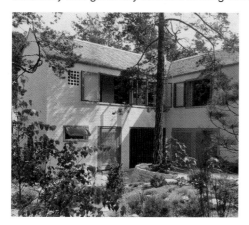

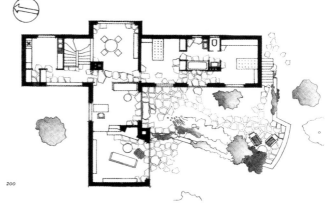

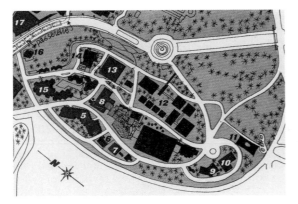

8. (left) German Pavilion at Brussels, site plan, number 12.
9. (above) Model of the group of pavilions plus entry bridge.

their time, but the commission for the Brussels Pavilion called for a special performance. We have chosen it as our main example because, in forcing Eiermann away from the literally functional, it reveals the essential qualities of his architecture, including some crucial innovations. It also reveals the architectural values of the time: a period of triumph and consolidation for the Modern Movement. Pevsner called it *'a perfect blend of crisp clear, cubic transparent blocks and their grouping in a landscape setting'*. [22]

The Brussels Expo
The Belgian government approached that of the German Federal Republic in 1954, inviting a German presence at the World Expo. Two architects were approached: Eiermann and Sep Ruf, another respected architect in the Miesian direction.[23] They both produced designs in 1956, Eiermann offering two versions. Their ideas were very similar, and they were asked to proceed in partnership, though the reins seem to have been left largely in Eiermann's hands.[24] The building needed to show the rest of the world the spirit of the new West Germany at a time when Hitler and the war were still relatively fresh memories. The over-scaled monumentality of Albert Speer's Pavilion at the Paris Exhibition of 1937 obviously had to be avoided, but Mies's Barcelona Pavilion of 1929 would be more appropriate to emulate. The brief, though, was considerably larger. The site was a part of the former royal park with sloping lawns and mature trees, all of which were to be retained. Both Ruf and Eiermann in their initial projects had pursued the idea of a series of linked pavilions which could fit the site while avoiding the trees. The final version had eight, all square, in three different sizes, and linked by elevated walkways

to maintain a horizontal datum in contrast with the falling ground. The squareness of the pavilions reflects a desire for purity and universality, entering that exclusive architectural territory where the same thing happens in both axes.[25] The pavilions were made in steel with flat roofs and glass walls, and with two, three or four supporting columns in each direction depending on size. They stood one to three storeys above base. The system was universal, details were repeated, but the variations were skilfully played, sufficient to avoid a repetitive impression. Entry points and bridge links were asymmetrically placed, never on a pavilion's axis, and the blue painted plywood doors – the one touch of applied colour – were centrally pivoted, forcing visitors to pass to either side. The complete circuit of pavilions formed a neat rectangle in plan, but was broken by a change of level. It was entered from a high-level road on the east side via a bridge elegantly supported on a single pylon, which met the longest of the open decks with its descending stair. The largest pavilion at the north end was dedicated to education, but also contained the library and conference room. The one next to it with the change in level was the restaurant. The south-east pavilion was for industry, the south-west for housing and town planning. The four small pavilions to the west housed a wine-bar and exhibitions about recreation, health and welfare. The exhibitions varied in layout, exploiting the essential flexibility of the spaces. Just as central axes were denied by entrances and links (and by a central column in the case of the middle-sized pavilions), so the interiors were divided asymmetrically in various ways, and passage from one to the next offered fresh views and new discoveries. The largest pavilion had an open well asymmetrically placed to the north-west: a square

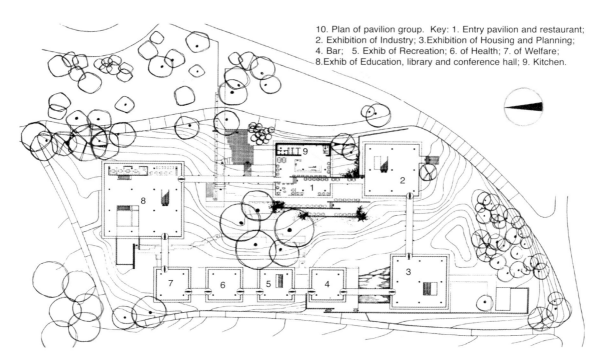

10. Plan of pavilion group. Key: 1. Entry pavilion and restaurant; 2. Exhibition of Industry; 3.Exhibition of Housing and Planning; 4. Bar; 5. Exhib of Recreation; 6. of Health; 7. of Welfare; 8.Exhib of Education, library and conference hall; 9. Kitchen.

within a square. The use of steel columns and steel beams in the floor and roof plates allowed a very slender structure, made highly transparent by single glazing in the largest possible sheets of plate glass, with narrow mullions and concealed frames top and bottom. The effect was radically improved by setting the glass a metre inside the floor edge to create an open gallery around each building. If few visitors actually chose to walk the perimeter, the mere presence of these galleries made the buildings more generous and inviting. It also stressed the open connection with the park, creating a liminal place at once inside and out. By shading the glass, the gallery cut solar gain and reduced the reflections that make glass seem more solid.[26] In a further refinement, Eiermann added delicate venetian blinds around the perimeter, motorised to drop as soon as the sun came round, and fully hidden when retracted apart from fine vertical nylon guide wires. The blinds transformed the facade and made it translucent to the inside. Protecting them, and supporting the minimal tubular handrail, were a series of vertical steel tubes on the outer face, which stated the constructive rhythm. While the bearing columns and window mullions within the perimeter were painted black to recede, these outer tubes were picked out in white to become the dominant verticals. The effect was graceful, for

they stood in for structure, yet were too impossibly thin ever to hold the building up. If Mies's small I sections on the almost contemporary Seagram Building stated a similar fiction, Eiermann's tubes pushed the idea further, and the external gallery, which Mies never developed in this way, was Eiermann's principal legacy to the developing vocabulary of architecture.[27] Equally lightweight were the bridge-link shelters, made again with steel tubes over which sail-like plastic fabric was stretched. The guard rails on the bridge sides used minimal steel tension wires, a detail familiar today that was then quite new.

Steel and precision

Steel allowed a machine-like precision that amply represented the technical prowess of the new Germany and the pinnacle of the new construction methods that had supplanted handcraft. The extreme expression of lightness and transparency could hardly make a stronger contrast with traditional load-bearing construction, and the organising geometry showed total control, rigorous rationality and order. With Eiermann the choice of steel was almost a religious conviction:

Steel buildings demand the best knowledge, demand logical clarity down to the last detail and classical level-

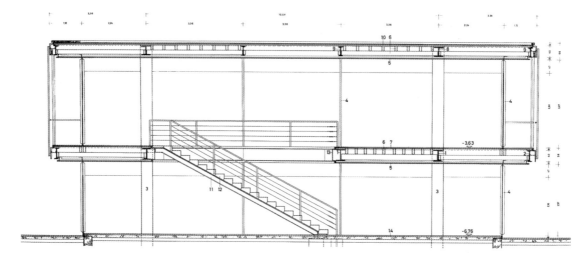

headedness, which expresses itself not least in the use of the right angle as the optimum ratio... As a lover of steel I would like to say that for me steel building shows the aristocratic principle of building... It fills me with a high ethical and aesthetic sense, for as an architect I also must submit to the material with which I have to work... Therefore I would take the trouble to show it in its extreme purity... The French and German Pavilions in the last Brussels Exhibition owed their conception to this... In these buildings the constructions show their natural profile. Columns stand freely visible before the wall. Scientists and engineers should look at such things to feel the most advanced spirit in which architects work with steel. [28]

In contrast, working with concrete was a messy affair taken up by architects interested in *'wasteful Baroque form making, which resembles sculpture more than building'.* Concrete was *'a mushy mass which, introduced into a mould, lets itself bend and turn, slowly set, and even then requires a backbone of steel'.* Furthermore, steel had the moral virtue that it could be removed, while Eiermann claimed to *'look with dismay at the concrete bunker, for I know it can never disappear'.* [29] Lightness meant flexibility, adaptability. He also took a decidedly moral stance over mixed construction:

Mixing means lack of clarity, it introduces chance like a card game. It brings together things that are essentially unrelated. When I see thousands of embedded bolts to transfer loads from concrete to steel I am unconvinced. It may be economical to do it. But it does not – how should I put it? – really make sense (ist nicht im Sinne). [30]

Eiermann was acutely aware of the problems of executing buildings, and therefore always put a high priority on questions of assembly and detail: on buildability. With the Pavilion, speed was of the essence, and the use of steel in construction that was largely dry allowed a high degree of prefabrication, ease of removal, and potential re-assembly. The steel elements were all welded up in Germany and brought to site in good time, so that the German Pavilion was ready and waiting to be unveiled while in some others work was going on frantically until the eleventh hour. [31] The fanatical planning of every detail in Eiermann's office left nothing to chance, and the building expressed this precision of control.

Public reaction

Eiermann and Ruf's Pavilion met with huge critical success, not merely counted among the top half -dozen contributions but consistently published first and given the most space. Commentators remarked that the glass box pavilions had been the most impressive, that they evidently showed the influence of Mies, but that in their refinement they showed this architectural language being played with a new maturity. Although the Japanese and Yugoslav pavilions were also praised, the West German one led the field. *Architectural Forum* remarked that it was *'to many visitors the most polished performance of the fair',* [32] and J.M. Richards, writing in *The Architectural Review,* called it *'the most sophisticated work of architecture in the exhibition',* noting *'the precise elegance of its steel-framed structure, the aptness*

11. (opposite top) Section through a middle-sized pavilion showing gallery treatment and stair. Also visible is the relationship between the steel main structure and the timber sub-structure.

12. (above) Large pavilion and approaching two-level walkway with light canvas roof.

13. (left) Axial view from pavilion to walkway through centrally pivoting blue-painted door. The entry steps from the high-level passage around the exhibition are visible on the right.

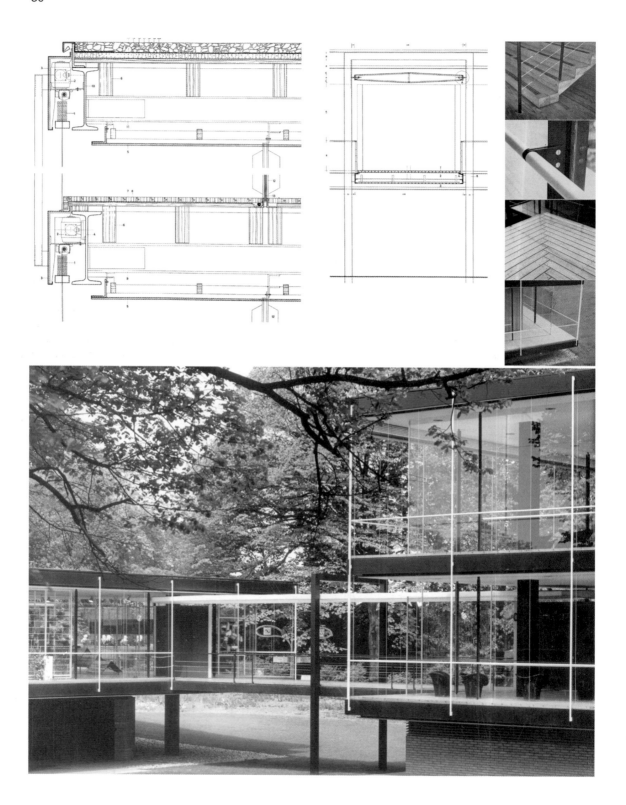

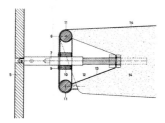

14. (opposite top left) Detail section of floor and roof at the edge of a typical pavilion, showing hidden blind, glass detail and hidden construction.
15. (opposite top middle) Walkway section.
16. (opposite top right) Details shown in *The Architectural Review*.
17. (opposite bottom) Pavilions linked by walkway.
18. (above) Tensioning device on fabric awning.

and thoroughness with which every detail, and every juxtaposition of materials has been worked out, and the poetic effect of its transparency, revealing the internal geometry to the external eye'.[33] Julius Posener later remarked that it had been the task of Eiermann's generation to refine modern architecture to the last detail, and that he knew of *'no other who has followed this goal so stubbornly'*.[34] Yet it is clear from statements by Eiermann, like those cited above, that his rationality was not at all the same as that of contemporary system builders. It was not primarily to do with efficient and economical construction *per se*, but with an architectural statement on ethical and aesthetic grounds. In this he shared territory with Mies, whom he openly admired,[35] and Eiermann certainly could be said to have sought God in the details.

In fact there was much of the art of concealing art, which made it all seem misleadingly effortless. Eiermann was lucky to be able to avoid the clumsy apparatus of a heating system or air-conditioning: ventilation was effected by leaving a narrow gap at the top of the glass panels throughout. However, he could not avoid the basic facts of construction. Square structures symmetrical in both axes are perverse in attempting to deny the asymmetry of reciprocal layers universal in building, by which members running in one direction transfer loads hierarchically to larger ones running in the other. The flat roof decks of the pavilions were in fact supported by timber joists running in one direction that rested on steels running in the other, but

this was not made evident, for the suspended ceiling concealed all. Rainwater was presumably conducted from the felt roof down the hollow box-section main structural columns, but the published details show none of this, not even the slope needed to drain it. Also very largely suppressed – and cleverly so – was the fact of prefabrication. Little evidence of the assembly process was allowed to persist: few visible joints or bolt heads. Everything was remarkably clean and clear: the steel must have been welded, ground off, then meticulously painted.

A commanding architecture
There were good grounds both for the prefabrication and the provision of a flexible building, for there was an intention that it be reused as a school, but there was no pretence at the exhibition about the buildings being neutral containers in the sense of a supporting trellis on which life might grow.[36] Far from being prepared to let the exhibition take its course, Eiermann was deeply concerned that the Pavilion would be let down by its content, and he sought both to introduce and to eliminate material, at a late stage seeking to pare it down.[37] The abiding impression given both by the architect and his work is of obsessive control. The *Architects Journal* commented: *'The only criticism which can be made is that the architectural diagram is everywhere so strong that it tends to eclipse the exhibits: though these are always well conceived it is difficult to remember any of them.'*[38] In photos of the Brussels Pavilion the presence of the buildings is very dominant, and the exhibition itself almost fades into the background. The whole thing was dismantled straight after the show, and for its reputation this was perhaps even an advantage. It was always new, and remains so in photographs, the paintwork unsullied and with no stains on the fabric. As one of Eiermann's apologists put it: *'One can think of no better solution for making visible Germany's return to the circle of Western states in a way at once simple and spotless.'*[39]

While his struggle to avoid and eliminate errors – to get everything right – can be regarded as laudable and exemplary, the control he imposed seems exclusive rather than liberal, indicating a state of mind anxious about mess and disorder.[40] Eiermann was intolerant of the work of architects who did not share his lust for clarity of construction, rejecting their relatively broader vocabulary as individualistic or wilful,[41] and perhaps if he had

32

19. German Embassy Washington D.C. 1958-64, corner showing layering of facade.

20. (below) Max Planck Institute for Atomic Physics, Heidelberg 1959, unbuilt competition project; plan and elevation of three linked laboratory blocks.

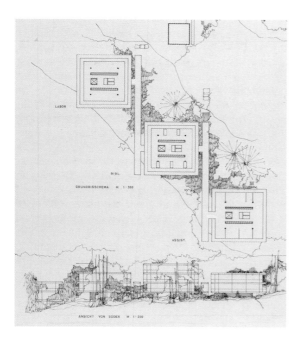

respected Mendelsohn more, he would not have been a party to the destruction of the Schocken Store in Stuttgart.[42]

Eiermann's architecture was also exclusive in its relationship with the landscape, showing by this both the strengths and the weaknesses of the period. The park-like setting with mature trees was gently landscaped by Walter Rossow, with beds of pebbles to define the territories of the buildings where no one should step, a limited network of more inviting paths allowing access across the lawns, and places to sit out to eat and drink. But Eiermann believed in the opposition of architecture and landscape, so nature was treated as a backdrop for the object-like buildings, a contemplative vista more than an outdoor room. The buildings were also detached from the ground, hanging in the air on modestly receding brick plinths and linked by horizontal bridges that played against the slope. The poised galleries hanging just above the landscape recalled the effect of the Katsura Palace in Japan, an influence acknowledged by Eiermann, but they lacked the Katsura's invitation to partake of the garden.

The raised position of the pavilions followed the Miesian precedent of the Farnsworth House – detached on stilts – rather than of the Barcelona Pavilion, which had a full groundwork like a classical base, or the later Neue Nationalgalerie (Blundell Jones 2002, Ch. 14) which is conceptually similar. Because of his modernist training, Eiermann's work was less obviously neo-classical than that of Mies, but his belief in rational order, geometry, symmetry and proportion grew directly out of traditional classical academic teaching. Eiermann became professor and the dominating presence at a school of architecture with a neo-classical background in radially-planned Baroque Karlsruhe, the city where Weinbrenner had built and Friedrich Ostendorf had launched his re-classicising attacks on Hermann Muthesius.[43] Arguably, it was a neo-classical tendency to seek a design complete in itself and replete in its own ordering system.

A weakness of self-sufficient pavilions like those at Brussels was that they encouraged the tendency to make buildings detached entities set off against a green setting, which was anti-urban. Eiermann went on to design many projects in pavilion form, including a student centre in Kiel of 1958, the Max Planck Institute in Heidelberg of 1959, Mannheim Town Hall of 1959-60 and the College for Social Science at Linz in 1961. Pavilion thinking

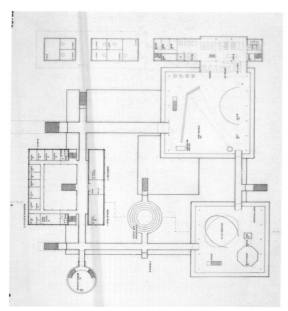

21 Student union and Mensa for Kiel, 1958, unbuilt competition project; plan showing organisation of linked square pavilions.

22. Kaiser Wilhelm Memorial Church, Berlin-Charlottenburg 1957-63.

even extended to his best religious building, the Kaiser Wilhelm Memorial Church at the centre of West Berlin, where the pure geometric volumes were disposed on a stepped platform in a dense urban situation. The preservation of the half-ruined Baroque tower as yet another element in the composition was a late addition,[44] and contemporary commentators found it compromising and uncomfortable.[45] Yet that very contrast is the now outstanding feature of Eiermann's best known building, perhaps because it breaks the self-sufficiency of the new elements to force a relationship, and because it acknowledges the historical layering. It is a certainly disquieting, yet it breaks through Eiermann's autistic perfection: that quality of completeness, of limpid order, that we can no longer strive for quite so innocently. One of Eiermann's most perceptive assistants, the architect Helmut Striffler whose work appears in Chapter 7, shed light on this in a reminiscence about zero hour and the new beginnings after 1945:

The dream that industry, hitherto dedicated to the most efficient techniques of extermination, could turn instead to rebuilding, made us intoxicated with loud possibilities as Egon Eiermann put it. In this condition of "professional drunkenness", he could dismiss the rubble heaps, the bizarre mountains of detritus, the twisted beams and

broken columns, replacing them with a clean rectangular world. Through sheer self-control he arrived at a discipline which acknowledged no more than the minimal products of industry: bricks, steel beams, sheets of glass, and also the virgin board. He discovered his architectural language in the effort to make buildings out of these elements, buildings which also expressed some complexity of content. He handed on this relentless rationality but not the spirit of the forms produced, for he knew in the end a hint of poetry would melt this collection of ideas together into a whole. [46]

Through sincere, dogged determination, and by limiting the frame of his operation to that which was controllable, Eiermann achieved the high quality of work that he strove for. This stance doubtless reflected the natural essence of his personality and attitude, but it also helped him come to terms with his times through disengagement. First he disengaged himself from the Nazis, their policies and their architectural restrictions. Later he disengaged himself again from the physical and economic chaos left by their war. The aesthetic and ethical convictions to which he held must have given him great comfort and a firm sense of direction in a fast-changing and difficult world.

PBJ

34

Notes

1. He does not appear in Frampton's *Critical History* (Frampton 1985). He is mentioned once by Jencks who calls his work *'unmistakably Germanic in its tough efficiency'* but manages to misspell his name (Jencks 1973, p. 320).

2. Klotz 1977, p. 54.

3. Hatje 1963, article on Germany by Wolfgang Pehnt, p.127.

4. Blundell Jones 2002, pp. 14, 203.

5. See for example the write-up of the Brussels exhibition in *L'Architecture d'aujourd' hui* no. 81 December 1958, p. 94: *'Certain works of architecture of high intrinsic quality, perfection, and pursuit of established techniques exploited with elegance and brio to their ultimate consequences .. derive from the teachings of Mies van der Rohe'*: my translation.

6. Schirmer 1984, p. 11.

7. Posener 1995, p. 199; Klotz 1977, p. 140. Hentrich was founding partner of Hentrich and Petschnigg, another leading German firm of the 1960s on the Miesian side.

8. See account by Hentrich in Klotz 1977, p. 139.

9. Posener 1970, p. 10.

10. Posener 1995, p. 200.

11. Ibid, p. 199.

12. Bricks laid on edge in basketweave pattern with reinforcing bars laid both ways in alternate joints. It is thin and strong, and the lack of interlock between the bricks indicates the reinforcement. It was used by Poelzig in his chemical factory at Luban of 1912, and by many other Berlin architects in the 1920s, including Hugo Häring and Max Taut.

13. *'Das zeitgemässe Eigenhaus' Bauwelt* 1931 and Das wachsende Haus 1932, see Schirmer 1984, pp. 28, 29.

14. See Schirmer 1984, pp. 30-49.

15. On the Scharoun houses see Blundell Jones *'Hans Scharoun's private houses' The Architectural Review* 1983, pp. 59-67. In a recent booklet on Scharoun's Möller house of 1937, Andreas Ruby describes in detail the long struggles with the Baupolizei.

16. Rudolf Büchner in Schirmer 1984, pp. 19-20.

17. 'Gebt mir vier Jahre Zeit', Schirmer 1984, p. 34.

18. Shown in Schirmer 1984, p. 56. His office and records were destroyed in the war, so the list of works may be incomplete.

19. Hitler praised 'true practicality' and 'crystal-clear functionalism'. See Lane 1968, p. 204.

20. Factory and boiler house for Degea, Berlin-Wedding 1938, extension for Foerstner in Apolda 1938-9, and Factory for Märkische Metallbau 1939-41: see Schirmer 1984, pp. 44, 50-53.

21. Büchner calls the houses 'timeless' rather than the factories, see Schirmer 1984, p. 21.

22. Pevsner (presumably) in John Fleming, Hugh Honour, and Nikolaus Pevsner, *The Penguin Dictionary of Architecture* Harmondsworth, 1966.

23. Ruf was born in Munich in 1908, remaining there to study, practice and become professor; his buildings include the management school in Speyer (1954), the Art Academy (1955) and National Museum (1967) in Nuremberg. His most famous work is the German President's House in Bonn of 1964, see Pehnt 1970, pp. 50-51. He died in 1982.

24. Correspondence reproduced in Eiermann 1994, pp. 79-87, indicates a cordial relationship, but with Eiermann suggesting the division of work and also intruding quite heavily into the content and organisation of the exhibition, for which Hans Schwippert, architect of the Bonn Parliament, had been commissioned. His perfectionist zeal would leave nothing untouched.

25. As with Mies's New National Gallery, see Blundell Jones 2002, Ch. 14.

26. Norman Foster's Willis Faber & Dumas building in Ipswich (Chapter 12) seems like a solid black castle in the daytime, quite unimpregnable by comparison.

27. The layering and the lightness were taken up powerfully by Günter Behnisch in the 1970s and 1980s, see Chapter 8.

28. Eiermann, speech at Steel Congress, Luxemburg, 1964, reproduced in Schirmer 1984, p. 146: my translation.

29. Ibid.

30. Ibid.

31. *Architectural Forum*, June 1958, p. 79.

32. Ibid

33. *Architectural Review*, vol. 124, no. 739, 1958, p. 91.

34. Posener 1995, p. 201: my translation.

35. After the opening of the Neue Nationalgalerie he expressed disappointment in a letter that press reports about it not been entirely positive: Eiermann 1994, p. 204.

36. The Miesian paradox: see Blundell Jones 2002, Ch. 14 (pp. 203-214).

37. See correspondence in Eiermann 1994, pp. 79-87.

38. *Architects Journal* Vol. 127, No. 3300, 29 May 1958, p. 814

39. Klaus Lankheit in Schirmer 1984, p. 12.

40. On the symbolic basis of pollution ideas, see Douglas 1966.

41. In letters he was sour about the rising Philharmonie and accused both Scharoun and Aalto of setting a bad example to younger architects: see Eiermann 1994, pp. 174-175. He also criticised Le Corbusier's Ronchamp, see Schirmer 1984, p. 11.

42. He replaced it with a much poorer work of his own, excusing himself on the basis that it had become unworkable due to lack of escalators and air conditioning: see Schirmer 1984, pp. 162, 306.

43. Posener 1972.

44. The first versions tried to do without it: see Schirmer 1984, pp. 166-167.

45. Pehnt 1970, p. 30.

46. Striffler, *'Gewehrkügeln fliegen gerade' Werk und Zeit* no. 2/3, 1985, published in translation as *'Bullets travel in straight lines', The Architectural Review* February 1992, p. 37.

Chapter 3. Aldo van Eyck: Orphanage, Amsterdam, 1954-59

Aldo van Eyck was born in the Netherlands in 1918, but was educated in England before studying architecture at the ETH in Zurich. He worked with Jan Rietveld and 'de 8 en Opbouw' (the Dutch CIAM group) before setting up on his own in the early 1950s, but the most important achievement of his early career was a long series of children's playgrounds built across Amsterdam from 1947 onward under city architect Cornelis van Eesteren. Van Eyck designed them at first as an employee of the city but later as an independent architect, using a repetitive but endlessly varied vocabulary of climbing frames, sandpits, rails, benches, trees and paving. Apart from their primary social purpose, the playgrounds were also devices to heal the city fabric, rescuing street corners, forgotten squares and vacant sites, and over thirty years no less than 734 of them were built.[1] They had to be functional as well as offering pleasing compositions, and each site offered a different kind of space requiring a different response: they were linking spaces, pieces of the public 'in-betweenness' that was later to become an explicit van Eyck theme. At the same time they were a kind of architecture that not only offered but positively required interaction with the

user, for a dead playground is pointless. The architect may suggests uses, but children and their parents must first decide to enter and then discover how to take possession: there is an open endedness here that helped inform van Eyck's critique of narrow functionalism and went on to colour his whole career, as well as that of his protégé Herman Hertzberger.[2] Children were the theme in another early work, a series of primary schools (one built) at the new town of Nagele in the Noordoostpolder, which van Eyck had also helped to plan. Executed in 1954-6, these were modest asymmetrically planned single-storey structures. They had separately articulated classrooms, stepped corners, and an emphasis on exterior play and garden spaces. So keen was van Eyck to achieve the free-standing porches that marked the 'unfunctional' threshold structures between the classroom groups and the main courtyard, that he paid for them himself.[3]

In 1954 the city of Amsterdam decided to build a new orphanage on open ground south of the city, and van Eyck was given the commission because of his rising reputation with the playgrounds. It came at the right moment for the 36 year old architect, catching the wave of post-war welfare-

1. (below left) Dijkstraat playground by van Eyck, Amsterdam,1954.
2. (below) Plan of primary school by van Eyck at Nagele, 1956.

36

3. The orphanage inner courtyard and bridging upper wing. The circular enclosure was intended for a sculpture.

4. (below) Interior detail of Hendrik Berlage's Amsterdam Beurs, 1897-1910, showing the strongly expressed construction.

state idealism before it had lost its impetus, and providing him with sympathetic and imaginative clients and a relatively generous budget. This ideal project for a socially-minded architect also became the main vehicle for van Eyck's burgeoning architectural sensibility, a kind of built manifesto in which his ideas, the fruit of his own researches and debates with colleagues, could be tested. Completed in 1959, it established him as a leading figure across the world, adding to a reputation already gained at home as an articulate commentator and one of the Dutch representatives at CIAM. He had also been a founder member of Team Ten, the group deputed to organise the tenth conference of CIAM, whose critical stance soon led them to develop a break away organisation of their own that filled the gap when CIAM died. It was more modest and informal than CIAM, without great venues or recorded proceedings, but it was a key centre of architectural debate, and van Eyck was a leading contributor.[4] Other members with work discussed in this book are Alison and Peter

Smithson (Chapter 5), Ralph Erskine (Chapter 11) and Giancarlo De Carlo (Chapter 13). Van Eyck consolidated his intellectual position in 1960 as editor of the leading Dutch architectural magazine *Forum*, which he dominated for years. The orphanage therefore marked the establishment of his reputation and a peak in his career, for he never again managed to complete so large a project under such ideal circumstances, nor was he able to offer so radical a reinterpretation of space and technique. Although the social context has changed radically, the orphanage still offers hints for a child-centred architecture, and it stands out from the rest of van Eyck's oeuvre as his masterpiece and work most significant for architectural history.

Unity and variety

The orphanage is impressive for the sheer number of architectural issues that it engages, abreast of if not ahead of its time. Presented as an example in Reyner Banham's *The New Brutalism* of 1966, it certainly marks the prevalent rediscovery of texture and material, contrasting exposed brick-work with concrete that was sometimes in-situ and sometimes precast.[5] But this was far more profound than a mere issue of style: it reflected the effort to use a rational system without being overwhelmed by it. The inevitability of serial production had been one of the main assumptions of the modernists. The repetition of standard components meant adherence to an orthogonal grid and a strict module.[6] In Holland this 'module consciousness' was even stronger than elsewhere, as the landscape was dead flat and had long been planned out artificially in a grid, while brick, which is modular by nature, was the primary building material. At the beginning of the twentieth century, the leading proto-modernist Hendrik Berlage had set a strong precedent in modular planning with his famous Amsterdam Stock Exchange – in brick – which memorably put its construction on display. The virtues of geometric discipline were backed up by aesthetic theories advanced by Lauweriks and others, and later embraced by De Stijl. Clearly van Eyck was touched by this, regarding himself as a primary inheritor of the Dutch Modern Movement.[7] But as many architects of the 1950s and 1960s found out to their cost, a module can also be a strait-jacket, constraining the design from responding to anything other than its own technical process. Van Eyck saw this danger and avoided it with panache.

5. View from the outer courtyard through to the inner.

6. (below) The roofscape of small domes, some with central rooflights. This dictated a small scale, appropriate to children.

The orphanage was planned out on a strict grid with a module of 3.6 metres which set the basic scale of the whole institution to that of a domestic room-sized unit, but allowed these units to be combined into spaces up to four units long and four units wide. The basic module was small for a public building, but it set everything to the scale of the child, a policy carried through also in the vertical dimension, so that steps, seats and tables were set to children's heights and glazing bars were arranged to give the best view to them, rather than to adults. The unit could have columns at its corners or be bounded by a brick wall, but the visible edge of the building everywhere was unified by a series of precast lintels. There was something fundamental about this simple trabeated construction of regular columns supporting regular beams, almost as if van Eyck was suggesting a new column order: certainly he was echoing the classical idea that column and architrave are the essence of architecture. Each lintel had a long horizontal slot, usually glazed, which served both to make it recognisable as a symmetrical entity and to add a sense of fragility. The lintels assured the rhythm of the composition and set a continuous horizontal datum. As we shall see, the true structure was a grid of in-situ concrete beams running both ways behind, but it was the columns and lintels that made the system visible at its edges, also stating the basic 'room' or aedicule.

The decision to confine the building largely to a single floor made the roof hugely important, both as a source of light – daylight everywhere – and as a reminder of its sheltering nature. Van Eyck introduced no flat and neutral ceiling: instead there was an embracing canopy, a shallow dome over each unit, sometimes with a central skylight at its climax. The repeated domes carry the rhythm through like giant coffering, but each cell is centred on its own concavity. Domes tended to be seen as archaic forms associated with religious buildings and massive forms of construction, so it was notoriously difficult to use them in the twentieth century without seeming anachronistic,[8] but van Eyck's dome avoided these associations through pursuing its own technical logic, which made it modern. He invented a building system using repeated precast concrete domes as permanent shuttering, then putting steel reinforcement in the troughs between them before spraying concrete over the whole. The standard set of forms could run identically through, but long-spanning beams could be made to run unsupported across up to four units merely by increasing the reinforcement. This meant that the network of squares did not need supporting at every node, but only sporadically, allowing relatively free planning and the omission of inconvenient columns. In a further bid for variety, van Eyck introduced an occasional larger dome 10.8 metres square, covering three units in both directions. Also of sprayed reinforced concrete construction, and including rings of small skylights, these large domes were used exclusively to articulate the centre of each 'family' house occupied by a group of children. For younger children at ground level on the east side, they covered the main living spaces, while in the 'houses' of older children to the west they covered upper storey groups of bedrooms. The only other part of the complex permitted two storeys was the linear tract of staff quarters bridging the front courtyard. Columns supporting two floors remained of standard girth, additional strength again achieved with reinforcement.

A house is a small city and a city is a big house
Van Eyck's essay presenting the orphanage in *Forum* was entitled 'The Medicine of Reciprocity', in which he repeatedly criticised the way in which polarised thinking has led to things being divided and compartmentalised in a destructive way – individual and collective, architecture and urbanism, part and whole, unity and diversity:

The time has come to conceive of architecture urbanistically and of urbanism architecturally (this makes sensible nonsense of both terms), i.e. to arrive at the singular through plurality, and vice versa. As for this home for children, the idea was to persuade it to become both 'house' and 'city'; a city-like house, and a house-like city. I came to the conclusion that whatever space and time mean, place and occasion mean more, for space in the image of man is place, and time in the image of man is occasion. Split apart by the schizophrenic mechanism of deterministic thinking, time and space remain frozen abstractions. Place and occasion constitute each other's realisation in human terms. Since man is both the subject and object of architecture, it follows that its primary job is to provide the former for the sake of the latter. Furthermore, since place and occasion imply participation in what exists, lack of place – and thus of occasion – will cause loss of identity, isolation and frustration. A house should therefore be a cluster of places, and the same applies no less to a city.[9]

7. One of the external courts formed as part of the territory of a 'family' of children.
8. Edge of the orphanage giving way to garden as seen in restored and modified form in the 1990s.

At a time when architects were inclined to think of buildings as sculptural objects surrounded by a carpet of green space, the orphanage was hard to see as a whole except from the air. Not only would you have to walk right around to see its different parts, it was also subdivided by internal courtyards and its 'houses' were linked by what were consciously intended as internal streets. These in-between spaces were left in rough brick like the exterior, as opposed to plastered surfaces within the 'houses'. Van Eyck made comparisons with a coconut – rough and brown on the outside, milky white and soft within – and with a winter coat, its soft lining facing the body.[10] The 'streets' also had street-like lighting at night, and *'no lux meter was allowed to prove the advantages of an even distribution of light'*.[11] Not until nearly twenty years later did Colin Rowe publish in *Collage City* his famous observation that the modern city inverts figure and ground, the Corbusian Unité more or less fitting the space that is the focal court of the Uffizi,[12] but such figure-ground inversion, or ambiguity, was already evident in van Eyck's thinking. The mat-like orphanage plan binds together internal and external spaces in a free exchange. It was a kasbah-like structure, and van Eyck is reported actually to have pinned up a photograph of such a place in the orphanage.[13]

The recovery of the street as a place of public interaction was a strong theme of Team Ten which will be discussed further with respect to the Smithsons in Chapter 5. The group also shared an interest in mat-like plans, in which a warp and weft of primary and secondary streets could serve a series of static intermediate squares housing specialised activities. This idea reached its ultimate expression in the work of Team Ten's Candilis, Josic & Woods with their prize-winning but unbuilt planning proposal for Frankfurt-Römerberg of 1963 and the disappointingly labyrinthine Berlin Free University of 1963-73.[14] Even Giancarlo De Carlo proposed a mat-like organisation for a hospital in Mirano won in a competition of 1969, later built in reduced form.[15] If tied to this intellectual context, van Eyck was nonetheless both early and sophisticated in his response. Though part of the lure of the mat-like plan was its supposed flexibility, he had little sympathy for the 'flexophiles' and one aspect of 'reciprocity' was not to allow the organising system to prevent the creation of highly specific places.[16] He planned separate 'houses' for the eight family-like groups, each marked by a large dome and each with a courtyard, but those for the older groups of children differed from those for the younger. With bedrooms upstairs and views out over the surrounding suburb, they had more contact with the outside world, and their external courtyards were only semi-enclosed, encouraging use of the garden beyond. In the houses for children under ten, by contrast, the fully enclosed courtyard was more of a focal point, and was accompanied by a living room of the same size covered by one of the large domes, while sleeping quarters were off to the side. Further differentation was applied within the range of houses for younger children according to age-group (2-4, 4-6 etc.), in terms of courtyard treatment, subdivisions of the sleeping wing, and the treatment of the main domed room. To preserve child scale and to add a sense of centre, each main room had a sunken floor-well with built-in seating and a tiny playhouse, a room within a room. For the older children, sitting alcoves, a dining space and puppet theatre provided similar micro-worlds.

If we look to the plan as a whole in terms of content, there is again a strongly articulated organisation. The clear formal 'front' to the street and north contrasts with an informal back dissolving into the garden. The youngest, babies under two, occupy the rearmost house, while the oldest boys aged 14-20 are nearest the street, girls of the same age behind them. The territory of the orphanage is entered via a protective enclave, a long courtyard bridged by the staff accommodation as a second threshold, with reception and offices on its west open side, services and staff flats behind a wall to east. Only beyond the courtyard do internal streets lead off to the two groups of houses, each set on a diagonal line which provokes an echelon of corners both inside and out. This staggered arrangement has been compared with the planning of Frank Lloyd Wright and traditional Japanese architecture such as the Katsura Palace,[17] but it also invites comparison with the corner obsession of Erich Mendelsohn (see Blundell Jones 2002 Ch. 6). This reflected a struggle by pioneer modernists to avoid automatic recourse to the Beaux Arts type of classical plan in which they had been trained, with its central axis and symmetrically disposed wings. Although there are hints of large-scale symmetry in the orphanage's organisation, such as in the two splayed lines of house groups or the basic rectangular shape of the entrance court, axial formality is reserved mainly for the very small scale, within the room or court, and rooms are rarely axially

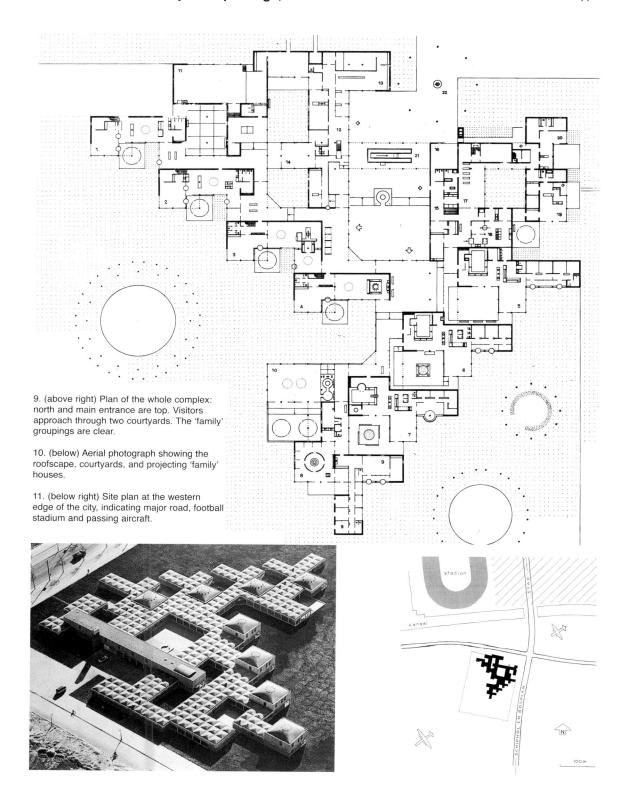

9. (above right) Plan of the whole complex: north and main entrance are top. Visitors approach through two courtyards. The 'family' groupings are clear.

10. (below) Aerial photograph showing the roofscape, courtyards, and projecting 'family' houses.

11. (below right) Site plan at the western edge of the city, indicating major road, football stadium and passing aircraft.

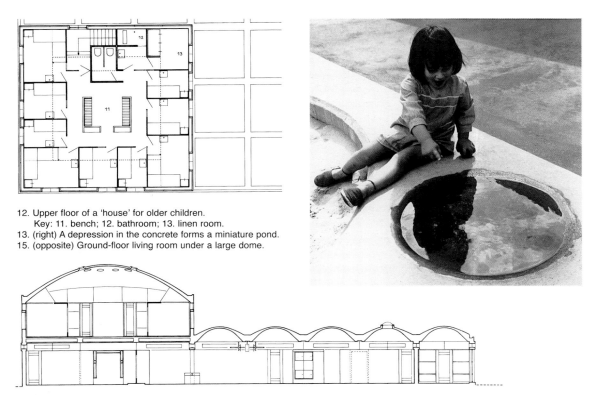

12. Upper floor of a 'house' for older children.
   Key: 11. bench; 12. bathroom; 13. linen room.
13. (right) A depression in the concrete forms a miniature pond.
15. (opposite) Ground-floor living room under a large dome.

14. Section and (below) lower floor plan of the 'house' for older children. Key: 1. living room; 2. tea-kitchen; 3. study; 4. reading corner; 5. cupboard; 6. wardrobe; 7. WC; 8. shower; 9. ring of lamps; 10. double bench.

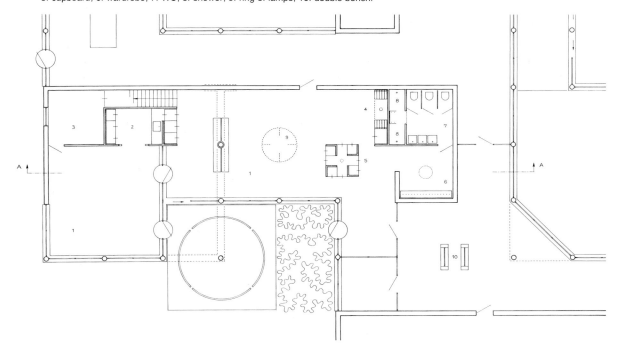

entered. There is even a game of axial shifts anotated by van Eyck in a published drawing.[18] He relished the way the routes around the building could play against the modular system, and he was also deeply sensitive about thresholds:

It seemed best to anchor the children's large house – little city – to the street, i.e. to the public sphere where they enter and leave it, by introducing a large open square as a transition between the reality outside and that inside. It is an in-between domain leading the trail gradually, in stages, helping to mitigate the anxiety that abrupt transition causes, especially in these children. Leaving home and going home are often difficult matters; to go in or out, to enter, leave or stay, are sometimes painful alternatives. Though architecture cannot do away with this truth it can still counteract it by mitigating instead of aggravating its effects. It is human to tarry.[19]

The arriving visitor first encounters the open corner of a court where the building steps back from the street. The path here was intended to pass through a ring of trees which would more or less fill the corner with shade in summer.[20] The outer court could be entered by outsiders, and by officials requiring to speak with staff or the head, via the glass wall to west; but the route for residents carried on through to an inner court with entrances to west and south leading to the two groups of children's houses. The threshold between the two courts was the bridge of the staff wing set on columns, and beneath it was the ramp down to the basement bicycle park. To give the inner court some focus and sense of arrival, a special circular setting was made for an intended sculpture by Carel Visser. The glass walls of the cloister-like passages on two sides meant that visitors would be observed and could be challenged visually before they reached the door. For the returning children on the other hand, the penetration of so many thresholds made them feel deep within the heart of the building, well protected. After entering the internal street space, there were further thresholds marked by turns in the route and also by one or two step level changes which reduced the ceiling height, making the area beyond seem more private and intimate and marking boundaries within the complex. These subtle changes of level were quite unprompted by the site, which, being sand like much of Holland, was relentlessly flat.

Drawing on anthropology

Van Eyck has been widely credited with drawing architects' attention to social anthropology as a source of knowledge about human beliefs and behaviours, and certainly his article in *Forum* on the Dogon people of Mali, later reprinted in English by Jencks and Baird, marked the beginning of a new interest in the way architecture has been employed to help make sense of the world.[21] In fact the publication about the Dogon and the visit to Africa that prompted it post-dated the building of the orphanage, but van Eyck was already widely read and well-travelled, and he presumably already knew Marcel Griaule's book *Dieu d'Eau: entretiens avec Ogotemmêli* with its rich descriptions of the cosmic resonances of Dogon village and house, published as early as 1948.[22] Van Eyck was not the only member of Team Ten interested in peasant or vernacular architecture: his friend De Carlo had organised the exhibition 'Spontaneous architecture' at the Milan Triennale of 1951; but van Eyck gained a special insight which allowed a critical addendum to orthodox modernist funct-ionalism. This was certainly reflected in the matter of thresholds discussed above, for in most if not all traditional societies these are foci of ritual and symbolic interest. Anthropological influence is also felt in van Eyck's archetypal use of the circle to make spaces of gathering and concentration, potential social foci of many kinds, in contrast with the neutrality of the rectangular grid. But perhaps most important of all was the awareness, vividly exemplified in the orphanage, that a social institution may exemplify its entire structure in its deployment of rooms and spaces. This was an idea to which lip-service had been paid by the modernists, but usually without it being consistently carried through. The articulation of Gropius's Bau-haus building, for example, differentiated between workshop, classroom and residential blocks, but suppressed the identity of the socially important theatre and library (Blundell Jones 2002, pp. 61-72). Only Hugo Häring and Hans Scharoun seriously tried to articulate all parts fully and hierarchically, a practice best illustrated in Scharoun's unbuilt design for a school in Darmstadt of 1951, but realised in a modified form with the Geschwister Scholl School, Lünen, of 1958-62 (Blundell Jones 2002, pp. 59-60).[23] The main difference between these works and van Eyck's orphanage is that Scharoun permitted himself a broader planning vocabulary, exaggerating the differences between elements with changes of dimension, shape and orientation, and with frequent departures from the right angle. Van Eyck, in contrast, worked within the discipline of his module. He managed none-theless to articulate 'family' groups, to differentiate between them, to provide a sense of centre, to respect front and back, and to set everything in a meaningful hierarchical sequence of oppositions or adjacencies.

Van Eyck's anthropological studies must have confirmed the validity of the idea, for in traditional pre-industrial societies the layouts of buildings and settlements commonly reflect social structure: this might even be considered a dominant principle.[24] Among the Dogon of Mali, the family house on a standard square plan represents symbolically the union of husband and wife, while its facade of 10 x 8 squares is a memorial to the ancestors. Walls tie the house to a family compound which includes separately articulated granaries, celebrated with sculpted decoration and pointed roofs. They are models of the universe, and hold in four compart-ments the four sacred crops on which life depends. The village as a whole represents a human body with the smithy and elders' parliament at its head, an altar for its male member and the oil mortar for its vagina.[25] The explicit connections between ploughing, weaving, laying out a square house or granary, and providing a gridded facade to house the ancestors, may have suggested to van Eyck an archetypal justification for his modular unit as reflecting the starting point for architecture, quite apart from the nesting symbolic series which ties house and village to universe, inspiring van Eyck's house/city reciprocity.

Anthropology was in its structuralist phase at the time of van Eyck's interest, and he is usually credited along with Herman Hertzberger for having invented 'Dutch Structuralism'. At a physical building level this had to do with creating a structural system that would make rational sense of production and building processes, accepting the imperatives of the factory, while at the same time allowing life to play as many variations as possible, including those quite unforeseen by the designers.[26] But as an intellectual movement in anthropology, psychology and linguistics, structur-alism was about the pursuit of implicit underlying structures in human knowledge and in manifest-ations of culture. This could mean the underlying structures of language sought by Noam Chomsky, which seem to be built into every child's mind,

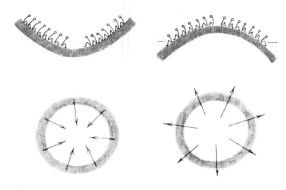

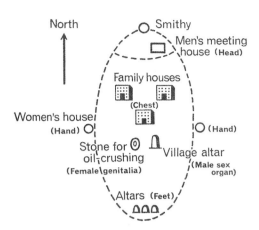

16. Van Eyck's diagrams of the social use of a circle, inward- and outward-looking.
17. (right) Diagram of the symbolism of a Dogon village, from Marcel Griaule, *Conversations with Ogotemmêli.*

allowing it to discover and construct its own speech from what it hears around it. On the other hand, it could be the kind of underlying structures in a myth, a song, a village layout or a kinship structure which Claude Lévi-Strauss was analysing to such effect and which seemed to offer a key to a universal understanding of mankind.[27] Van Eyck shared this bid for universality, and for a reintegration of modern life with what humanity has always been:

Architecture is a constant rediscovering of constant human proportions translated into space. Man is always and everywhere essentially the same. He has the same mental equipment though he uses it differently according to his cultural or social back-ground, according to the particular life-pattern of which he happens to be a part. Modern architects have been harping continually on what is different in our time to such an extent even that it has lost touch with what is not different, with what is always essentially the same.[28]

The orphanage began with enthusiasm and ended in collapse. Intended landscaping and artworks were never funded, and many of van Eyck's light-hearted and perceptive gestures to entertain and stimulate the children, like the distorting mirrors built into the floor, were later removed as danger-ous distractions, while interior details were lost by thoughtless modifications and overpainting. Mean-while expert opinion everywhere bemoaned the effect of institutions and institutionalisation, so pop-ular wisdom came to accept that unwanted children were best fostered singly in ordinary families. By the 1980s, after only twenty years of use, the

building had lost its original purpose, and in 1986 it was even threatened with demolition. Herman Hertzberger launched a campaign to save it, and it now houses the Berlage Institute, a school of architecture, along with other municipal functions. It seems ironic that this most social of architects, who desperately sought to reconnect the art of building with the rituals of everyday life, should have expended so much energy on a building type so soon and so completely doomed. Van Eyck's enthusiasm for a programme that involved creating a house or city for a whole society was understandable, yet despite all his good intentions it ended up closer to social engineering than to the spontaneous architecture he so admired in the anthropological record.

Twenty years after the orphanage, van Eyck gained a chance to make another institution, Hubertus House of the late 1970s, a home for unmarried mothers and their children in central Amsterdam.[29] It was half new-build and half conversion, and there was much more debate with those who were to run it, resulting in a more harmonious fit. It was well received both by the clients and the press, and it well exemplifies van Eyck's architectural sensitivity, his continuing interests in place-making, articulation of social relationships and elaborated thresholds. It also allowed him an opportunity for bold experiments with colour and an urban facade, but the whole nature of the building was contingent: that is to say it was highly specific in its response to site and programme, and therefore it needs to be understood within its own terms, not as a general proposition. Also it is the very nature of the institution it houses to be private and protective, a

18. Van Eyck's Hubertus House for mothers and their children, Amsterdam, 1980.

world where abused women can retreat into safety, so its virtues are not for public display. This intense specificity, both social and architectural, limited its exemplary relevance, even if it was suggesting a noble way of pursuing the art of architecture – perhaps the most noble way.[30] The orphanage, by contrast, was breathtakingly daring in its general concept and gave the world a crucial demonstration that a large house could be a small city just when that message was most needed. It seemed for a moment that the technical imperative of modernism could be allied with a full sense, as van Eyck liked to put it, of 'welcoming one's homecoming'.

PBJ

Notes

1. For a history of the playgrounds see Lefaivre and de Roode 2002, shorter version in Lefaivre and Tzonis 1999, pp.13-78.
2. See Hertzberger 1991, original texts Hertzberger 1973: the key project was his Diagon housing in Delft, a framework encouraging the inhabitants to add gestures of their own.
3. See Ligtelijn 1999, p. 86.
4. For the story of Team Ten see Risselada and den Heuvel 2005.
5. Reyner Banham coined the term in an article for *The Architectural Review* in December 1955: the eponymous book did not appear until 1966. There Banham illustrated the orphanage on pp. 158-163, though he wrote only one paragraph about it on p. 128. His parting apologia calls Brutalism *'an ethical stand, the persistence of an idea that the relationships of the parts and materials of a building are a working morality',* p.135.
6. This was the essence of Gropius's Weissenhof house of 1927 designed on a 1.06 metre grid: see Blundell Jones 2002, pp. 16-17.
7. He pursued many projects connected with painting and sculpture: famously the sculpture pavilion at Arnhem of 1965-6, and he often declared allegiance with 'The Great Gang', the leaders of the Modern Movement. He loved the works of Arp and Brancusi, and commented that Rietveld: *'could really make a square laugh'*. He rehabilitated Jan Duiker as a Modernist hero in a special edition of Forum.
8. Notable exceptions include Kahn's Kimbell Museum and Lewerentz's Church at Klippan, both in Blundell Jones 2002 pp. 229-240 and 215-228. Both Le Corbusier and Hugo Häring suggested vaults for domestic construction, the former with his Petite Maison de Weekend of 1935, the latter in a house for an exhibition in 1930, see Blundell Jones 1999, pp. 123-125.
9. This most famous of van Eyck's essays was first published in *Forum* 1960-61 no. 6-7, then in English in *Architect's Year Book,* 1962, pp. 173-178, and reprinted in Ligtelijn 1999, pp. 88-89. Another version, as presented by van Eyck at the CIAM conference in Otterlo, appeared in Newman 1961, pp. 26-34.
10. *'The Medicine of Reciprocity'*, Ligtelijn 1999, p. 89.
11. Ibid.
12. Rowe and Koetter 1978.
13. Lefaivre and Tzonis 1999, p. 101.
14. Both discussed in Frampton 1980, pp. 277-278.
15. See *The Architectural Review* March 2002, pp. 64-67.
16. *'The Medicine of Reciprocity'*, Ligtelijn 1999, p. 88.
17. Lefaivre and Tzonis 1999, p. 104.
18. Ligtelijn 1999, p. 98.
19. *'The Medicine of Reciprocity'*, Ligtelijn 1999, p. 89.
20. This gentle device anticipated Kahn's grove of trees at the Kimbell Museum (Blundell Jones 2002, pp. 229-240).
21. *'Architecture of Dogon' Architectural Forum* September 1961, pp. 116-121. Baird and Jencks 1969, pp. 170-213.
22. English edition *Conversations with Ogotemmêli*, Oxford University Press 1965. Kenneth Frampton reports that van Eyck's interest in anthropology dated from the early 1940s, Frampton 1980, p. 276.
23. See Blundell Jones 1995, pp. 136-151.
24. *'In every instance that we have seen, social relationships rather than geometrical order appear to be the major determinant in the placing of buildings',* Fraser 1968, p. 47.
25. For all this see Griaule 1965.
26. Herman Hertzberger particularly developed this, creating half a gesture to be filled in by users, see Hertzberger 1973.
27. See Lévi-Strauss 1970.
28. Van Eyck, statement at the CIAM Otterlo congress of 1959, published in Newman 1961, p. 27.
29. See van Eyck 1982.
30. This is a constant paradox with the organic tradition of modernism, that is the architecture of specificity, for the more unique the response to circumstances, the less can a work provide a clear paradigm.

Chapter 4. Gottfried Böhm: Town Hall, Bensberg, 1962-71

Though internationally respected for a long series of good buildings and decorated with prestigious awards such as the Pritzker Prize,[1] Gottfried Böhm (b. 1920) has remained a marginal figure in the architectural debates of the last forty years. This is partly because he himself has chosen to be neither a theorist nor a propagandist, talking about his own work only modestly in an unpretentious and largely descriptive fashion. He could speak movingly about place and light, about routes and thresholds, about how people use a room and which materials seem appropriate, but he has generally eschewed philosophical parallels and complicated intellectual alibis.[2] Despite holding the title of professor for some years at Aachen, he founded no school or style, and always fought shy of the cult of personality that goes with the star system, preferring if possible to let his architectural and artistic work speak for itself.[3] But most of all, he has remained a marginal figure because neither in the modernist nor in the postmodernist periods did his work fit the trends and categories established by architectural critics and historians: chameleon-like, it was too complex, too changeable, too multi-faceted, but also too specific for repetition or direct emulation. If one had to place him in relation to the key modernist polarity identified at the start of Blundell Jones 2002, the universal versus the specific, he would definitely fall on the side of the specific – that of Häring, Scharoun, Asplund and Aalto – though he did not lack admiration for the work of Mies.

The reason is his great sensitivity to site and region, attending to land form, building profile and local style, the building being shaped by its context. The work examined here is typical, for without the presence of its old castle, Bensberg's modern town hall would be unthinkable.

Gottfried Böhm's independence is not unconnected with that of his father Dominikus Böhm (1880-1955), one of the leading German Roman Catholic church architects of the previous generation. Usually categorised as an expressionist, Dominikus Böhm was in fact trained by Theodor Fischer at Stuttgart, imbibing that great teacher's commitment to *genius loci* and regional style.[4] The elder Böhm went on to make his name in the early 1920s with buildings for the Benedictines at Vaals. Here he pursued a bold reinterpretation of bricky gothic, with polychromatic banding and daring corbels, and this sense of tactility and material realism ran on right through his *oeuvre*.[5] By the late 1920s he was making bold experiments with variations on concrete vaults and with church layouts reinterpreting liturgical space. In the era of the 'new objectivity' churches were perhaps something of a contradiction, clinging to an old mysticism with forms that could be dismissed as 'irrational'. Between 1930 and 1970 they suffered a marked tendency towards formal indulgence and experiment, so that any new building with a markedly unusual or irregular form standing out among the boxes was likely to be a church.[6]

1. (left) Gottfried Böhm, sketch of Bensberg Town Hall.
2. (right) Dominikus Böhm, Benedictine monastery at Vaals, 1923.

48

3. Town hall as seen from a street in the old town.
4. (below) Plan showing town hall in relation to market place.

Yet at the same time, the need to respect their sacred purpose reserved for churches parts of architecture's traditional role that were being squeezed out elsewhere by the 'merely functional'. The church architect had somehow to continue supplying atmosphere, sensitivity: the aesthetic

continued to matter. Gottfried grew up with this, trained first in architecture from 1942-46 at the T.U. Munich and then additionally in fine art as a sculptor. He started to work in his father's practice in 1947, but he also worked under Rudolf Schwarz, another great German church architect whom he later called his teacher. The task was the post-war replanning of Cologne.[7] After a short period in the United States Böhm returned to work for his father, inheriting the office on the latter's death in 1955. He continued to work with the same Roman Catholic clients, for whom he built social buildings and further churches, including his masterpiece in that form, the Cathedral at Neviges of 1964. The Böhm family practice was based in Cologne, and almost all of Gottfried's early work was carried out in that locality. It is fitting that an architect with a 'regionalist' heritage and such concern for *genius loci* should have such a geographically specific field of operation.

The place

Bensberg is a small town a few kilometres from Cologne, part of Bergisch-Gladbach. It grew up around a thirteenth-century castle, the residence of the Dukes of Berg, which served a defensive purpose until the end of the Thirty Years War in 1648. Subsequently it fell into ruins, while the Dukes built themselves a magnificent new Baroque palace on a classical plan further up the hill. In 1859 the old castle's remains were converted into a monastery which was extended in 1897 as a hospital, these additions masking the forms of the older historic structures. In 1961 the municipality decided to bring together its various departments, which had been scattered across the town, on to the old castle site. They set up a limited architectural competition

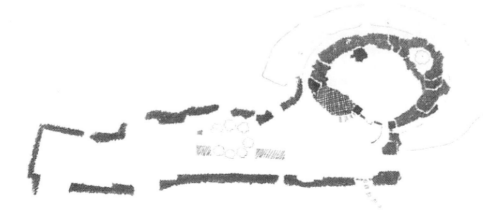

5. View at entrance to the castle courtyard, with old castle towers to left and new one to right: Bergfried tower, behind, has pointed roof.
6. (below) Section through main court, showing changing ground level.

among twelve architects, emphasising the importance of respecting the old castle.[8] In December 1962 Gottfried Böhm was awarded first prize and complimented on his artistic sensitivity. He gained the commission and the building went ahead very largely as planned, the first stage being completed in 1967 and the second in 1971.[9]

Böhm's first key decision was to demolish the nineteenth century buildings in order to expose the original castle walls, whose circuit became the basis for the new plan. This was a highly selective move, abolishing signs of an intermediate history, but Böhm considered it necessary for the clarity of his reinterpretation. The one high remaining piece of medieval wall on the north-west side was retained, along with a substantial tower, the Bergfried, and two lesser medieval towers also on the west side, which he used to flank and define the

7. Town Hall seen from the east across the valley, and the later Baroque Schloss to right further up the hill.

new entrance. Böhm decided to retain the steeply sloping castle courtyard, letting the horizontally layered new building play against it. From the south-western entry the plan seemed now to wind up in a spiral, culminating in the curved piece of thick castle wall set between two existing towers: this was the obvious place hierarchically to set the council chamber, the social and political heart. The tail of the building could unwind clockwise around and down the hill, stepping down gradually from seven storeys to three. The numerous offices and meeting rooms of the civic departments could be distributed at several levels to either side of a broad internal passage, enlivened by angular turns and occasional open bays with views to the outside world. At the south-east corner, where the castle outline projected, it was possible to short-circuit the loop with an extra wing of offices, opening the spinal passage into a small courtyard with a new pentagonal corner stair. The crucial remaining decision was where to place the main entrance and hub of vertical circulation. Böhm set it to the north east, at the highest point of the rising courtyard, directly opposite the gap in the west wall through which the building was to be approached. Placed at the centre of the tallest part of the office tract, this allowed convenient distribution in both directions and a slightly raised entrance from the car park at the rear, while the piece of building linking it through to the council chamber could be developed

as foyer and vestibule. The entrance was turned into a tower, projecting it up to compete with the remaining castle towers among other medieval and baroque towers in the Bensberg skyline.

The tower

Böhm's tower is the key gesture for the whole project. It follows medieval precedent in providing the main vertical circulation with its stepped spiral stair. This is made visible on the courtyard side by the spiral glazing, which steps up in the same direction as the hill in contrast with the horizontal layers of offices. The tower also tapers towards the top, both exaggerating vertical perspective and expressing the reduction in pedestrian traffic. It continues to rise a full five storeys beyond top office level, in order to exceed the slate-clad cap of the Bergfried tower, establishing its priority in the skyline. This upper part is entirely unfunctional, containing no room or viewing gallery, its faceted concrete form developed intuitively through delicate sketches and clay models. Critics have inevitably called it 'sculptural', stressing the personal touch. It was perhaps due to his engagement with church architecture that Böhm retained such sensitivity to the importance of towers as messengers of a building's role and aspirations, but it was becoming a rare concern. The 1960s was for towers perhaps the most banal period in the whole of architectural history. Bell towers had lost their

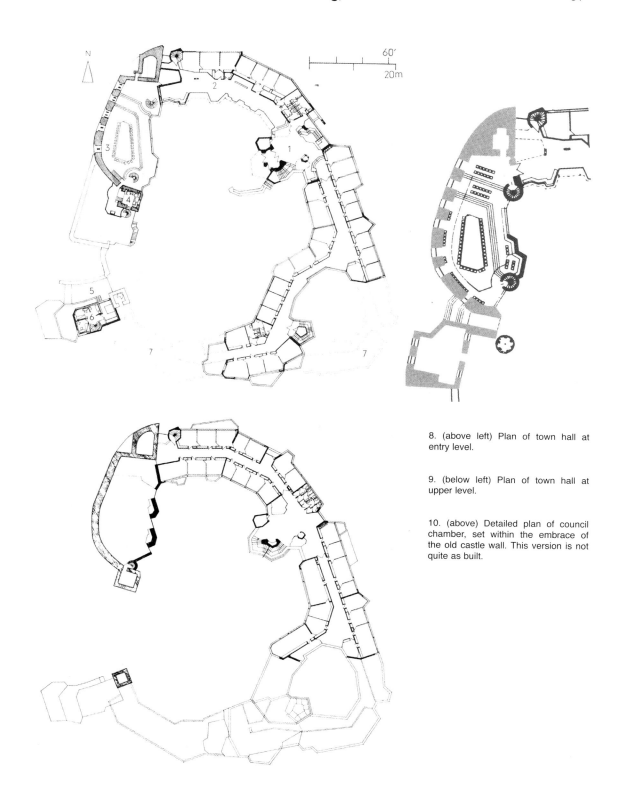

8. (above left) Plan of town hall at entry level.

9. (below left) Plan of town hall at upper level.

10. (above) Detailed plan of council chamber, set within the embrace of the old castle wall. This version is not quite as built.

11. Tower and main entrance.

12. (below left) Gottfried Böhm, Church of St Gertrud, Cologne 1962-65 street view.

13. (below right) Gottfried Böhm, Pilgrimage Cathedral at Neviges near Cologne, 1964, pinnacle of the main roof.

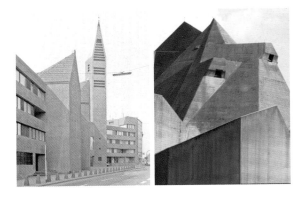

acoustic command in an increasingly noisy world, and the hierarchical distinction hitherto reserved for churches and palaces – or even for the competing families of San Gimignano – had been usurped by corporations. Mies's famous Seagram building of 1957 had provided the international precedent for glass office blocks. Its inhabited storeys were largely identical, the sky scraped merely by the rational cage covering the air-conditioning apparatus, not even the functional lightning conductors being made visible. At the same time residential tower blocks were rising across the world, their forms dictated by no more than the reach of the crane and the logic of prefabricated assembly, their effect on the skyline left almost accidental. Gaston Bachelard's famous book *La poétique de l'espace*, pointed out the universal polarity of the cellar and the attic, the lure of the philosopher's tower and of our deeply-lodged ideas about the opposed properties of earth and sky, but it was not yet widely known.[10] In this context, not only was it daring of Böhm to propose spending money on a completely anti-functional tower: it was extraordinary that he had the compositional skill to achieve it so convincingly, thereby winning the competition outright.

Consider the problem. The importance of a tower's termination had long been recognised with the spires, lanterns, and domes that in earlier centuries had received great elaboration, yet in the twentieth century repeating almost any kind of traditional elaboration came to appear eclectic, or worse still kitsch. Old crafts like the slatework on the Baroque helmet of the Bergfried tower were no longer available, and the new technologies seemed to demand simplicity and directness. Böhm's answer was to use solid concrete, exploiting its affinity with stone and its capacity to take on the shape of the mould. But while the material was simple and monolithic, the form could be complex, sometimes echoing the roof geometry of earlier towers, sometimes suggestive of a rock formation, but rising to a pure pyramid. Door-sized openings and balconies beneath the summit restated the human scale and suggested a human presence, but the tower remained a mysterious place, unavailable for visits. Böhm's sketches and models show that it was always multifaceted, rising to a point from the spiral stair and lift shaft, but the shape developed through many versions. The monolithic nature of the concrete enhanced the play of light and shadow, changing across the day. The success of this tower is not unrelated to a whole series of

14. (above) View within court looking across towards the glazed wall of the council chamber. The effect of the cobbled sloping ground played against the horizontal layers of the building is surprisingly powerful.

15. (right) Details of the council chamber glazing, with frameless vertical joints and separation of the structure.

16. (below right) Details of the foyer glazing, with frameless vertical and horizontal joints and the same level maintained right through.

17. (below) View up the side of the tower showing its changing shape and dimensions.

other projects in which Böhm was engaged around the same time, including the churches of St Gertrud in Cologne and St Matthew in Düsseldorf-Garath, the Cathedral at Neviges, and the chapel of the children's home at Bergisch Gladbach-Refrath. All had faceted concrete roofs rising to one or more points, the three-dimensional effects of which were repeatedly explored in sketches and models.[11]

Despite the context of medieval remains, the building has also been called 'futuristic' and the strongly emphasised horizontal glazing is a hallmark of modernism – one of Le Corbusier's Five Points in fact, but in this case more reminiscent of the work of Mendelsohn (see Blundell Jones 2002, Ch. 6). It was only possible by cantilevering the concrete edges out from the inner structure, though the metal-framed windows are set back to create an impression of solidity that was actually due to the insulated cavity construction.

Looking at the whole, the breaking of the horizontals at bays and corners, which occurs at different heights on different levels, is of great importance for the compositional balance. It also reflects the presence of different kinds of room within, as with the lavatories on the back where the cill is raised but the horizontal line of the head runs through. There are two important exceptions to the mainly horizontal waist to ceiling glazing. One is on the ground floor stretching from the entrance to the council chamber, where faceted glass runs from floor to ceiling. In the council chamber itself the glass wall reaches a height of two storeys, expressing the desire for maximum continuity between inside and out, and stressing that council business is public business. Here Böhm took the trouble to minimise the cills and to keep internal paving at the same level as external to stress spatial continuity.

The other exceptional piece of glazing is on the tower, whose spiral progress is marked by glass not only set flush with the outside wall, but also frameless at its vertical joints. This daring usage stretched the available technology to the limit in 1964, ten years before the breakthrough in completely frameless glazing made by Norman Foster at Ipswich (see p. 159), but we should notice that unlike Foster's work the different types of glazing used by Böhm are not applied to the whole building but used instead to articulate certain parts, set at the service of the spatial experience.

Culmination of a route

The building needed a formal presence in the town, and its well-judged massing is important, but Böhm was interested in much more than sculptural form. In the 1960s, as buildings became increasingly like packaging, and gridded plans with endless blind corridors made visitors dependent on written signs for navigation, he was among those architects who insisted on the value of legible routes, of an architecture that tells you where to go and celebrates progress along a route. Both his father and his teacher Rudolf Schwarz had been deeply concerned with the reinterpretation of liturgical space, and Schwarz's theories were summarised in a book *Vom Bau der Kirche*.[12] His spatial diagrams point back to two archetypes, the circular concentric space of 'holy intimacy' and the linear axial space of 'holy journey', which are perhaps the archetypes of all architecture.[13] He went on to explore in further diagrams the various ways in which these might meaningfully be combined. A very early church project by Dominikus Böhm from 1923 showed concern with the same theme, with an oval linear space leading towards a circular sanctuary defined by 12 columns explicitly named 'Circumstantes', the apostles standing around their Lord. Forty years later, in one of his most important projects – the Cathedral at Neviges – his son Gottfried had to deal with the most intense combination of the linear and the central. It is a pilgrimage church dedicated to the Virgin Mary and the holy journey is the journey of a lifetime, an intensified experience whose stages must be registered by the pilgrim, but which must also culminate in a holy of holies, a place of arrival. The final part of the route winding around up the hill was therefore designed as a series of stages divided periodically by broad waves of steps, and the mountainous cathedral beyond reveals itself gradually as the corner is turned. When they finally reach the building, the pilgrims are plunged into a mystic gloom relieved only by candles and a handful of stained glass windows, the space having become unfathomable due to its complex irregular geometry.[14] It is a place of intense contemplation and togetherness, under a great echoing void which amplifies and merges all sounds, and bids one keep one's peace.

This example shows at its extreme a sense of spatial progression and focus that can be found throughout Böhm's work. In his housing projects he always showed concern with threshold, and the houses of his children's village are entered by tiny

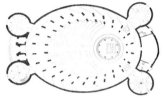

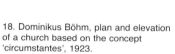

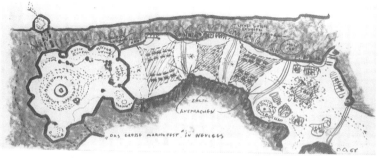

18. Dominikus Böhm, plan and elevation of a church based on the concept 'circumstantes', 1923.
19. (above right) Cathedral at Neviges: the end of the pilgrimage route, rising to the church.
20. (right) Böhm's sketch of the pilgrimage route animated like a market-place.

bridges meant to cross a little stream, though in execution it was reduced to a storm drain.[15]

Site sketches of Bensberg indicate Böhm's interest in the way the entrance to the castle courtyard, flanked by two medieval towers, relates to the existing town square running along the contour and punctuated by a ring of trees (Fig. 4). Initially he intended to bring the northern pedestrian entrance through the base of its tower, and the centre of the gap was to reveal a low part of the old castle wall interrupted by a sitting bay, while a narrow ramp at the south edge would provide access for service vehicles. In the revised version, existing walls within the northern side of the gap were retained to define the Ratskeller, a public restaurant mediating between the territory of the town hall and the public realm, while the rest of the gap was left open with the paving flowing out. Böhm placed the porter's flat traditionally to command the right hand side of the entrance. Stone paving unifies the sloping court and the tower-entrance

beckons, but glass to the left reveals the council chamber, as if the deliberations of representatives might spill into the court.

Böhm used the concave shape of the old castle wall to create an asymmetrical room (Fig. 10), reinforced with space-defining steps which also produce a pair of lower galleries, and with a polygonal table left seatless at its narrow end. This gives the chamber a centre of gravity opposite the tightest part of the castle's curve. It also means the whole space is inflected towards the courtyard, its focus set neither on the mayor as boss nor on a circle of councillors turned in upon themselves. As one might expect, this room is the tallest in the building and includes an upper gallery around one side. In the upper part of the old west wall Romanesque windows were reconstructed from the castle's earliest phase,[16] linking civic power today with the memory of feudal power eight hundred years ago.

21. West wall of the council chamber with Romanesque windows reconstructed from archaeological fragments. The Bergfried tower is to left.

22. South end of the complex ending in the porter's flat.

Crowning the town

Just as it would be wrong to talk about 'sculptural massing' without the accompanying spatial progression, so it would also be wrong to talk about the progression without considering the integration of the building into the town. Many commentators have pointed out the similarity between Böhm's town hall and Bruno Taut's idea of the *Stadtkrone* (city-crown) celebrated in his eponymous book.[17] Not only does Böhm's architecture seem formally to echo the crystalline towers of the expressionist period (and slightly the Einstein Tower of Mendelsohn), it is also the social building at the town centre, political and social hub. Both Bruno Taut and Böhm's father had been pupils of Theodor Fischer, who had began his career as a town planner in 1893, landing the job of planning the expansion of Munich and becoming one of the most successful exponents of the theories of Camilo Sitte. Fischer was obsessed with context, rejecting the geometric plans of predecessors to follow existing lanes, lines of trees and other local features, for the lines and wrinkles in the ground preserved the memories of previous generations. He followed Sitte's teaching about the charms of irregular old towns and the way one would be led visually down a curving street to a well-placed monument at the end, but his concern went beyond a taste for the picturesque. His acceptance of irregularities was more a response to *genius loci*. Buildings had to be planned to take advantage of the ground and to make appropriate neighbourly connections. Their massing had to be so handled that they were in an appropriate hiearachy: tall buildings along major streets, shorter ones along minor, with buildings of appropriate public importance sited at junctions.[18] Gottfried Böhm's handling of routes and massing stood directly in this tradition. In a period where the rational grid was the universally assumed ordering device, his ability not only to accept irregular planforms and constantly mutating sections, but also to turn them from problems to advantages, showed in updated form precisely the skill that Fischer had extolled.

Bensberg Town Hall pulled the ailing Bensberg together. It gave the few remaining fragments of the old castle – surprisingly few in view of the powerful effect – a vibrant new life. Through Böhm's deft reinterpretation it also showed how a large and potentially dull bureaucratic complex could be absorbed into the old town without overwhelming it. Building on the outskirts for easy access and

23. (above) Entrance to the castle courtyard with old structures and entrance to the Ratskeller (the town hall restaurant) to left.

24. (below) Marl Town Hall, result of a competition in 1958 won by van den Broek and Bakema. This is what a new town hall on a virgin site could become with a typical brief of the time. Van den Broek and Bakema designed it with four identical office towers allowing for expansion, but only two were built.

25. (overleaf) One of Böhm's sketches for the tower.

freedom of approach, with the inevitable effect of sucking life and money away from the centre, was happily avoided. At the same time the question of providing an identity for the town hall was brilliantly solved. That this was not easy is shown by comparison with the contemporary case of Marl Town Hall, a brutalist complex by van den Broek and Bakema resulting from a competition win of 1958. Despite the provision of a boldly folded concrete box to signal the council chamber, the overwhelming impression for the visitor was the pair of office towers, rigidly square, evenly fenestrated, and declaring nothing more than a hanging construction principle. Unsuccessful organic entries to the competition by Hans Scharoun and Alvar Aalto attempted a more dynamic and spatially based articulation of parts, and both were more promising in terms of spatial progression, but even these masters could not avoid the dominant bulk of offices.[19] At Bensberg the offices are enlivened by numerous variations and are difficult to see together in a single view, but their saving grace is the unique role of mimicking and replacing the castle wall. This required an architect able to work with complex, asymmetrical, and non-rectangular compositions,

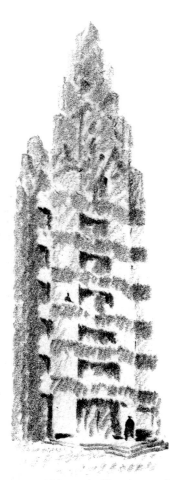

exploiting old irregularities to create new accents, and creating new elements in balance with old. Such work would scarcely have been possible without an open attitude towards the material, a broad vocabulary, and a powerful imagination to visualise the potentialities. Certainly intuitive control and artistic judgement were also needed, but since all work had to be carried out in close dialogue with the given, it could hardly be that selfish whimsical imposition of the personal touch so often caricatured as 'expressionism' or implied with faint praise in the designation 'sculptural'. Equally, to dismiss Böhm's work as 'irrational' is to refuse even to begin to understand, while to discuss it merely in terms of its 'form-language'[20] is to miss most of the point, especially fifty years later when the style is at its weakest, tarnished but not yet quaint. Bensberg is much more a question of place, and here lie the important lessons for today.

PBJ

Notes

1. 1986: the citation is available at www.pritzkerprize.com/boehm.htm
2. See lectures published in Raev 1988, with English translation.
3. Heinrich Klotz, in his book of interviews with leading German architects, mentions a refusal from Böhm to take part, though he was presumably not encouraged by Klotz's general antipathy to the organic/expressionist direction; see Klotz 1977, p.10.
4. You can read it either way: Pehnt (1973, pp. 152-154) convincingly connects his work to the social concepts of other 'expressionists', while Nerdinger (1988, pp. 86, 94) sees his churches with their mixture of Gothic and reinforced concrete as a Fischerian legacy.
5. The term 'material realism' was coined by the Swedish architectural historian Björn Linn to characterise the early twentieth-century work in Scandinavia usually called 'National Romantic'. It identifies an intensified concern with the nature and textures of materials and the associated craftsmanship.
6. This tendency was epitomised by Le Corbusier's chapel at Ronchamp, which upset many of his followers in its 'irrationality': see James Stirling, 'Ronchamp, Le Corbusier's Chapel and the Crisis of Rationalism' *Architectural Review,* vol. 119, March 1956.
7. Rudolf Schwarz (1897-1961) was Chief Planner for the City of Cologne from 1946-1952.
8. The invited architects, listed in Darius 1988, p. 42, were mainly local. They included Joachim Schürmann, Emil Steffan and Oswald Matthias Ungers.
9. Information from Darius 1988, pp. 34-42, the best general source (in German).
10. Bachelard 1969 (first published in English in 1964).
11. In the churches the interior spaces were as important as the exterior, soaring into mystical gloom, and intended to recall tents.
12. Würzburg 1938, English edition, *The Church Incarnate* Chicago, 1958.
13. Greek theatre or roundhouse versus basilica and axis.
14. Essentially the effects parallel those of Hans Scharoun with his theory of 'aperspectivity', see Blundell Jones 2002, Ch. 13.
15. It was planned along the contours to allow a little water to be diverted from the adjacent brook then returned at the end, rather like old villages where a rivulet of cleansing water runs alongside the pavement, as in Thorverton, Devon.
16. Böhm's competition elevations show two lines of later windows: the five Romanesque ones were presumably rediscovered and restored during operations.
17. Bruno Taut, *Die Stadtkrone*, Jena 1919.
18. The main German monograph on Fischer is Nerdinger 1988. For an English summary of his life and work see Blundell Jones 1989.
19. Both are shown in Wilson 1995, pp. 81-86.
20. 'Formensprache', Klotz 1977.

Chapter 5. Alison and Peter Smithson: The Economist Building, London, 1964

Post-war London presented the visitor with a prospect substantially changed from that recorded by Steen Eileer Rasmussen in *London: The Unique City* of 1937.[1] The effects of aerial bombardment had been extensive, but changes in architectural taste had had a yet more profound effect on the skyline. During the early years of the war Sir Edwin Lutyens had headed a Royal Academy Committee which envisioned reconstruction in the grand manner of an imperial capital. But by the time resources became available, not only had he and others of his generation died, but the whole imperial system was in retreat, allowing an altogether more difficult form of city slowly to take shape. This affected even its most conservative areas. Running between Piccadilly and St James's Palace, St James's Street hosts one of the most provocative but sensitive interventions of this period of reconfiguration. The footprint of this area of the city had largely been a product of Georgian development, a gridiron adjacent to some of the great aristocratic houses gathered near the royal pleasure ground of St. James's Park, and in the later Georgian period host to the palazzi of the gentlemen's clubs.[2] The political and economic power of the membership of clubland had attracted commercial development in the Victorian and Edwardian periods, which substantially increased the scale and density. By the 1960s the *habitué* of Swinging London, proceeding down a street of eclectically classical facades, encountered a new bank building which followed the scale, height and material of its neighbours, but was devoid of ornament and largely enclosed in plate glass. Behind this frontispiece a squat tower in the same architectural language broke the skyline. This could be approached by a ramp and stair to the left of the bank, which negotiated the half-level rise to an irregular plaza defined by the tower's perimeter colonnade. Here one became aware of another tower, shorter and more slender, occupying another corner of the ambiguously defined space. This was the new public realm as presented to London by the husband and wife architectural partnership of Alison and Peter Smithson. Built as the head-

quarters for *The Economist* magazine, it expressed in sober and condensed form many of their radical ideas about architecture and the city.

The Smithsons bestrode the British architectural stage between the 1950s and 1970s, both as building architects and as critics. Unlike the marginal pre-war modernism imported by émigrés such as Mendelsohn, Lubetkin and Gropius, the arena of post-war modernism in which they performed was mainstream, and part of an international trend. Links with Europe were particularly strong, but there was also much intercourse with the developing architectural culture of North America.

Alison (1928-93) and Peter Smithson (1923-2003) met while studying architecture in Newcastle, and came to prominence as brilliant young architects with Hunstanton Secondary School in Norfolk, won in competition in 1949 and completed in 1954. This flexible steel-framed building was essentially Miesian in inspiration, but it was also radical in putting materials and services on display, and

1. Promenade through the Economist Plaza.

2. School at Hunstanton in Norfolk, 1949-54.

it later became the founding example for the historian and critic Reyner Banham's definition of new brutalism, a canonisation that did much to establish the Smithsons' high reputation.[3] In the 1950s they joined the Independent Group of artists, and 'pop' influences entered their work, notably in their contributions to the *This is Tomorrow* exhibition at the Institute of Contemporary Arts of 1956.[4] Along with artists like Richard Hamilton and Eduardo Paolozzi, and especially with the photographer Nigel Henderson, they eulogised the social patterns of the working class as a model for the synthesis of art and life.[5]

To this specifically British context was added the broader international experience as founding members of Team Ten, the breakaway movement from CIAM which they shared with contemporaries Giancarlo De Carlo (Chapter 13), Aldo van Eyck (Chapter 3) and Ralph Erskine (Chapter 10) as already mentioned in Chapter 3, p. 36. This group of young architects became increasingly critical of the old guard, and started their own debate, unleashing a stream of polemic on the architectural world to a degree unheard of since Le Corbusier's

pre-war heyday. Although the principal tenets of modernism, rationality and abstraction had been widely accepted, Team Ten, like all self-appointed avant-gardists, saw the need for a new beginning:

This new beginning, and the long build-up that followed, has been concerned with inducing, as it were into the bloodstream of the architect, an understanding and feeling for the patterns, the aspirations, the artefacts, the tools, the modes of transportation and communications of present-day society, so that he can as a natural thing build towards that society's realisation of itself.
In this sense Team Ten is Utopian, but Utopian about the present. Thus their aim is not to theorise but to build, for only through construction can a Utopia of the present be realised.[6]

The subtext of Team Ten's critique was the transformation in the concerns of the architectural avant-garde which took place a few years after the Second World War. After initial uncertainties following the war, it became apparent that the language to be used for reconstruction, especially

3. UR Grid presented by the Smithsons at CIAM 9, Otterlo, on the theme house, street, district, city, illustrated with their work.

4. View down St James's Street with Boodle's Club and the Economist tower behind. The club's Georgian proportions are replicated in the bank building which fronts onto the street.

in the countries embraced by the NATO Alliance of 1949, was to be the idealistic modernism advocated by the pioneers of the International Style twenty years earlier, although the cultural as well as military centre of gravity had shifted from Europe to the United States. That the virtually unopposed supremacy for the patriarchs of modernism – Le Corbusier, Mies van der Rohe, Gropius, and even Aalto – might provoke a form of reaction from a younger generation is perhaps now no surprise. We are familiar with juvenile rebellion and its acceptance as a form of cultural and commercial expression epitomised in these years by the advent of rock 'n' roll. To claim a direct connection would be to overstate the case, but there is some parallel in the falling off of purity and clarity, and the consequent rise in dissonance and even wilful cacophony represented by brutalism's desire to be 'with it'. This surely was symptomatic of a deeper problem than the limited availability of resources in the post-war years that had brought about the use of *béton brut,* for example, in Le Corbusier's Unité d'Habitation at Marseilles (1946-52). The technology

destructively evident in the First World War, which early modernists had sought to harness to Utopian aesthetic and social purposes, had in the Second World War run almost beyond human control. After the Holocaust and Hiroshima, the perfectibility of humankind proposed by modernists became a virtually worthless enterprise, persuading architects that their work should respond to a rather more complex context than the *tabula rasa* still advocated by CIAM. This rift, between what had come to be seen as orthodox and 'official' modernism, and a less obviously photogenic, even deliberately 'ordinary' approach to design, is represented by the Economist Building. Indeed it is almost a piece of propaganda in this direction. To achieve their return to reality the Smithsons and their collaborators sought an architecture less obviously sophisticated, more related to the directness of modern experience and contemporary anthropological studies. This search for the essential led to a preference for a supposed naturalness of expression associated with the term 'new brutalism', which was coined by Alison Smithson in 1953 before being adopted by Banham.[7]

The Economist Building

The Economist Group, or Economist Building as it has come to be known, housed *The Economist* Magazine and its research arm, the Economist Intelligence Unit, besides including lettable commercial space. The complex brief was conceived in 1959 and was commissioned at the behest of the company chairman Geoffrey Crowther to gather together the different elements on one site and to provide him with a penthouse. Peter Dallas-Smith, the joint manager, acquired the site and chose the architects on the basis of their entry for the Churchill College, Cambridge competition from the previous year.[8] Design work began in 1960, and the complex was completed in 1964. The site included an existing house occupied by the chambers of Boodle's Club, housed in a delicately proportioned building fronting St James's Street. This building by John Crunden, dating from 1775, was according to Summerson *'a witty re-hash of Adam's facade of the Royal Society of Arts in the Adelphi'.*[9] An agreement was reached between the magazine and the Club, allowing the chambers to be replaced and the plot to be considered as part of a larger overall scheme. The combination of residential, office and commercial accommodation, a plot ratio of 5:1, and the aspect of the building

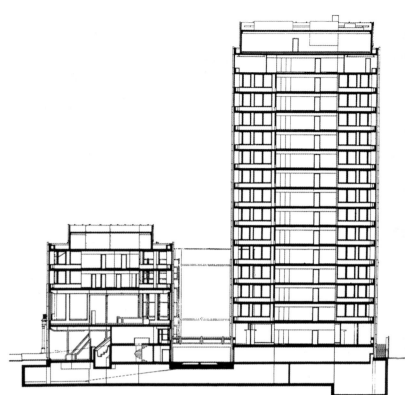

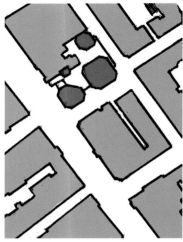

5. (left) Section through the bank and main tower, which contrasts the varied room heights of the bank in response to the context with the serial repetition of the office tower.

6. (above) Site plan.

7. (below) Photomontage applying the urban model of the Economist across a wider area of central London.

8. Upper level plan showing, clockwise from top left, Boodle's Club with the additional bay window, the small tower for the club's chambers, the Economist's offices, and the diagonally arranged bank building.

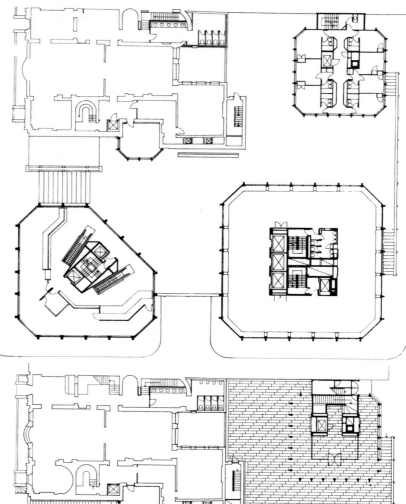

9. Plaza level plan, showing the intention to create a unified datum for the individual buildings, the paving extending through the colonnades and beyond the glazing around the entrance lobbies.

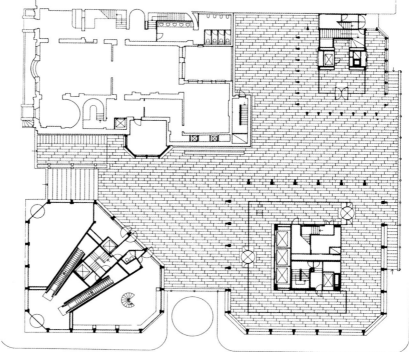

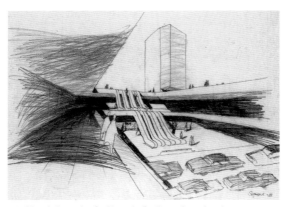

10. Sketch from the Smithson's Berlin project showing separation of traffic and pedestrian plaza, the latter dominated by a tower.
11. (opposite) View across St James's Street showing the unified articulation of bank building and tower.

from St James's Street and St James's Park, had to be juggled in order to provide an acceptable solution. The Smithsons' proposal was to pare down the brief into its constituent parts and express each separately, with the resulting elements sitting around a raised public plaza. Besides reflecting the same kind of will for functional articulation seen at the contemporary Leicester Engineering Building (next chapter), this was revolutionary in returning part of the site to public use, the normal procedure with such valuable land being to fill it from edge to edge. The family of buildings consisted, as if in mathematical progression, of a four-storey block for the commercial element – principally a banking hall; an eight-storey tower for the residential component; and a sixteen-storey office tower for the magazine and its research department. As commentators pointed out, there was an effective fourth member to the family in the new three-storey bay attached to the existing club. Beneath the podium were a further two storeys linking these elements with services and parking.

The Plaza as unifying base combined several ideas. It clearly referred to the base of Mies's Seagram building in New York, both in the provision of public space and in the formation of an artificial plateau raised above the street, a device used with equal effect by Mies at the Barcelona Pavilion of 1929 and at his gallery in Berlin. Besides its formal value, this plateau allowed a reconcilliation of the various levels of the sloping site, including an entry ramp for vehicles. The Smithsons had also long dreamed about a two-level city with streets in the air, whose ideal

form was expressed in their Haupstadt Berlin competition entry of 1958. Separation of vehicles and pedestrians was then advocated by traffic planners and widely accepted, leading to the hope of a free pedestrian realm where urban life could flourish free of noise and exhaust fumes. The largest exemplars of this tendency in London were the Barbican development by Chamberlin Powell and Bonn and the Foundling Estate by Leslie Martin and Patrick Hodgkinson, both completed later. The Smithsons showed how it might develop in a more subtle and piecemeal manner by repeating the Economist development several times over in a tempting collage suggesting a pedestrian network that could grow and spread. As the development was sited on the street corner between St James's Street and Ryder Street, the bank building was placed on the diagonal, setting up a symmetrical relation between the upward pedestrian staircase to the left and the downward vehicle ramp to the right. The bank's corner entry was connected by escalators to shop and office entrances from the plaza. The switch to 45° seems to have inspired a general chamfering of corners, as also happened with Leicester Engineering Building (next chapter). Internally, each block was organised in a different way. While the bank followed its diagonal axis, the office tower was arranged around a central square core with toilets, lifts and stairs. This left a circuit of office accommodation to be subdivided into cellular offices as best suited the users. The residential tower had a central axis of symmetry, with individual rooms either side of a corridor running across the block on the first-floor floors, and four levels of individual flats above. Despite these internal differences, the external treatment was almost uniform. Each building was clad in large areas of glazing articulated by stone ribs.[10] The rhythm of these units varied between the towers, with an office bay width of 10 feet 6 inches (3.20 m), appropriate for two persons, while in the residential tower it was a more domestic 5 feet 3 inches (1.60 m). The architects' comments about the cladding reveal concerns beyond the immediate life of the buildings:

The space available on this site is small, which suggests that the cladding material should be light-coloured so as to reflect light into the courtyard-like spaces between the buildings. This material also had to be capable of being worked in large units, which could sustain the scale of the building and

provide an obviously support-cladding architecture, more or less in the way that the columns and entablatures are applied to the outside of the structural frame of a Roman amphitheatre.

Roach-bed Portland stone was chosen as it fulfills these conditions and an attempt has been made to control the flow of waterborne dirt over the stone by a system of gutters at the cills and down the sides of the columns so that the final weathering pattern over the facades is predictable.

It is hoped that the building, so far as colour is concerned, will eventually resemble Archer's Church, St. Paul's, Deptford, that is, with a strong black and white contrast according to orientation (The Economist tower has the same orientation as the tower of this church). [11]

Ostensibly the concern to admit light to the plaza lay at the heart of the architects' vision. As a compositional device this intention was the basis of the decision to chamfer the corners, maximum site coverage not being allowed to reduce lighting standards. A classical reference is cited for the use of an *'obviously support-cladding architecture'*, while an expressive English Baroque precedent is evoked in the weathering of the material. These elements of urban design, historical concern, the desire for expressiveness and the sense of community, are common to many of the buildings and projects produced by members of Team Ten, as are the twin desires to deal more comprehensively with urban situations (particularly the integration of architecture into the planning infrastructure), and to be more contextually sensitive. Understandably, they were searching for an effective system to ensure both uniformity and variety, and the ambivalence of this position is understandable when one reads the townscape-based criticism of the project by Gordon Cullen in the pages of *The Architectural Review*, a voice more familiarly heard describing historic centres.[12] The Economist Group was seen as rather finely balanced between sensitive refinement and blunt certainties. In another assessment, Kenneth Frampton emphasised these ambiguities, especially in relation to the apparently mannered use of scale:

The question of integrity of expression with regard to accommodation simply does not arise. It is suppressed by the interplay of scale set up between the two 'towers'. This change of scale between

12. View towards the plaza with additional bay of Boodle's club on the left and the base of the Economist tower on the right.
13. (top opposite) Rear of the plaza with the colonnade of the chambers' building.
14. (below opposite) View along Park Place showing tower.

the two buildings has resulted in a giant trompe-l'oeil *with which one is only to experience further perceptual difficulty as one enters the centre of the plaza. In the centre of the plaza, the 'photographic' reduction in scale of the residential block vis-à-vis the main tower has the optical effect of 'zooming' this block away from the observer, with a consequent dramatic enlargement in the apparent space of the plaza. This perceptual sleight-of-hand is brilliant but not in the last instance felicitous, for the observer does not remain rooted in the centre, and on moving around he quickly discovers the deception. Once the illusion of the residential building has been exposed, the whole assembly is open to a 'theatrical' interpretation, and this interpretation does not help in sustaining belief in the true monumentality of the major office tower. Seeing may be believing, but once one has been duped a state of 'visual trust' can only be re-established with considerable difficulty.*[13]

As urban setting, though, the grouping of the buildings pursued a scenographic path in which scale played its part. The aesthetic task was to maintain visual coherence throughout the project, as perceived from various positions and angles. The configuration of buildings produced two urban spaces, one essentially triangular between the sides of the bank and the office building, and a smaller rectangular one bounded by the colonnades of the office and the residential towers. These spaces maintain a sense of civic order in tension with the self-sufficiency of the building forms, but their separation from the general ground plane and removal from the principal surrounding streets distances them from the urban network. As a result they remain relatively dead spaces, at least in public terms. It seems ironic that spaces which the architects created rhetorically precisely to represent their civic intentions should fall so short. That the usefulness of the plazas became problematic for the owners is indicated by the later glazing-in of the arcades. The pictorial composition of a work that tries so hard to be pragmatic and even banal in its expression also seems curious.

15. Contemporary office interior of the bank.

The 'rhetoric' which the Smithsons so loudly proclaimed that they could do without[14] is so cleverly and knowingly muted, so confined to subtleties of scale and detail, that they defeat anyone but the hardened architectural detective. The rhetoric of the deserted arcades that the architects chose to illustrate speaks volumes, especially when contrasted with their stated intentions:

In a small way our Economist Building can be seen to be struggling with the idea of continuation and regeneration; continuation of an existing pattern quite specific and quite unique at the same time as struggling to establish a mode for the present. [15]

The confident statements with which the Smithsons described the significance of their built and drawn work are quietly dismissive of aspects outside the concerns of their circle. But the urban impact of the project should be studied to discern the true impact of the Smithsons' 'small way'. They respected the roof line of St James's Street and their bank building reflected the Georgian scale of Boodle's, particularly at *piano nobile* level. The social conservatism of this gesture, flattering to the streetscape of St James's Street, had the broader urban consequence of increasing dramatically the scale of the main tower at the rear of the site, which dominated longer views. Despite the discontinuity due to the different sized elements, the application of a system to frame variety lends the development a rather monotonous quality. A clue to the virtues they were seeking lies perhaps in their interest in repetition, and the economic basis of the culture to which it adhered, where the rhetoric spoke the language of financial power.

The identifying characteristic of a technological culture would seem to be that its key objects appear as a by-product of concentration not on 'old-world' notions like the discipline, but on perfection of process and of detail. Certainly the strongest hints of the emergence of another architecture are in multi-storey buildings with a great deal of repetition, where what Americans know most about in their bones – mass-production, process, control, etc. – becomes the control, rather than any notions of composition, or art.[16]

This statement disingenuously suggests that the architects' role is a humble one of organising components, although the specificity with which they are handled is, of course, entirely dependent on the traditional values of composition, as Frampton identified at the time. Important in retrospect, though, was the way modular systems were applied to a variety of purposes. These included the integration of services into the architectural language of the frame, horizontal runs being expressed externally by the stone spandrel panels between vertical fins. The economic consequence of a system which might accommodate some flexibility, redolent of the scale of American building which the Smithsons so admired, could be exploited to bring together commercial, office and residential uses in a unified way. In turn, the desire for repetition seems to reflect creation of objects responsive to internal logic rather than external context, so the rhythmic facades are set apart, disrupting the primacy of the plaza. The chamfered corners make each element yet more self-sufficient, further undermining the creation of a defined urban space.

The balance of arcades and penetrated blocks, which the Smithsons considered such an important element of the local urban pattern, suggested a degree of aesthetically integrated variety that might rival Georgian London, an alluring promise in a bomb-damaged city where a new comprehensive vision was decidedly lacking. The repetitive modular forms relied on the traditional compositional values of good proportion if their endless replication was not to produce a sterile effect. The subtlety of architectural proportion, however, remained somewhat arcane to an audience beyond the professional, so successfully did the architects pare down the elements. The stone cladding was used, beyond its light-reflecting function, to lend an equal honorific quality to all the buildings, confusing the hierarchies of scale. The application of motifs

16. Collage of Golden Lane housing as if under construction.

17. Park Hill, Sheffield.

like the perimeter colonnades, though aesthetically consistent, failed to distinguish entrance facades from side elevations. Such traditional distinctions were criticised at the time for being socially divisive, but lack of them simply made it difficult to know where to enter. Curiously the colonnades' direct engagement with the plaza, which was intended to encourage a variety of spatial uses, seems to have had the reverse effect of inhibiting occupation. Instead of the promised continuity and regeneration, contemporary photographs of the interiors suggest only discontinuity and isolation.

The Economist Group could hardly be described as being a prima facie case of brutalism, unlike Sheffield's Park Hill flats by Sheffield City Architects (1961), a project heavily influenced by the Smithsons' Golden Lane project of 1952. The attempt to recreate the life of working-class terrace streets, which the Smithsons had observed in the East End of London, and which they reified through Henderson's photographs in presentations during their struggles with CIAM, resulted in the disastrous social experiment of 'streets in the sky', the most widely accessible form of brutalism in deck-access housing projects.[17] The implementation of these experimental forms was the responsibility of others, although the Smithsons did eventually produce their own contribution to the genre with Robin Hood Gardens, London, 1972. For socially more privileged clients and users, and in a more prestigious location, they evidently preferred more conservative forms. Distancing itself from the usual quarters in which it was deployed, brutalism's presence in clubland required The Economist to adopt a subtler coding, emphasizing classical propriety against rawness of effect. So the mathematical sophistication of the heights and proportions of the different elements

could be related to the influential studies of Rudolph Wittkower published in his *Architectural Principles in the Age of Humanism* of 1949, a popular source of aesthetic justification for many of that generation.[18] For the uninitiated, the finished effect of unrelated discontinuities caused by changes of scale and isolation of individual buildings could be mistaken for a less self-conscious, or even a truly banal form of practice. For example, although the design of the main tower was supposedly indebted to the work of Ludwig Mies van der Rohe, progenitor of the aesthetic of urban transparency, the reflective effect was disrupted by overemphasis on the stone fins, which reduced the perceived penetrability of the block, especially in oblique views, and fulfilled a preference for animated surface effects. Lastly, the skills of the architects created some expressively alienating effects, like the use of stone that looked like concrete and the desolate character of the elevated plaza. The public was asked to accept a vision of the urban experience as hard, gritty and engaged: an unlikely prospect for the denizens of St James's.

18. Robin Hood Gardens.

Later work

The completion of the Economist complex marked the high-watermark of the Smithsons' career. Disappointments followed, both in the form of thwarted commissions like the 1978 Pahlavi National Library in Tehran, awarded just before the Islamic Revolution swept away the Shah of Iran's regime, and in the disastrous reception of Robin Hood Gardens, where a major accumulation of ideas was finally realised, but their inappropriateness in practice was exposed.[19] It seems ironic in view of their obsessive interest in contemporaneity that the Smithsons in their last decades seemed to become masters of a vanished age. The avant-garde stance, set against the background of war and commitment to the social values of reconstruction, seemed to suit the Smithsons better than any of their British contemporaries. In the United States, the Eameses presented some kind of equivalent, but their restless self-promotion revealed a more obvious commercial commitment, and did not depend on the same kind of acknowledgement as intellectuals. The Smithsons' uncompromising stance challenged visitors trying to come to terms with their buildings. Despite the invocation of social patterns, their work favoured an abstraction which became frozen and repelled other uses or interpretations. Their idolisation of the ordinary neutralised the disquieting power of the genuinely ordinary, leaving instead only a dry arrangement of enigmatic forms. What the work did promote, however, was an attention to context and to the form of urban architecture which enjoyed a legacy in the work of other architects. The urban space they favoured, easily distinguishable from the anti-contextual model of their predecessors, and exemplified above all by the Economist's plaza, makes a real attempt to maintain a sense of civic order in tension with the self-sufficiency of the building forms. But its separation from the general ground plane, and removal from the principal streets which bound the plot, distance it from the urban network to which it demands connection, instead creating a form of dead public space. This space was created as propaganda for the civic intentions of the architects, but its general usefulness became problematic for the owners because of the ambiguity, as the later glazing-in of the arcades demonstrates. Notwithstanding this change to the urban configuration, the buildings have survived with their status enhanced, as Frampton observed:

The Economist Building emerges today as that rare example of a modern building that has withstood the 'flow of time' where the quality of the work has improved rather than the reverse. In retrospect this structure would seem to come closest to Peter Smithson's archaeological ideal of a building that could, in some future time, be reconstructed from its ruined fragment. [19]

EC

Notes

1. Steen Eileer Rasmussen, *London: The Unique City,* Jonathan Cape, London, 1937.
2. John Summerson, *Georgian London,* Barrie & Jenkins, London, 1962.
3. Banham 1966.
4. Anne Massey, *The Independent Group: modernism and mass culture in Britain, 1945-59,* Manchester University Press, Manchester, 1995.
5. Victoria Walsh, *Nigel Henderson: Parallel of Life and Art,* Thames & Hudson, London, 2001.
6. Alison Smithson, *Team 10 Primer,* Studio Vista, London 1968.
7. Harwood 2003, p. 634.
8. Ibid, pp. 634-637. The Smithsons were not the only architects considered: Stirling and Gowan were also interviewed: verbal information from James Gowan, February 2006.
9. Summerson 1962, p. 153.
10. This may have been inspired by Hendrik Berlage's nearby Holland House, which has similarly spaced vertical mullions in terracotta. James Gowan challenged Peter Smithson on this and reports that 'he knew all about it'; verbal information from Gowan, February 2006.
11. Alison & Peter Smithson 'The Economist Group St James's Street, London', *Architectural Design,* Vol. XXXV, February 1965, pp. 63-86.
12. Gordon Cullen, 'The Economist Buildings St James's', *The Architectural Review,* 137:819 (February 1965) pp. 114-24.
13. Kenneth Frampton, 'The Economist and the Haupstadt', *Architectural Design,* Vol. XXXV, February 1965, pp. 61-2.
14. Alison and Peter Smithson, *Without Rhetoric – An Architectural Aesthetic 1955 -1972,* Latimer New Dimensions, London, 1973.
15. Ibid, p. 91.
16. Ibid, p. 28.
17. Eric Mumford, *The C.I.A.M. Discourse on Urbanism 1928-1960,* M.I.T. Press, Cambridge, Massachusetts, 2000, pp. 238-57.
18. Wittkower 1949.
19. For Robin Hood Gardens and the Pahlavi National Library see Alison and Peter Smithson, *The Charged Void: Architecture,* Monacelli Press, New York, 2001, pp. 296-313 and 426-431 respectively.
20. Frampton 1995 p. 365.

Chapter 6. Stirling and Gowan: Leicester University Engineering Building, 1959-64

The Leicester University Engineering Building stands out in British architecture as a work of extraordinary novelty and inventiveness, considered in its time the single most important British work since the Second World War.[1] It was revolutionary both in creating a new architectural language derived from many unfamiliar sources and in its virtuoso handling of form, space and constructive possibilities. It also marked the peak of collaboration between two influential British architects, James Stirling and James Gowan. Because of Stirling's later world renown, and because he appropriated the vocabulary of Leicester by repetition in subsequent work alone, Gowan has increasingly been written out of the story, but his contribution both to Leicester and to Stirling's development should not be underestimated.[2] They had complimentary strengths, and though Stirling's later work was highly acclaimed, neither alone repeated the sheer originality of Leicester.

James Stirling (1924-92) was born and educated in Liverpool. He reached his teens at the outbreak of the Second World War, was called up to fight before the end, and was wounded in the D-Day landings. This delayed his education at the Liverpool School of Architecture until 1945-50. There he soon developed a cosmopolitan air, variously ascribed to his father's career as a captain of ocean liners, the legacy of Sir Charles Reilly at the Liverpool School, the presence there of a Polish School of Architecture-in-exile during the Second World War, an early experience of working in New York, and the influence of his thesis tutor Colin Rowe. Although not alone among his

generation in having such experiences, he seemed especially able to synthesise their influences. He graduated while working at the modernist architectural practice of Lyons Israel Ellis, where he met James Gowan (b.1923). Gowan was born and educated in Glasgow and saw war service as a radar operator before studying architecture at the Kingston School of Art. He had earlier worked for Powell and Moya on the Skylon for the Festival of Britain. He and Stirling formed a partnership in 1956, and for most of the next seven years worked closely together.

Projects for the expanding University sector had dominated the early part of Stirling's career. A competition project for Sheffield University in 1953 transformed to educational purposes the language of Le Corbusier's recently completed Unité d'Habitation at Marseilles. The building's entry was raised above the ground plane, and the centre of the linear block was dominated by the expression of stacked interlocking lecture theatres. A proposal with Gowan for Churchill College, Cambridge of 1958 featured an elemental and fortress-like character, possibly influenced by exposure to the work of Louis Kahn in the United States. A further project for Selwyn College, Cambridge of 1959, also with Gowan, provided the opportunity for dramatic contrasts between glazed walls and masonry surfaces animated by service towers. Elements of these unbuilt projects surfaced again in the design for the building at Leicester, and then in the subsequent buildings by Stirling alone for Cambridge University History Faculty 1964-67, the Florey Building at Queen's College, Oxford, 1966-

1. Competition entry by James Stirling for the University of Sheffield 1953, with exterally articulated lecture theatres.

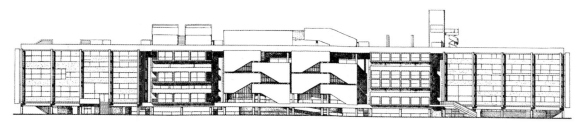

71, and St Andrews University Halls of residence 1964-68, all completed after the partnership with Gowan was dissolved in 1963. The Leicester building was the pivotal design in the transformation of architectural concepts into physical form.

Genesis of the Engineering Building

It was 1959 and the newly upgraded University of Leicester was expanding. The decision had been made to start an engineering department, and Leslie Martin, advisory architect for the whole campus, recommended Stirling and Gowan for the job. The site was an irregular piece of ground surrounded on three sides by the neo-Georgian buildings of the former University College, but the fourth, north-east facing, side opened onto the downhill sloping Victoria Park and became the front. Here the swinging curve of a service road opened up a triangle of space in the northern corner, prompting the 45° swing of the building's entry ramp. The client was effectively Edward Parkes, who had been lured away from Cambridge to head up the new department. He produced a fairly matter-of-fact brief and demanded efficient operation, but left it up to the architects what it looked like.[3] However, the functionalist approach that they seemed to be taking was in line both with his way of thinking and with modernist principles

then still fully in force.[4] The main part of the building was a big workshop which Parkes wanted as a single columned space in the interest of flexibility. This was divided about two thirds to one third between general workshop and specialised hydraulic and structures areas, displacing the main cross axis of the service passage into an asymmetrical position. The whole space was to be daylit like a factory with a glazed northlight roof, but as the site stood at about 45° to north, the roof needed to be set diagonally: a radical move for the time, but with clear functional justification. Similarly radical functional thinking also developed in other details. Gowan conceived the idea of laying the floor as a series of great concrete slabs placed directly on the ground, so that any one could be lifted in future to make a foundation to a machine, and one can imagine Parkes's delight at the pragmatic logic.[5] Along the rear edge an extra storey was added for the lighter and smaller electrical and aerodynamics workshops, and it was made to overhang to allow a long loading bay at the rear directly accessible from above using cranes within the building.

The decision about daylight provision meant that a large part of the site was single storey, so the remaining teaching and administration rooms had to be stacked at the front edge, but there was a further starting point for the tower: a large water tank needed for hydraulic tests, which had to be at least 60 feet in the air and was built 100 feet up. Between its legs the offices could be placed, and at its foot were added a series of separate buildings housing lecture theatres and a lower but still elevated wing of laboratories. The theatres had raked seating for good sightlines, which produced wedge-shaped forms.[6] The smaller one was fully cantilevered, part of a muscular structural demonstration that was arguably appropriate to an engineering building and was worked out by the rising engineer Frank Newby. The larger one had a glazed spiral stair for rear entry. While the offices were totally glazed, the laboratories had horizontal bands of projecting triangular section windows to stress their ventilation function.[7] The stair and lift shafts required to service this group of elements were also articulated as separate turrets, the two main ones standing within the territory of the workshops to tie the complex together. In line with the idea that circulation space should diminish with reducing traffic,[8] the upper landings were cut back and the glazing was allowed to fall in a polygonal cascade. Here functional logic gave rise to forms neither cheap

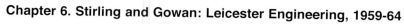

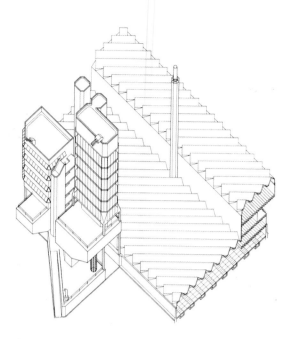

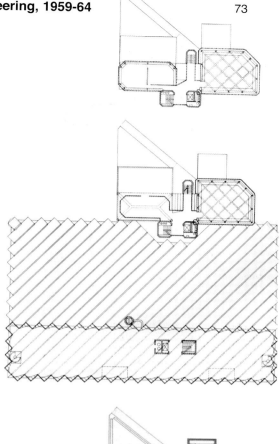

2. (opposite) Original photo of the tower by James Gowan.

3. (above) Axonometric projection, from approach side, with cut-off end to show section.

4. (below) Site plan. The park slopes away towards top.

5,6,7,8. (right bottom to top) Floor plans at ground level; at lecture theatre level; fourth floor with laboratories and offices; and sixth floor. All these line drawings are derived from the original Stirling and Gowan publication drawings.

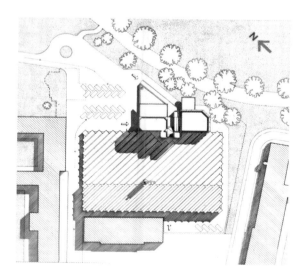

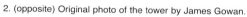

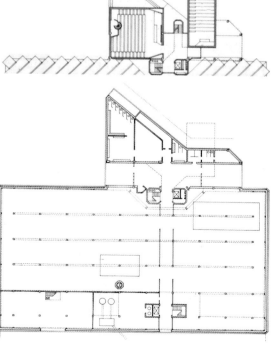

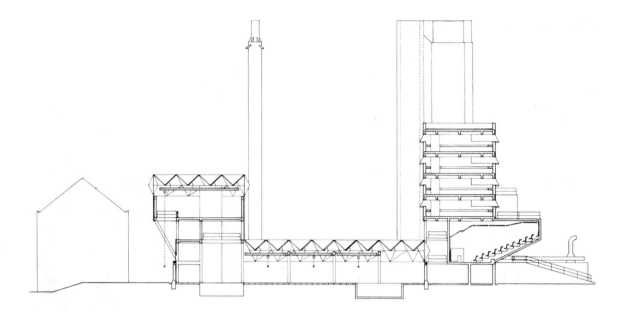

nor easy to construct. Finally, cloakrooms were grouped in a blind triangular base pulled away from from the workshop block to create an axial passage for main entrance and vestibule, a slot of space closed only by glazed walls. The outer edge of this base incorporated a ramp to allow a secondary entrance at first floor level.

This ramp, remembering both the Villa Savoye (Blundell Jones 2002, Ch. 7) and the more recent Carpenter Centre, reflected both architects' obsession with Le Corbusier, but otherwise the two compulsory references of the age, Mies and Corb, remained remarkably absent. The visual language of the building broke away sharply from the modernist canon, which was perhaps why Nikolaus Pevsner was so deeply upset by it.[9] The lecture theatres and corkscrew spiral stair came from Konstantin Melnikov,[10] the former having earlier appeared in Stirling's entry for the Sheffield University competition of 1953, and the structural play also seemed constructivist. Another important source was the industrial vernacular of the nineteenth century which Stirling had grown up with in Liverpool. Both architects had admired and photographed the tough direct construction, visible materials and clear abstract forms of warehouses, and the unexpectedly sculptural shapes of buildings like kilns, maltings and oast-houses.[11] The pure shapes and builderly logic

of such unadorned structures had long been a source of form for modernists, but the functional rationale behind the forms was also of interest, and it was surely appropriate to make a functional/structural demonstration out of an engineering department.[12] Another quality of old industrial work was the virtuoso use of brick for all surfaces: cills and string-courses would be integrated, wall and buttress would blend into gutter and paving. The mechanisation of brick-making with the development of the Hoffmann kiln in the late nineteenth century had increased the ease with which a huge range of brick specials could be produced, getting round any kind of corner, cill or step, and making the material beautifully continuous and durable. Stirling and Gowan repeated this appearance to great effect with their interplay of colour-matched bricks and tiles.[13]

Revolutionary also was the break with the right angle, for it had become ubiquitous in post-war British architecture, resulting in rectangular buildings despite the shape of the site. The 45° swing prompted by the irregularity and orientation at Leicester was taken up by the architects with relish. It became the excuse for chamfering the corners of tower and laboratory and later, with Frank Newby's help, for adopting a 45° floor structure in the latter. Its other prominent effect, the staggered ends to the northlight roofs not present in the first version of 1960, was the happy result of late and inspired detailing by Gowan. Both architects were clearly fascinated by the effects of the complex geometry produced by their shifts onto the diagonal, but there is no reason therefore to doubt the seriousness of their intention to articulate content, which had long been a stated concern of Stirling's.[14] This tendency not only related to early modernist works and industrial buildings as already described, but also to the Gothic Revival, whose principal theorist A.W.N. Pugin demanded in the name of 'propriety' that the internal organisation of a building be readable on the exterior.[15] The other great Gothic theorist, John Ruskin, also stressed the articulation of parts, and made aesthetic virtues of asymmetry and irregularity, with great effect on the next generation.[16] The ruthless articulation and constructive logic of architects like William Butterfield and Philip Webb produced a kind of rugged integrity, resulting in arrestingly asymmetrical compositions that Summerson, the great apologist for Georgian architecture, could not help but admire, and even called 'the glory of ugliness'.[17] Gowan can still open his Ruskin at the appropriate page: that Stirling was equally familiar with all this is clear from his quoting Lethaby in an article of 1957.[18]

Composition and proportion

If the Leicester building echoed Ruskinian change-fulness and Butterfieldian ruthlessness, its genesis was rather less anarchic, for beneath the apparent irregularity is system. Gowan insists that the starting point for the whole building was a 10-foot module which ran consistently through in both plan and section, confirming the square as guiding principle.[19] This was standard practice for the time, as such a grid not only helped rationalise construction but also placed a controlling frame on the composition, to preserve a network of relations

9, 10, 11. (previous spread) James Gowan's original slides of the tower as first completed.
12. (opposite top) Section taken through smaller lecture theatre.
13. (above) Tower and projecting lecture theatres photographed by PBJ c.1970.
14. (bottom left) Rusakov Club Moscow, 1927, by Konstantin Melnikov, photo David Wild 1970.
15. (below) Hoffmann kiln at William Thomas brickworks, Wellington, Somerset, c. 1880, photo by PBJ 1976 (demolished).

78

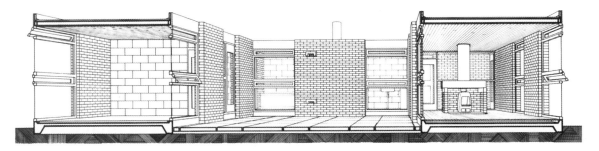

16. House on the Isle of Wight, 1957, the project that Gowan brought to the incipient practice. This drawing combining perspective view with constructional section shows the relish for texture and components that lay at the heart of the brutalist movement. What is less obvious, though confirmed by other drawings, is that the building followed a strict proportion system.

despite the irregularities. The use of the square was linked with beliefs in the aesthetic benefits of geometry held by both architects and derived from several sources. Le Corbusier had developed and published his *Modulor* in 1945: a proportion system based on the golden section and the height of a man, which was regarded for the next two decades as a key to the aesthetic quality of his work.[20]

At more or less the same time, Rudolf Wittkower made his analysis of Renaissance architecture, not just revealing the hidden geometric system of Palladio and others and relating it to ideas of mathematical order and musical harmony, but implying a universal cross-cultural aesthetic system.[21] This was taken up in an exhibition at the Milan Triennale of 1951, which read geometric systems into a wide range of architectures to discover, as Le Corbusier put it, *'the disciplines which are at the root of every plastic work'*.[22] Gowan was steeped in all this, had read Wittkower avidly, and even absorbed the more arcane aspects of the 'maniera tedesca',

the Gothic regulating system described in *Gothic Versus Classic*.[23] Proportional principles were strictly applied in the building he brought with him to the joint practice, the Isle of Wight house of 1957. Stirling, meanwhile, had been tutored at the Liverpool school by Colin Rowe, whose seminal *Mathematics of the Ideal Villa* of 1947 directly linked Wittkower's principles with the villas of Le Corbusier, and Rowe remained Stirling's mentor. This was not all, for both architects were interested in the geometric compositional principles of Dutch De Stijl, particularly of Theo van Doesburg.[24] Early on in practice together they experimented somewhat abstractly with a series of siteless and almost functionless houses asymmetrically composed of geometric solids.[25] The geometrical regulation was applied to a combination of straight and rounded forms, while the preferred drawing technique was the axo- or isometric projection. Gowan observes that one of these studies, a loose arrangement of juxtaposed masses, ramp and

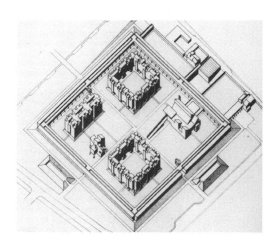

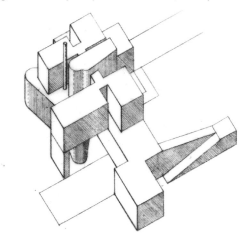

17. (bottom opposite left) Churchill College, Cambridge, competition project 1958.
18. (bottom opposite right) One of the experimental house projects inspired by van Doesburg drawn by Gowan in the late 1950s.
19. (below) Sectional isometric drawing of Ham Common flats 1959-60, showing the strong contrast between in-situ concrete and brick infill, and the continuity between inside and out.
20. (right) Detail of the base block at Leicester containing cloakrooms and of the handrail/seat above. Red brick gave way to red tile to create a continuous red clay surface.
21. (below right) Detail of the terminal to the boiler flue.

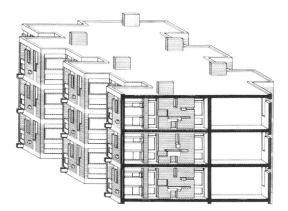

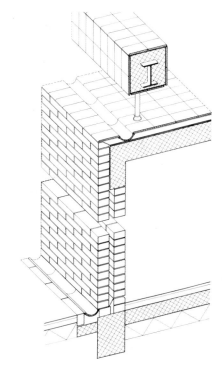

funnel, seems to prepare the way for the tower composition at Leicester, though 'the latter is a tighter assembly, ad quadratum throughout, more mechanical, engineered'. [26]

Brutalism and expressed materials

Part of the brutality in the new brutalism was a kind of bloody-mindedness epitomised by Jimmy Porter in John Osborne's play *Look Back in Anger*, which gave rise to the phrase 'angry young man' applied to Stirling and Gowan's generation. Stirling certainly and repeatedly showed this irreverent quality, and Gowan criticised the establishment as bitingly, if with a more dry and subtle wit.[27] They probably both enjoyed irritating Pevsner. But the dominant theme of the so-called movement docu-mented by Reyner Banham was the expression of materials, which had supposedly been led by Le Corbusier with his use of *béton brut* at the Unité in Marseilles.[28] Stirling visited the new Le Corbusier buildings in the 1950s and wrote about them, prob-ably at Banham's request, in *The Architectural Review*.[29] Among others he saw the Maisons Jaoul with their rough brickwork and concrete vaults, and this resulted in an act of homage in the partner-ship's most important work before Leicester: Ham

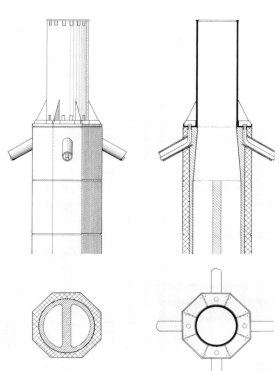

Common flats. Here the contrast between concrete and raw brickwork was played out inside and out in every detail with many small accents. The precision of the construction reveals the same taste for material realism evident in the Isle of Wight house, even if parts are more daringly abstract. The contrast between brick, in-situ concrete and precast concrete places Ham Common right at the heart of Banham's book. Leicester, though, occupies its very end, as though it also ended brutalism. The celebration of the boiler chimney with its exposed draught tubes seems fully and straightforwardly brutalist, but the water tank so crucial to the building's genesis lies invisible beneath a skin of red tiling. Contrast this with Banham's opening example, the Smithsons' school at Hunstanton (see p. 60), where the water tank became a major accent despite its lack of programmatic significance. Stirling and Gowan had more reason for such play with a panelled steel tank, but they were selective. They chose not to, just as they chose not to expose the lecture theatres' concrete, again covered in red tiles. The most crucial piece of material suppression was the roof of the ground floor service block, made as a terrace and covered with the same red tiles. The lavatories within could

do without windows, and ventilation with a ship's snorkel was a happy piece of functional ornament, but necessary service doors were covered with deceptive brick slips like a book-covered door in a Baroque library. Even more telling is the base's balustrade, not treated as an added fence like those higher up, but made as a solid bar which could also be used as a seat (see Fig. 20). Clad with red tiles, it was suitably abstracted and could blend in with the volume, but the presence of a steel RSJ as its heart and support could only be guessed at. The service block needed to be read as solid, with the ramp on its side an integral part, just as implied in the earlier house compositions. When approaching the building via the main ground floor entrances, this treatment further gives the sense of entering a canyon of brick/tile, whose continuity is hardly interrupted by the flimsy glass walls constituting the envelope. These were of another material employed as a ubiquitous skin.

Developed for greenhouses and factory roofs, patent glazing was a linear system of vertical aluminium glazing bars normally set at two foot (600 mm) centres to be spanned by thin glass sheets. It was the obvious candidate for the north-light roof and could also be used for its opaque parts, with fibreglass sheets sandwiched between glass panels. The solution of the angled ends to the roof provoked a doubling of the projecting triangles, resulting in a series of stepped diamond shapes in crystal-like formation, which turned a constructive problem into a formal gain. Equally imaginative and unprecedented was the application of patent glazing to the rest of the building, which Stirling at first resisted as he wanted plate glass for the offices, but economy prevailed.[30] Having covered offices and rooflights, patent glazing could also be draped over the circulation system of the tower, and it proved versatile in its ability to change angle and direction, tailored to the space on site. This created not just the glass cascade over the staircase and landings that excited the first visitors, but a totally new sense of solid and void, an ambiguity of inside and outside. The view upwards in the entrance hall at the crossing of the building's main axes was complex and unprecedented (Figs 10,11). It was greatly helped by the simple contrast between two kinds of skin: the red tiled solids and the gossamer patent glazing. The latter allowed a new freedom of form, for the frameless glazing familiar today was not to arrive for another dozen years, introduced by Norman Foster (see Chapter 12). Stirling loved the effect of patent glazing versus red tile so much that he went on to repeat it in his first two buildings after the dissolution of the joint practice in 1963.

24. (above) Looking across from tower towards elevated workshop, period photo by Gowan.
25. (below) Original design drawing by Gowan of the northlight glazed roof and its edges, showing an alternative solution to the geometry of the projecting ends. Note the strong underlying grid.

22. (opposite top) An early perspective as seen from the park. Neither the ends to the rooflights nor the tower glazing are as built.
23. (below) Retrospective sketch by James Gowan showing the proportion system on which the Leicester building was based: a 10-foot square.

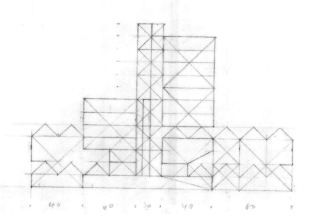

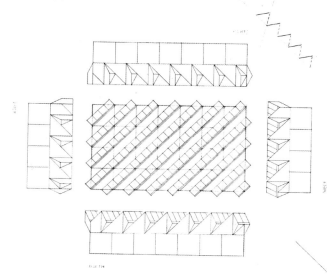

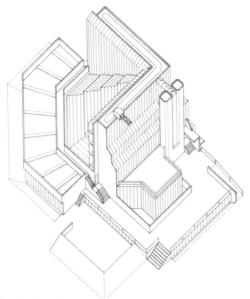

26. (left) James Stirling, History Faculty, Cambridge, 1960-64, axonometric projection.
27. (above) History Faculty photographed on the diagonal axis, c. 1980 and prior to remedial works. The stepped glass roofs cover the library, which is fan-shaped with central supervision of bookstacks. Offices and seminar rooms occupy the L-shaped framing block.

After Leicester

Until the building of Leicester, Stirling and Gowan's office was very small and they worked closely together, sometimes even swapping places at the same board, but success precipitated changes. It brought bigger jobs requiring a larger team, but also teaching opportunities abroad, and Stirling was absent at Yale for several months during the development of Leicester. A proliferation of jobs also divided their energies, so while Gowan concentrated on housing at Greenwich, the Cambridge History Faculty was left largely to Stirling, who brilliantly reused and extended the discoveries of Leicester. Gowan criticised what he had done, but offered no ready alternative, for the project had already gone too far.[31] It turned out both a triumph and a disaster: a triumph because it consolidated Stirling's formal and spatial vision through seductive drawings and sunny photographs propagated internationally, a disaster because it was dogged by technical and environmental problems.[32] The slightly later Oxford Florey Building was no less flawed.[33] These technical failures not only meant that Stirling for a long time ceased to receive commissions in Britain, but fuelled prejudice against architects generally by exposing a yawning gap between the world of architectural discourse and that of everyday life.[34]

When the client of Leicester, Edward Parkes, wanted a summer house, it was to Gowan rather than Stirling that he turned, and he was delighted by the pill-box-like form, which had nothing to do with Leicester and seemed almost a return to the 1930s. At the same time Gowan was working on his masterpiece, the castle-like house in Hampstead for the furniture manufacturer Chaim Schreiber, completed in 1968. Extraordinarily restrained for a luxury mansion, it seemed in its volumetric composition to hark back to the partnership's proposal for Churchill College. Execution was fastidious in the extreme, with materials expressed and every detail thought through. Gowan even designed a range of furniture in laminated wood made by the client's firm, and later added a circular swimming pool with a domed roof, again detailed to perfection.[35] While Stirling was concerned primarily with the appearance and formal effect of details, Gowan's drawings speak more of assembly and the nature of material *per se*. He was perhaps at his happiest with small projects for discerning clients where everything could be carefully controlled, and he remained committed to the idea that one should find 'the style for the job', a phrase repeatedly used by Banham in describing the work of the partnership, which that critic later thought applied more to Gowan alone. Stirling's repetition of the same formula for different situations after the break-up certainly suggests a less acute sense of propriety.

But there is no denying Stirling's extraordinary gift for formal and spatial thinking and for capturing it in drawings, particularly in selective axonometric

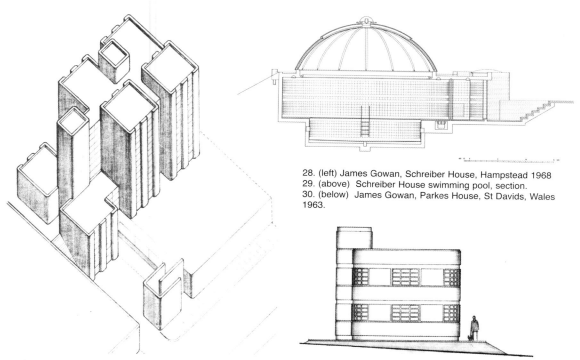

28. (left) James Gowan, Schreiber House, Hampstead 1968
29. (above) Schreiber House swimming pool, section.
30. (below) James Gowan, Parkes House, St Davids, Wales 1963.

projections. For a couple of decades he held the readers of architectural weeklies in thrall, for the publication of a new Stirling project was always an event. On the other hand his spoken explanations of his buildings tended to be deadpan, often falling back on pragmatic alibis. Although he had lived in an extraordinarily fertile architectural milieu and had undoubtedly absorbed much,[36] he was no theorist.[37] His personal sensibility was more directly visual/spatial and less verbal than that of Gowan, and it was precisely the immediate connection of hand and eye through the drawing that made his vision so compelling, even letting it run away with him, and seducing critics who perhaps should have questioned it more.[38] A friend and client claimed: *'He rarely mentioned the sociological background of buildings. He was interested in their formal and aesthetic qualities'.*[39] Gowan on the other hand was a precise thinker and a stickler for detail, in analytical intelligence and knowledge of architectural history at least the equal of Stirling. He was the more articulate, and beyond his undoubted creative and builderly input he fulfilled a crucial critical role. Stirling's later partner Michael Wilford, who joined the office in the Leicester phase, reports that they argued constantly.[40] A typical instance near the end of their association concerns the

History Faculty. Stirling had put the cycle park on the roof of the lower part, doubtless to create a *raison d'être* for the beloved Corbusian ramp. Still indignant ten years later, Gowan remarked: *'Can you imagine: all those students wheeling their bicycles up there! - It took me three months to talk him out of that'.* [41]

The world-wide reputation of the Leicester building tends to obscure its original status as a humdrum and relatively minor university project built within the then current cost yardstick. Photographs greatly exaggerate the tower which is really quite small, with only four small offices per floor in the office part, for example. The subtle mix of ideas, the way they were integrated, and the enhancement of formal effect during the development and detailing of the design, all contribute to its paradigm-shifting originality and justify its high historical reputation. But the success of Leicester destroyed the intimate conditions of the two partners' work together, and Stirling adapted better to their sudden fame, which fed his extrovert personality and allowed it to flower. His later work showed equal inventiveness and fluency, but lacked the sense of propriety and critical distance shown by the work with Gowan.

PBJ/EC

Postscript: The Stuttgart Staatsgalerie, 1981-84

The masterpiece of James Stirling's later *oeuvre*, the extension to the Staatsgalerie at Stuttgart designed with his later partner Michael Wilford, was so influential and remains so central to the story of postmodernism that it cannot be omitted from this book. It would have deserved a chapter of its own but for our rule about one work per architect. Its importance is fourfold: a new and more ambitious borrowing from history, a revived interest in urban context, a subversion of the earlier 'functionalist' position, and a conscious display of irony. Stirling's engagement with German museums began in 1975, when he was invited to take part in a limited competition for Düsseldorf. This went unplaced, but in the same year he was invited to a second competition for Cologne, in which he developed the ideas further. He finally won the Stuttgart competition in 1977, which was completed to inter-national acclaim in 1984. The three projects can be regarded as a theme and variations: that for Düsseldorf already contained the main ingredients of Stuttgart, particularly the central drum as anchor for the composition and the idea of a public through route which passes through the site without passing through the building. Already, too, a complex of differently shaped buildings was deployed in relation to the geometry of the site, seeking continuity with the surrounding city rather than object-like status. This approach to the city developed the Smithsons' treatment at the Economist (Chapter 5), but was more immediately attributable to influences from a brilliant young assistant and an old mentor. The assistant was Leon Krier, later classical revivalist, who worked for Stirling between 1968 and 1970, and played a leading role in his Derby Civic Centre project which pioneered the contextual approach. The mentor was Colin Rowe, who had just summed up advances in his thinking with *Collage City* (Rowe and Koetter 1978), and Stirling certainly fulfilled his idea of 'collage' besides extending brilliantly the compositional sensibility of Le Corbusier, the hero of Rowe's whole generation. For Rowe and other historians, Stirling's work also fulfilled the idea of a phase growing from and reacting to orthodox Modernism just as Mannerism had grown from the Renaissance.

Stirling must have been delighted when he discovered among the clauses of the brief for the Stuttgart Museum the need to preserve a right of way across the site. This became the *leitmotiv* for the whole design, taking the form of a pedestrian route which ramped up to the initial platform, ramped up again to enter the central drum, rose spirally around half of it to regain the axis at the north, then passed out sideways into the upper street. It did not really matter that the route was used mainly by tourists wanting to see the building: a masterly statement had been made about forming a *promenade architecturale* and about creating a new relationship between the institution and the public realm, whose spaces were coming increasingly under threat.[42] A museum was the ideal vehicle for such a demonstration, not only because of its acknowledged public role and duty, but also because of the new emphasis on commercialisation and visitor numbers, at which the Staatsgalerie proved particularly successful. The promenade acted almost like a film trailer for a visit, offering tempting glimpses and enrolling the passer-by as spectator.

Many critics have pointed out the obvious kinship of plan between the Staatsgalerie and Schinkel's famous Altes Museum in Berlin, a venerable German precedent. Both centred on a focal drum, but while in Schinkel's building this was the distributor and place of arrival, Stirling's court was an open-air void, crossed laterally by visitors with tickets proceeding to the upper courts, but possessed visually by the public on the through route. The galleries were efficient rectangular toplit white rooms confined to the upper level perimeter, and getting to them involved an irregular route through the asymmetrical foyer with its wavy glass wall, around a ramped passage in the wall of the drum, and up an axial stair at the back with a blind turn. This modernist promenade playing around the central drum owed something to Asplund, whose work Stirling had long admired, but unlike the Swedish master it contradicted a traditional axial progression, bringing an element of 'complexity and contradiction' that aptly fulfilled Venturi's postmodernist programme.[43] The way the principal internal route was underplayed in favour of the external one was regarded as ironic and playful.[44]

Although the ramps and cylinders were Corbusian in inspiration and could have been left in an abstract white render or raw concrete, Stirling wanted a stone cladding in striped layers, celebrating arches with fake voussoirs and adding a huge Egyptian cornice. This quotation of archaic elements was cleverly generic, producing a monumental impression reminiscent of Asplund's Stockholm City Library (Blundell Jones 2002,

31. (below) James Stirling and Michael Wilford, Staatsgalerie
Stuttgart, 1984, upper floor plan showing central drum with
ramp, upper courts, and peripheral gallery rooms.
32. (bottom) Staatsgalerie, lower floor plan, with entrance
terrace off ramp from street at bottom, foyer, temporary
exhibition gallery to left of central drum, and start of upper ramp.
33. (right) Staatsgalerie, axonometric drawing of central part
showing juxtaposition of parts and progress of ramp.

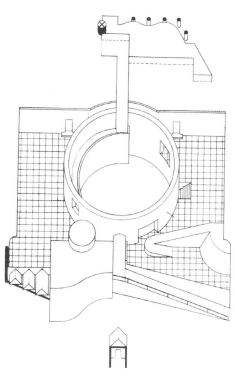

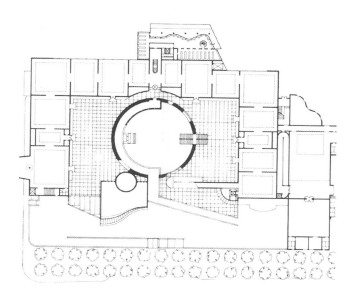

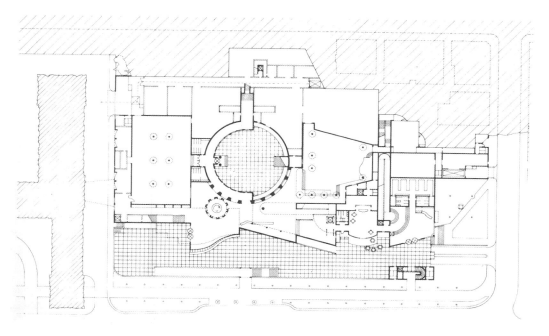

pp.123-7) a building long familiar to Stirling.[45] But the illusion of heavy construction was immediately undermined, for the stonework joints were visibly open and the thinness of material made evident. As if this were not enough, the front wall was built as a broken opening, with fallen stones embedded in the grass. The former brutalist, brought up to the idea that materials should be 'honestly expressed' relished the fakery, the breaking of rules. This was part of a timely irony that tickled the fancy of a whole generation of critics, and led to the flattering sobriquet *Vitruvius Ludens* from Sir John Summerson, the grand old man of architectural history.[46] Unlike a younger generation of sincere classical revivalists intent on building with solid walls and lime mortar, Stirling was well aware of the problems of anachronism. Had not his pseudo-monumentality been suitably distanced from the realities of antiquity, it would have been more problematic to 'collage' the archaic elements with the quasi high-tech of the exposed lift mechanism, the giant metal handrails, the steel supports of the canopies, and a wavy glass wall; but Stirling synthesised all this most convincingly.

Through so perfectly representing the 1980s and postmodernism, the Staatsgalerie has inevitably become dated. Its sheer virtuosity has remained unequalled, but its style was imitated across the world in the following two decades, and one sees the drum, the stripey cladding, and the wavy glass wall in unexpected places. Its somewhat cool treatment of the art collection, confined to the white boxes around the perimeter, makes the purely architectural gesture at the physical and metaphorical centre all the more important, and in retrospect it brought a new creative freedom to museum design. Museum buildings proliferated towards the end of the twentieth century, and many became less neutral containers than celebrations in and of themselves, visited for their own sake. Daniel Libeskind's Jewish Museum of 2001 almost displaced its content, exhibited at first completely empty. Frank Gehry's Guggenheim in Bilbao of 1997 is not lacking in artworks, but they, and the interior housing them, are of minor importance compared with the world-famous 'Bilbao Effect'.

PBJ

34, 35. (this page) Staatsgalerie, view on main axis at street level and where ramp enters drum.
36 - 43. (opposite) Procession of views: street and broken wall; entrance outside and in; drum from above; passage into drum and arrival at upper court.

88

Notes

1. Girouard claims it received *'an international acclaim unequalled by any previous British building since the Crystal Palace'*: Girouard 1998, p. 114.

2. John McKean's monograph on Leicester (McKean 1994), Irenée Scalbert's article in *Archis* (Scalbert 1994) and Girouard's biography of Stirling (Girouard 1998, p.115) are the noble exceptions to the general rule of Leicester being reascribed to Stirling. Girouard provides the most detailed retrospective account of the genesis of the building, though it was written without direct input from Gowan.

3. Girouard 1998, pp.106-115.

4. Even if not always obeyed, the idea that form should follow function was deeply ingrained as a starting point in architects' education and remained so until the end of the 1960s. Architects tended to explain their buildings in terms of pragmatic logic, leaving aesthetic justifications off the agenda. Girouard (1998) reports repeatedly how Stirling tended to speak in such terms.

5. Conversation between Gowan and PBJ, 13 April 2005.

6. This was also a functional element demanded in the very first briefing document from Parkes (copy in Gowan's possession).

7. There were opening louvres in the underside, which could admit a considerable draught.

8. A typical early modernist idea seen, for example, in Hannes Meyer's League of Nations proposal of 1927 and in earlier projects by Hugo Häring and Hans Scharoun.

9. Rightly he felt the paradigm shift, and famously described it in a radio broadcast as having exposed concrete volumes and blue bricks, a lapse that suggests he hardly dared to look. Printed as 'The anti-pioneers' in *The Listener*, 5 January 1967.

10. The Rusakov factory club of 1927 and the Makhorka Pavilion 1923, (see Starr 1978, pp. 61,134-8). That Stirling possessed Russian books is recorded in Girouard 1998, pp. 73-4. Gowan reports having a folio of drawings of Russian modernist work collected and published by Arthur Korn.

11. Stirling's friend Christopher Owtram had made a radical conversion of an oast-house, see Girouard 1998, pp. 77-79.

12. Crucially, the whole July 1957 edition of *The Architectural Review* was given over by J.M.Richards to a display of warehouses, wind- and watermills, textile factories, breweries, maltings and oast houses under the title *The Functional Tradition*. Shortly afterwards this was both cited and echoed by Stirling in his own version with his own photos published in *The Architects' Yearbook* Vol. 8, 1957, pp. 62-68.

13. There were two unforeseen technical problems here: the adhesion of the tiles and the frost resistance of the terracotta material. The durability of nineteenth-century bricks was difficult to repeat with faster mechanised kilns. The Leicester building suffered leaks and other damage, and was later submitted to a technically-based remedial programme which rode roughshod over many significant details.

14. The later disdain for functionalism has resulted in too summary a rejection on too simple a basis.

15. Pugin's *True Principles*, (first published 1841) at that time rare in the original and not yet published in facsimile, was certainly well known to Gowan.

16. John Ruskin 'The Stones of Venice', in Ruskin 1903-12.

17. *'William Butterfield or the Glory of Ugliness'* in the collection *Heavenly Mansions* (Summerson 1949). This was an intellectual landmark for Gowan.

18. 'Regional architecture', *Architects Yearbook*, Vol. 8, pp. 62-68.

19. Conversation with PBJ, 13 April 2005.

20. Le Corbusier 1951.

21. Wittkower 1949.

22. Le Corbusier 1951, introduction.

23. Wittkower 1974, cited by Gowan in conversation 13 April 2005. Since this was based on Wittkower's lectures of 1971/2, it post-dated Leicester, but it shows Gowan's engagement.

24. Scalbert (1994) confirms the importance of this from his conversations with Gowan, and identifies a particular van Doesburg composition that had been published by Zevi.

25. The house studies were prompted by a contribution to *House and Garden* called 'A house which grows' (April 1957, pp. 66-71). Gowan produced a series including the one illustrated, but *'Stirling was not taken by them and suggested clamping sequential quadrants to my service core'*: Gowan, letter to PBJ 16 January 2006.

26. Again Gowan letter of 16 January 2006.

27. His ironic essay on teaching at the Architectural Association is an entertaining example, see Gowan 1978, pp. 14-15.

28. Banham 1966.

29. Stirling's articles on Le Corbusier for *The Architectural Review* were entitled 'From Garches to Jaoul', September 1955, and 'Ronchamp – Le Corbusier's Chapel and the Crisis of Rationalism', March 1956.

30. According to Scalbert (1994) Parkes also objected to the idea of giving higher status to the offices through better glazing.

31. Gowan did not believe in the central supervision of book-stacks as a generative principle, and thought the readoption of the Leicester vocabulary inappropriate. Problems were already arising with Leicester's glazing, so he was amazed to see Stirling repeating it at much larger scale. Asked what he would have done instead, he remarked: *'Aalto designed a very good library at Viipuri, and if you can't think of anything better you should take that as a model'*: remembered conversations with Gowan 1972, PBJ.

32. There were endless leaks, and the university's confusion about ownership of the site – no fault of Stirling's – prompted a late change of orientation that turned the library into a solar collector. The patent glazing neither permitted adequate insulation nor acoustic isolation between adjacent rooms. One lecturer, despite everything a supporter of the building, told me, c. 1985: *'In the winter it's all right because I can put on lots of pullovers and jump up and down, but in summer when it gets above ninety I just have to leave.'* PBJ.

33. Again formally brilliant, and again prey to climatic and technical problems, but with the added pain that its internal transparency made an unwanted arena out of private rooms.

34. *'You want architecture? Look at the history faculty'* became the refrain of philistine clients in Cambridge in the 1980s.

35. Schreiber loved the house and lived there until his death in 1984. For several years the house was used as an office, but it has recently returned to residential use, lovingly restored.

36. Girouard 1998, ch. 5.

37. As Gowan put it: *'you couldn't argue architectural theory with him'*, conversation with PBJ, 13 April 2005.

38. Sir John Summerson dubbed Stirling 'Vitruvius Ludens', accepting every lapse from classical conformity as playful mannerism, see *The Architectural Review,* 1984.

39. Paul Manousso, son of the Ham Common client, reported in Girouard 1998, p. 73.

40. Girouard 1998, p.107.

41. Remembered conversations with Gowan 1972, PBJ.

42. The main theme of Richard Sennett, later expressed in *The Fall of Public Man* (Sennett 1977).

43. Venturi 1966.

44. The building's main axis, celebrated at street level with a glass-roofed portico, leads directly to the underground car park. The axis is marked again at high level by the entrance and exit of the through route in the drum then by the internal stairs, though nobody would know without a plan. The main cross-axis links the visitors' door to the central drum with the outdoor stairs opposite – architecturally the most prominent steps in the building – terminating in a locked door in the centre of the east gallery. See my critique 'Man or superman?' in *Architects Journal* 6 February 1985, pp. 44-55. PBJ.

45. He had even stolen a library copy of the 1950 Asplund monograph: see Girouard 1998, p. 64.

46. *The Architectural Review*, March 1983. The publication of the Staatsgalerie in *The Architectural Review*, December 1984 had critics queueing to praise Stirling: Alan Colquhoun, Reyner Banham, Emilio Ambasz, Oriol Bohigas and William Curtis.

Chapter 7. Helmut Striffler: Protestant Chapel at Dachau Concentration Camp, 1964-67

Helmut Striffler (b.1927) is perhaps the least internationally known architect in this book, and like Böhm and Schattner his work has mostly been concentrated in a single German region, in his case the city of Mannheim. But his masterpiece at Dachau is a building of world significance, confronting one of the toughest programmes an architect has ever had to face. At a time when much architecture across Europe had descended into a banal utilitarianism, this chapel's purpose was almost entirely representational, and that representation was of the most difficult kind imaginable: the remembering of and attempted reconciliation to the worst mass murder in history. Of all the works in this book, it has the greatest right to be called 'poetic', because of its dual appeal to head and heart, its evocation

of an appropriate mood under the most difficult conditions, and its great economy of means, with every detail contributing to the impact of the whole. Striffler has written articulately about his intentions, and his explanation of the building makes good sense, yet there is much more to it than can easily be explained, for the resonance is deep and intuitive. Also the great consistency between the building and its incorporated artworks reveals a remarkably unified sense of purpose. Striffler was a schoolboy at the start of the Second World War and a teenager at its end, serving for two years as assistant anti-aircraft gunner before being called up as a soldier. He reached adulthood at the time of chaos, deprivation, and huge ideological change which Germans call *Stunde null* (zero hour).

1. The downward main entrance to the chapel: a furrow of protective refuge. Photo by Robert Häusser.

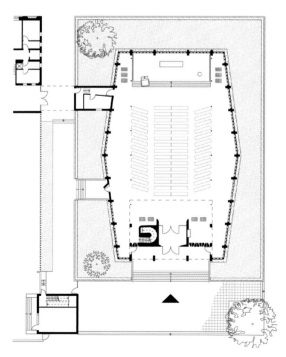

As order returned he went to study architecture in Karlsruhe under the rather strict and puritanical Egon Eiermann (see Chapter 2) whose office he worked in before graduating in 1955, and later again as assistant, helping to build the concrete St Matthew's Church at Pforzheim.[1] In 1956 he set up his own office in Mannheim with a commission for Trinity Church in the city centre, and he started to enter competitions. There followed various small domestic and commercial jobs, and a school won in a competition of 1960 was realised, but Striffler became best known for his churches, initiating a further four in the Mannheim area before being invited to the competition for Dachau in 1964.[2]

Trinity Church, Mannheim, his first independent work, shows the influence of Eiermann, as the master's geometric simplicity and clear expression of structure are directly carried over, and the use of stained glass in a concrete wall is again the main visual effect. But Striffler had already departed from Eiermann's extreme simplicity by producing a slightly lozenge-shaped space that was more centralised. He also made a more subtle and irregular reinterpretation of the stained glass detail. Perhaps because he was constrained by the intense rationality of Eiermann's teaching, Striffler burst out into a greater spatial freedom which the medium of cast concrete allowed without blurring of detail. He introduced curves and diagonals in his church at Blumenau and diagonals again at Ilvesheim, while the church at Rheinau completed in 1965 went a step further. It had an irregular outer wall developing into its triangular tower, and the space for worship was mainly defined by the corner altar and radial seating. By this point rational objectivity and rectangular geometry had given way to a more complex and ambiguous spatial language no longer bound by the structural frame or by conventional symmetry and axiality; in fact it was already 'aperspective'.[3] The corner entrance at Rheinau leads towards the tower, visually framed by the highly elaborated right wall, but the route then swings around towards the corner altar, which is defined by its curved steps and the bay in the back wall. Altar, seating, steps, gallery and entrance take up slightly different curves or angles in a kind of conversation amongst themselves rather than conforming to a discipline that would have them marching to the same tune. That this development in his architectural vocabulary had a spiritual meaning for Striffler is evident from his writing. While admitting the need for special places

Churches in and around Mannheim by Helmut Striffler:

2, 3. (opposite) Trinity Church, central Mannheim, 1956-59, photo and plan.
4. (above left and plan, left) Church at Blumenau 1960-62.
5. (below left) Church at Ilvesheim 1963-64, plan.
6, 7. (above and below) Church at Rheinau 1961-65, photo and plan.

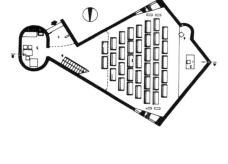

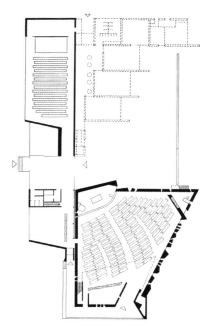

of religious observance, he opposed the tendency to dictate the forms too clearly:

The Church as institution has always delivered important themes for architecture. Whole epochs have been named accordingly. In contrast, the dominant impression today is as if there were no future and that therefore the role of the church as client were finished. This tendency has been strengthened – even directly produced – by the latest developments in church-building activity, which is characterised by a stressing of formal claims. In the process we have overlooked the importance of the role played in the practical bid for space. By stressing a distinctive kind of celebration, we pay for it increasingly by restricting the freedom of activity that architecture has the duty to deliver. Herr Funke speaks of a 'frozen Christmas atmosphere'.[4]

Without going to the opposite extreme of the totally flexible space, there had to be nonetheless room for the unexpected and the unpredictable, and for a dialogue to occur between the space and the events held within it. There also had to be margins within which the partially engaged could float without a sense of alienation:

A total milieu in which an open discourse can take place: this is what can be described as the basic principle of contact.

In the apportioning of space this means providing for enough 'overflow'. Only in still zones can one find the opportunity for conversation, to take somebody to one side, to withdraw with them. Enough opportunity must also be provided to allow one to stand apart, without being forced optically and spatially into the role of outsider or 'conspirator.' The built medium for this is called space, this includes space for movement, space of negotiation – in the sense defined above – and free space. I and my potential partners in discussion also need time for our decisions, time for the reflections which precede decisions about which direction to take.[5]

Striffler also lamented the increasing isolation of the Church, opposing the forces that tended to cut it off from the city and to make it just another private institution. He argued that on the contrary, it could offer a larger public role in mediating social and planning problems, and through acting as a catalyst

to bring different groups and ideologies together. He further noted that the Church as a body had a unique chance also to provide humanitarian and ethical respite in a world driven increasingly by a profane functional and economic view, from which ordinary people were being expropriated:

Where does the church stand when it comes to the question of making a new city?... [The development] evolves in phases: first comes obedience to the norm, then realised norm becomes monotony, and finally the legal state becomes a bureaucracy whose demands run unchallenged to the limit. Which body but the Church could be the advocate for those arriving later on the scene, and not earlier in a position to complain? It would be the role of the Church to engage itself as advocate of the humanitarian (with the help of specialist architects). She could perform this function best through those who understand the question of town planning, can help with the hurdles of the law, and so become catalysts. This would add to the spiritual and material position of the church, bringing a broader public engagement in an established territory of trust... To build for the church in this way would be unusually pertinent and would help to achieve a new reality to which architects would happily devote themselves.[6]

These extracts from Striffler's essay, 'Church and City', 1974, reveal the reasons for his commitment to working for the Church and his progressive stance. The four churches discussed above had given him chances to develop his spatial ideas and put them into practice, testing their public and liturgical effect. The invitation to the Dachau competition arrived therefore at the appropriate moment in the career of the 37-year-old architect for him to rise to the challenge.

8. Model of the camp diisplayed in the camp museum, with serried ranks of huts in centre and guard buildings surrounding Roll-call square on right. The main entrance was bottom right.

Dachau and its history

Though now known to most of the world primarily for its concentration camp, Dachau is an old town north of Munich with around 35,000 inhabitants. Its picturesque setting between rivers with views of distant mountains actually made it an artists' colony in the 1890s, but this paradise was lost in the First World War when it gained a large munitions factory. This major employer found no alternative role in peacetime, and by the end of the 1920s Dachau had the highest unemployment rate in Germany. Failing to attract private industry, the town lobbied the regional government in the early 1930s for re-use of the old works and workers' barracks as a labour camp. So when the Nazis came to power in 1933 and wanted to create camps to incarcerate their political opponents, it provided a ready opportunity.[7] They had long planned to make 'collection camps' for political prisoners, and the old works site was swiftly converted to this use, the first batch of around 200 prisoners being brought in less than three weeks after Hitler's takeover. Within a couple of months SS guards had taken over from regular police and violence had become institutionalised, including torture and murder. Because it was the first of the Nazi camps, Dachau was also the experiment and model for others, and its commandant Theodor Eicke was given the role of general inspector to all the camps.[8] It was Eicke who introduced the cruel work programmes in the name of prisoners' 'education' and the gate inscription 'Arbeit macht frei'. In 1937-8 the concentration camp was completely rebuilt within a new rectangular compound with ditch and watchtowers.

Most of the prisoners were kept in serried ranks of wooden sheds arranged around a north-south central spine which disgorged into a large Roll-call square embraced to south by the two-storey masonry control block. Initially it was not crowded, but the number of inmates doubled to 6000, then tripled to 18,000 in 1938 when Jews taken in the Kristallnacht pogroms and political prisoners who had tried to resist the takeover of Austria arrived.[9] As well as being a prison, the place became a national centre for the SS, with barracks, a special hospital, a factory for uniforms etc., so that by the outbreak of the Second World War the concentration camp constituted only about a quarter of the whole complex. Unlike Auschwitz, Dachau did not become a slaughter production line, and the gas chamber built and tested in 1942 remained unused,

9. The concentration camp in operation with inmates.

10. The preserved guard buildings now used as a museum.

11. (below) Reconstructed hut showing the cramped living conditions.

12. (left) Aerial photo showing procession at the opening of the Catholic memorial in August 1960.

13. (right) The drum-shaped Catholic memorial with its altar in the opening, which was built on the axis of the camp.

but cremation ovens operational by 1939 were augmented in 1940 and again in 1942, disposing of tens of thousands of corpses by 1945.[10] Quite apart from deaths through torture and execution by the SS and in medical experiments, disease was encouraged by overcrowding, food was short, and people were worked to death. Clergy were a special category of prisoner held at Dachau and better treated than most others, but 37 per cent of the 2500 held there had died by the end of the war.[11] Over 206,000 prisoners passed through Dachau and there were over 31,000 certified deaths: in the appalling conditions of early 1945 the death rate reached 100 per day.[12]

After liberation in 1945, the camp was used briefly to house survivors, then it served the Allies as a prison for war criminals, trials being held in the service building.[13] From 1948 to 1960 it became a refugee camp for fugitives from the East, Wohnsiedlung Dachau Ost, the barrack huts being cheaply converted into family housing.[14] In the deprived and chaotic post-war years the site was just a useful facility, and little thought was given to preserving memories of the atrocities, except by survivors who set up a small but unflinching museum in the camp's crematorium in 1945. By the early 1950s the will to forget was so strong that this museum had become regarded as a disgrace and an eyesore, and its founders were slandered and persecuted. In 1953 it was closed, and the local mayor even tried to get the crematorium itself destroyed.[15] Meanwhile, instead of focusing on the camp, early memorial activity had concentrated more safely on the mass graves at nearby Leiten Hill. A temple-like structure was planned before the end of 1945, but there were long and painful arguments about what could possibly be appropriate before a very plain memorial hall was finally

erected in 1952. Towards the end of the 1950s, attitudes were beginning to change. The publication of Anne Frank's diary and Alain Resnais' film *Nuit et Brouillard* helped open the question to a younger generation, and from 1954 onwards increasingly large commemorations were held at the camp each November by trades unionists to mark the anniversary of Kristallnacht.[16] Then in 1959 Bishop Johannes Neuhäusler launched an energetic initiative to build a Catholic memorial chapel within the site, accomplishing the building with his architect Josef Weidemann remarkably quickly. Taking the bull by the horns, they built their 14 metre high circular stone chapel – essentially an altar – right on the main axis of the camp at the north end, making the 'mortal agony of Christ' the new focus. To sharpen the outline of the camp, the fence, ditch and watchtowers were repaired or rebuilt. At the chapel's dedication in August 1960 the original barrack huts were still present, but because of their poor condition and the compromises of conversion, they were demolished in 1964. Just two at the south end were rebuilt to the original form, with bunks three-deep to demonstrate former conditions in the camp, but they were effectively sanitised, made permanent and museum-like through more enduring materials. Memories of the remaining huts were reduced to mere lines in the ground.

The Protestant Chapel

Catholic Bishop Neuhäusler's initiative spurred on the Jews and Protestants to make memorials of their own, taking sites to right and left of the Catholic chapel.[17] The Protestants drew up their brief and invited seven known church architects to produce designs in a competition of 1964 including Egon Eiermann, who planned simple boxes for the three

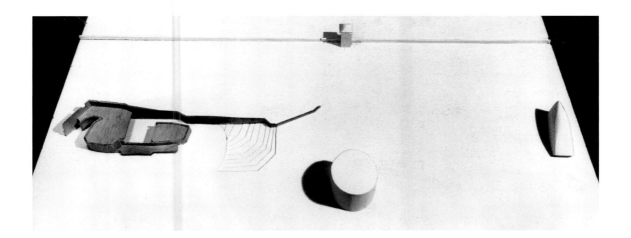

elements of the brief linked by a free-standing wall, his chapel enclosed by stained glass in concrete frames like his Kaiser Wilhelm Memorial Church in Berlin. That this was more than a gesture of sober simplicity was shown by his intended placing of the entire group on the diagonal, breaking with the order of the camp to follow the angle of the adjacent crematorium complex, and thus forging a spatial link between the two. Striffler, however, was much more radical in his rejection of the camp's basic geometry:

The monotony of the camp's schematic rect-angular layout is an insistent symbol of its deadly policing order, for rectangularity was an essential part of the murder system... Bullets travel in straight lines. With a few machine-gun posts along the four straight perimeter fences the security of Dachau concentration camp was assured, in murderous perfection. The same goes for the arrangement of the accommodation huts: in each block were sleeping-places for 2000 people, unbelievably cramped, and all organised through rational rectangular subdivision. The poplars of the axial street in the camp seemed at first as innocent as hundreds of other such trees in the Dachau landscape, but they became instruments of brutality when – as frequently happened – the guards forced the prisoners to collect all the fallen leaves into a pile. The grass strips along the inside of the fence were death strips: those daring to venture on to them were 'shot attempting to escape', and anyone reaching the fence was left hanging electrocuted on the wire. When the sun shone, punishment was increased by prolonging the daily line-up to

14. (above) Model showing north end of camp, with Protestant, Catholic and Jewish memorials from left to right. A watchtower marks the main axis behind.

15. (below) General plan of camp, north is top. Seventeen ranks of huts occupy the centre of the camp, deployed to either side of the axial street. Main entrance, Roll-call square and guard buildings are at bottom and the crematorium complex is outside main boundary top left. The three memorials can just be discerned across the top.

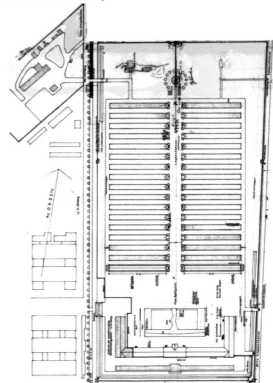

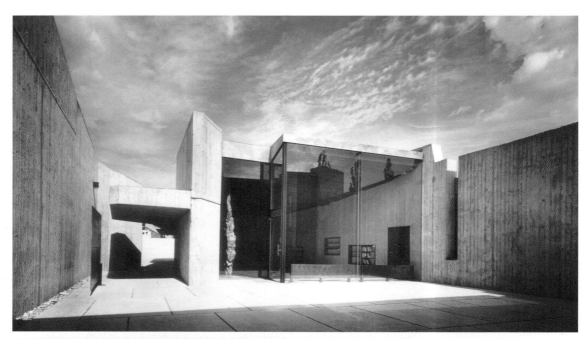

16-20. Photographs by Robert Häusser of the Protestant Chapel and plan showing route from right to left via sunken courtyard.

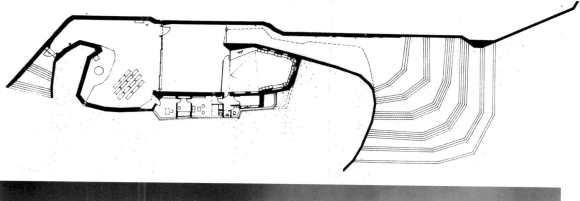

the point of torture, but rain, snow and wind all increased the hardship more automatically... After so much abuse, rectangularity therefore seemed to me impossible for a new building in the camp, and at first I thought I could not build anything without getting caught in its web. The new building needed to avoid all claims to monumentality yet at the same time it had to step beyond the camp's own primitive bid for order. [18]

The construction of the camp as a north/south orientated rectangle with central axis followed the same hierachical spatial order as the military camps of the Romans, and curiously the street arriving from the south was the Alte Römerstrasse, an old Roman road, though the south gate that would have linked it to the decumanus[19] was missing. Instead the main entrance arrived from the west across the canal which defined the west side of the site. Though not longitudinally central, this was effectively the cardo, for it ran across the centre of the main outdoor room where all inmates would collect, Roll-call square. Authority and control were vested there, and in the large symmetrical building embracing it to the south where guards and administration were based. This building also shielded off a separate territory beyond to the south, with cells for special prisoners which were also used for torture, and an execution wall. In setting up their memorial, the Catholics accepted this basic spatial order but attempted to trump it, equating the suffering in the camp with that of Christ. Effectively the whole camp became a church, for instead of progressing like prisoners down the spine to account to the SS in Roll-call square, worshippers would move up the axis to account to God at the altar. It was less an act of

memory than a radical reinterpretation credible only to Christian groups, and the Catholic appropriation of the axis left other faiths in a quandary about how to compete.

Striffler decided not only to deny all connection with the formal structure of the camp, but to dispense with symmetry and even with the right angle. He sought to make *'a counter-place (Gegenort) against all the apparatus of terror... a living trace (Spur) dug into in the merciless plain of the camp, as a protective furrow against the inhuman criminality which is still felt everywhere in the camp'.* [20] He sank the chapel into the ground, to be embraced by mother earth, *'which was present during the tyranny, but remained unaffected by its power. This embrace means protection from wind, heat, and enmity of all kinds'.* [21] The chapel and reading room, sacred and social spaces respectively, were placed to either side of a small square court which was left open to the sky to receive daylight and sun,[22] giving it to both spaces, but was completely cut off from views of the camp. Through glass walls the occupants of the two rooms look across at one another, and the chapel's sliding glass doors extend its active space into the court for large gatherings. Striffler intended that: *'embedded within is stillness and security (Geborgenheit)... the group of buildings should offer the camp's visitors the helpful gesture of a short period of relief. It should offer rooms which confirm that a bodily coming-to-rest is the prerequisite for reflection and prayer.'* [23]

The main architectural task then became the descent, something very unusual for entry into a church, as normally the progressions of steps at entrance, choir and altar lead ever upwards in celebration of heaven. This association is

21. (far left) Sunken entry passage with sculptural relief by Hubertus von Pilgrim.

22. (left) Sunken entry arrives at gate by Fritz Kühn, with the text *'I find refuge in the shadow of your wings'* written in the four languages spoken by the majority of inmates.

23. (right) Sunken courtyard with glass wall open to the chapel, with seating and altar visible within.

supported by a universal cross-cultural hierarchy that equates higher with 'superior', sets the most important persons in the highest chairs or at 'high table', gives them a 'rise' in salary, 'elevates' them to a peerage, or 'sends them down' from university in disgrace. The simple everyday differentiations between 'high quality' and 'low quality' or being 'at the top of the list' rather than at the bottom, show how difficult it is to escape this spatial metaphor. Downward entrances are further associated with crypts and tombs, with burial and death, with the terrors and mysteries of the underworld as opposed to the clarity of the heavens.[24]

Striffler could draw on these associations to underline the sombre terror of the camp, but he needed to make his entrance also gentle and inviting, a gradual embrace and deliverance from the camp and its menacing memories. His entrance starts very wide, radiating from south-west to north-east and dropping via groups of steps placed circumferentially, almost like a small amphitheatre. The steps are gravelled with stone-like edges and with stone steps indicating the way across the flats. They all lead down to a sunken passage which is paved at odd angles with very large slabs of concrete. A board-marked concrete wall to right and north embraces the whole complex and protects the route, expressing an inflection southward towards camp and sun. In a crucial gesture of asymmetry, this has its counterpart in a horizontal plane, the concrete extension of the ground which cantilevers out over the sunken passage, leaving just a light slit next to the wall. From all around, this concrete plane reads as mere ground, continuing the covering of small round pebbles used to neutralise and sanitise the camp, which Striffler saw as a kind of measureless desert or waste. But

the visitor approaching the chapel sees that this hanging plane conceals a secret refuge, which he or she is thus invited to explore. As Striffler himself put it: *'The covered part of the entranceway is the outermost counter-statement to the dramatic flatness of the camp. It mediates between the human dimension and the borderless expanse.'* [25]

The guiding north wall is mainly straight, but it kinks three times to break the view of the approaching visitor and to interlock the embrace of soffit and wall. Relief sculptures moulded into the wall's concrete show figure-like fragments by Hubertus von Pilgrim, the murmurs of the half forgotten, and the tough single-hinged stainless steel door at the end by Fritz Kühn repeats handwritten in four languages the lines of Psalm 17.8 *'I find refuge in the shadow of your wings'*. These and other artworks were remarkably well integrated. Arriving in the court, one rediscovers the free sky. The space can be read as square if one counts the glass walls as barriers, and rectangular paving slabs add to the sense of stability and calm. But one sees through the glass ahead to the chapel with its round altar, everything still enfolded by the womb-like concrete wall. One turns to discover the softly furnished reading room, a gentler and more inviting but profane foil to the chapel, allowing the chance of rest and contemplation. After attending a service or offering up a prayer, one finds a concealed door tucked around the corner that provides a discreet way up and out back to the camp. This exit is much played down to avoid confusion with the entry.

Externally the effect of the whole building is severe in the extreme, the boarded concrete unbroken at the back but for a narrow slot that marks the edge of the chapel. The concrete is tough and hard, but also stained and eroded by the weather, showing resistance but also suffering. The massing appropriately reflects the build up to a climax over chapel and altar, and the bell at the peak of the wall is contained in a louvred box as if it too needed protection from the unhappy spirits of the camp. The bleakness of the exterior and the reading of the camp as a kind of desert in which nothing could grow are apt metaphors for the extent of inhumanity that the place had known, metaphors that strike deep. The power of Striffler's architecture lies in the contrast between this unrelenting hardness and the relief within, mediated by that extraordinary downward entrance. The concrete wall could be called sculptural, but its free shaping is all at the service of the spatial progression, every kink and step in level carefully considered. The building was completed a year or two before postmodernism burst upon the world engendering a new enthusiasm for trivial and lightly applied symbolism, but it avoided this danger: it had fulfilled its symbolic programme not intellectually but viscerally. Even the tough Berlin critic Ulrich Conrads was moved to tears:

A work of architecture was recently erected that brings rest, peace, consolation in a place where the ground burns us through our soles, even when we haven't visited it... There is no building task, none before and – God willing – none to come, with which it can be compared. The dedication of effort required to bring a new building into existence in a place so poisoned from the depths of the earth to the heights of the sky can hardly be imagined. This dedication was required to attempt a reconciliation with the murdered and their executioners, who haunt us there like a thousand faces. Architecture, that earnest game, game in the highest sense, has given form to the plea for reconciliation, has changed the curse of the place into prayer, changed it into something new, as people arrive at that crypt under the open sky. It works with time, can appease time, perhaps even heal. That such works are again possible in Germany – works that defy criticism, that turn irony back on itself, that silence all accusation of vanity, defy all circumscription – indicates a new dimension of building... It shows that architecture is called to a new role in housing humanity. [26]

PBJ

Notes

1. One of Eiermann's better buildings: see Schirmer 1984, pp. 105-8. It was a precursor for his masterpiece, the Kaiser Wilhelm Memorial Church in Berlin.

2. Kirche auf der Blumenau bei Mannheim 1960-62, Evangelische Versöhnungskirche Mannheim-Rheinau 1961-65, Evangelische Kirche Ilvesheim bei Mannheim 1963-64, Evangelische Gemeindezentrum Gethsemane, Mannheim-Waldhof 1963-66, from work list in Flagge 1987, pp. 156-7.

3. The parallels with the theory and practice of Scharoun concerning departure from the perspective view, expressed in his competition entry for the National Theatre of Mannheim in 1953 (Blundell Jones 2002, Ch. 13), are striking, but Striffler had no direct or particular connection with Scharoun.

4. Flagge 1987, p. 21.

5. Ibid, pp. 21/22.

6. Ibid, pp. 22/23.

7. Marcuse 2001, pp.17-19.

8. Ibid, p. 26.

9. Ibid, pp. 34-36.

10. Ibid, pp. 41,45.

11. Ibid, pp. 43-4.

12. Ibid, p. 70.

13. Ibid, p. 69.

14. Ibid, p. 161.

15. Ibid, pp. 178-84.

16. Ibid, p. 203.

17. The political background is given in Marcuse 2001, pp. 276-289.

18. Conflation of two of Striffler's texts, one printed in Flagge 1987, p. 26, the other part of an article published in *Werk und Zeit* 1985: my translation.

19. Decumanus and cardo are the central north-south and east west streets of a Roman fort or town, linking the four gates to the central forum.

20. Striffler in Flagge 1987, p. 26.

21. Ibid.

22. Light is a major theme for Striffler, though it is not much discussed here. In an article of 1975 he wrote:
To enter a room means to follow its interplay of light and experience it as an opportunity to determine for oneself one's position in the spatial sequence. Thereby the connections between inside and out should never be destroyed... Connections between one part of a space and another arise through the changes in light conditions, which relate to our senses, and require a period of transition in accordance with the degree of change. Light leads us on. In spatial terms the leading of light is also essentially leading of route. Therefore light is our strongest most primary medium for reality. It regulates for us the defined edge of space. 'Licht artikuliert den Raum', Flagge 1987, pp. 100-2, my translation.

23. Striffler in Flagge 1987, p. 26.

24. The polarity of cellar and attic was famously explored in Bachelard's *Poetics of Space* (Bachelard 1969).

25. Striffler in Flagge 1987, p. 26.

26. Ulrich Conrads in Flagge 1987, p. 31, my translation.

Chapter 8. Günter Behnisch and Partners: Munich Olympics Complex, 1967-72

If one were looking for a single German firm to illustrate the changes in architecture between 1950 and 1990 there is hardly a better choice than Günter Behnisch's, for their work was exceptional for its extraordinarily wide range of approaches and in constantly keeping abreast of the times. But even more crucial to architectural history is the swing of their work away from a technically driven architecture of standardisation and towards a place-making responsive architecture which they called *Situationsarchitektur*. The Munich Olympics complex marks the very moment of transition, but far from accomplishing it by negating technology, the change was aided by pursuit of new and demanding techniques that led away from the grid, the right angle, and mindless repetition. As Behnisch himself reflected:

The competition came for us at just the right time. We were well prepared and had freed ourselves from strong formal ordering systems. We had experienced just how carefully the whole substance of architecture has to be handled and how easily it can be dominated and thrown off balance by certain forces. We had understood that we must take a fair and open attitude not only to people but also to things. [1]

Among the 'strong formal ordering systems' alluded to by Behnisch were the disciplines of prefabrication. Born in 1923, he had studied architecture at Stuttgart in the late 1940s before beginning to practise in the 1950s, but it was the prefabricated

1. Model of a prefabricated concrete school developed by Behnisch with Rostan c. 1960.

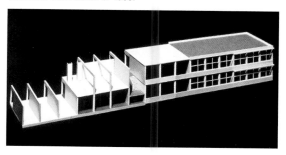

works of the 1960s that brought a national reputation, for Behnisch and his partners stood at the forefront in this developing field.[2] Ever since the 1920s, modernist architects had been convinced that the economies of Henry Ford's production line would inevitably be applied to architecture, for repetition would drastically reduce prices, and factories offered better and more predictable production conditions than building sites.[3] After the Second World War this became something of an obsession, helped along by books like *Mechanisation Takes Command*, and the need to put wartime factories to peaceful uses. There was therefore a widespread international effort to apply the rationale of serial production to building, which led to strict grid plans, a restricted range of components, and an appearance completely dominated by the production process. Behnisch struck up a relationship with the firm Rostan to produce a system in precast concrete for school buildings, at first with promising results and a certain elegance. The buildings could be constructed quicker and with less disruption by weather, and by adapting the system to different contexts the worst effects of repetition could be mitigated, but they were not significantly cheaper than traditional ones, and the price paid in terms of architectural limitation was too great. After three years or so the approach lost its appeal, and Behnisch came later to regard the whole excursion into prefabrication as a blind alley:

The geometric discipline became oppressive... Such ordering systems can become instruments of domination, first taking over design processes, then moving on to architecture and finally to life itself, whose vitality and variety comes to be regarded by the system-minded as a threat... The danger which later became a reality in new university buildings and massive hospitals was already beginning to show itself. We could see that if architecture followed this purely technical direction, it would necessarily become one-sided, unable to express wishes and requirements of a differentiated kind, unable to respond to and reflect the possible variety of our world. [4]

The alternative approach was to develop each work according to its own unique site and conditions. Günter Behnisch and his partners, Fritz Auer, Winfried Büxel, Erhard Tränkner and Carlo Weber,[5] had already produced some individualistic and site specific designs alongside more conventional work in the 1950s, but only around 1968 did this become the dominant design philosophy. The theoretical background lay in the writings of Hugo Häring, who laid the foundation for an organic architecture and warned of the dangers of standardisation, claiming that it *'helps the formally weak and the technically minded to take over, becoming not a strengthener of form, but merely a limiter of it'*.[6] The direct architectural example came from the late work of Hans Scharoun, who reached the height of his fame in the mid-1960s, pioneering an architecture of articulated parts and response to the site, which also deviated from the right angle.[7] Behnisch was also influenced by a more local organic architect, his teacher and former boss Rolf Gutbrod, best known for the Stuttgart Liederhalle.

Olympics in the Green
The buildings used for the Munich Olympics of 1972 were the result of a competition announced in 1967. It accompanied a period of wealth and good fortune brought by the economic miracle of post war recovery, expressing the pride and optimism of the Federal Republic. The design was made in 1968, a time of revolution and change, which saw the short-lived Prague Spring, the student revolt in Paris, worldwide protest against the Vietnam War, and the ascendancy of the new youth culture. The stage was therefore set for an Olympics that would represent the new democratic Germany in all its progressiveness, combining sport with the muses, intended to be 'casual, youthful, spirited, and open'.[8] It would celebrate the brotherhood and sisterhood of humanity as opposed to the dominance of the master race – the implicit theme of the previous Berlin Olympics in 1936. The kind of axial monumental layout planned by Werner March for that occasion was therefore altogether to be avoided, and the aim was instead an 'Olympics in the green' that would later serve equally well as a recreation park for the citizens of Munich.

The site was an unbuilt area north of the city that had been a military training ground and then an airfield. Through it the new motorway ring was destined to run, assuring good transport links. Munich's television tower already stood at the east end, along with a box-like skating hall. The whole area had originally been flat, but at the southern end lay a great spoil heap, made of rubble cleared from the city after wartime damage and of excavated material from the underground railway. Close by this artificial mountain was the diagonal line of the straight canal which conveyed water from the lakes and fountains of Schloss Nymphenburg, the old Royal Palace which lay to the south-west. Taking up the theme of 'Olympics in the green' Behnisch and his team conceived the idea of making an artificial landscape in which the seating banks of the great stadia would be set as ground-works like antique theatres. *'It is not a case of individual buildings but of an architectural landscape which covers the forms produced by individual uses'*.[9] The place had to work both for the Olympics with a crowd of 200,000 and afterwards with relatively smaller numbers casually enjoying the park, in summer or winter. The spoil mountain provided a welcome contrast with the flat ground and opened up long-distance views of the city skyline and the Alps beyond. It could be reshaped and spread to produce smaller hills and to absorb the seating of the larger stadia. It could also be used to provide elevated ridges leading to bridges which would effortlessly cross the motorway destined to divide the site, and which would continue guiding paths into the northern residential part. The changes of level would help to define a number of large outdoor rooms, breaking the site into more intimate areas, and in many places service provision could be included at the lower level while the park continued over the top. The other important given, the Nymphenburg canal, was opened up into an artificial lake to provide a focal valley. Within this landscape the three major arenas could be set: the great stadium for 80,000, the sports hall, and the swimming hall. With seating cut into the hillside and performance areas sunk into the ground, much of their volume could be absorbed, but they also needed to be roofed.

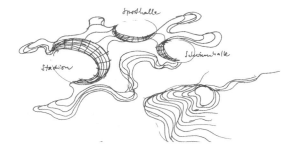

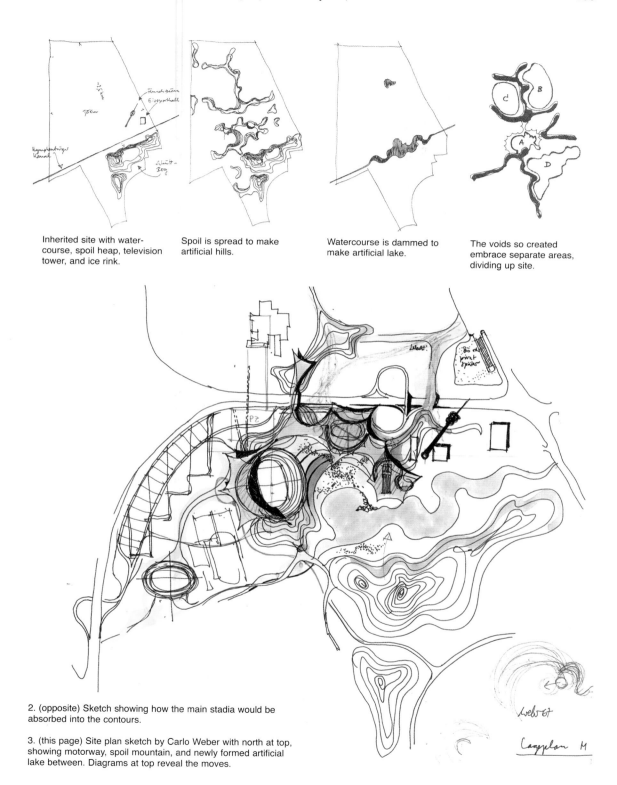

Inherited site with watercourse, spoil heap, television
tower, and ice rink.

Spoil is spread to make
artificial hills.

Watercourse is dammed to
make artificial lake.

The voids so created
embrace separate areas,
dividing up site.

2. (opposite) Sketch showing how the main stadia would be
absorbed into the contours.

3. (this page) Site plan sketch by Carlo Weber with north at top,
showing motorway, spoil mountain, and newly formed artificial
lake between. Diagrams at top reveal the moves.

The Tent Roofs

Behnisch's team explicitly wanted to avoid axes, great squares and monumental buildings,[10] but the three large arenas would inevitably present large volumes requiring conspicuous wide-span structures. To avoid the appearance of buildings as free-standing objects – a series of great boxes – it would be better if all were roofed together under a continuous skyscape to complement the ground-scape. So emerged the concept of a hanging cable net roof on steel masts. Frei Otto's Institute for Lightweight Structures was based at Stuttgart University where Behnisch had studied, and Otto had produced a hanging cable net roof for the German Pavilion at the World Expo in Montreal of 1968 with architect Rolf Gutbrod, a world-leading design that set the crucial precedent. Nonetheless, Otto was not part of Behnisch's competition team, the roof proposal being done instead by the engineer Heinz Isler.[11] Quite independently, he and the Behnisch team produced a plausible proposal in terms of shapes and loads, but it envisaged a hanging roof far larger than any so far built, with numerous technical problems to be solved: control of shape and distribution of weight,

anchorages, snow and wind loading, fire, durability, transparency, and so on. The judges of the competition, headed by Egon Eiermann (see Chapter 2), were enthusiastic about the general proposal but unsure about whether such a roof could be built, so although Behnisch and Partners were handed the project in March 1968, the decision on the roof was withheld until June while expert advice including Frei Otto's was sought and radically different roof forms were considered. Even after the principle was accepted there was much adjustment, for nearly a year and a half later, with foundations already laid, variants of the cable version were still being argued over.[12]

Finally, the structural breakthrough was made by Frei Otto. He and his institute carried out the crucial shape-defining work while the structural calculations and judgements were by Jörg Schlaich, then working for the Stuttgart firm of Leonhardt and Andrä, and now a world-famous engineer in his own right.[13] There were many unknowns. First of all, such a cable net has to be contrived so that every surface is in tension, and since it hangs, the shape is a result of the distribution of load, and can easily be distorted by wind or snow. The complex

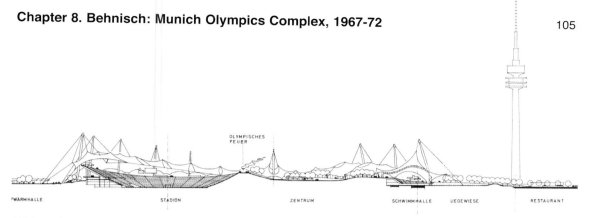

4,5. (opposite) Panoramic views of landscape with cable roofs.
7. (below) Panoramic view within main stadium.

6. (above) Section through site showing main stadium and swimming hall.

and changing curved surface is liable to a certain degree of movement which must be controlled, both in the detail of the covering and in the joint with any partition brought up against it. There are colossal compression pressures on the masts and lateral tensions on the anchors to the cables, and everything must be adjusted so that the load is evenly shared: make a cable very slightly too short and it relieves the others, overloading itself. It is difficult even to define the precise shape that such a roof will take. The roof of the swimming hall was done in Otto's institute by building and loading a scale model, then measuring it accurately through photogrammetry using stereo cameras. Computers were used for some of the calculation work, but they were primitive in comparison even to a PC of today. Numerous firms and experts were involved, always working against the clock, and there were frequent unexpected new problems to be solved. Initial plans to cover the cable net with a flexible wood deck, for example, were halted by the demands of German television, who demanded that the roof be translucent to prevent excessive contrast between lit and shaded areas that would upset their new colour cameras. The translucent

version then threatened to be too hot, necessitating varying degrees of opacity for the different parts, and the proposed acrylic sheet also had to be proved for fire, particularly to avoid melting and dripping on those beneath.[14]

The three stadia were placed in the southern part of the site, between the motorway and the spoil mountain, while the northern part was reserved for the Olympic village built by others. The motorway bridges were therefore critical links, particularly the western one leading through to the main stadium. It was made to disgorge into a space that dropped towards the widest part of the lake, meeting the water with theatre-like steps. This space became an outdoor room defined by the open side of the main stadium to west, the sports hall to north, and the swimming hall to east. Since only the western half of the great stadium was covered, the roof inflected it towards the central space, and the focal Olympic flame was set on the cross axis at the eastern side. Hung between eight rear masts and a horseshoe-shaped tension cable in front, the main stadium roof thus provided both boundary and visible symbol toward the outside world, while it also screened off the prevailing wind. This roof

was made to continue around the north side of the central space with smaller cable nets that covered and celebrated the incoming path from the bridge. It continued further into the masted structure of the sports hall and ran on to terminate in the swimming hall. Mountain, lake and the continuous roof over the three main buildings thus came to define the central room.

The choice of a cable net roof was essential for the kind of informality that the Behnisch team wanted to achieve, and the alternative roof types with arcs and segments explored during the development phase all look like compromises.[15] The dynamic and constantly varying form of the cable net is the complete reverse of orthogonal trabeated architecture: it simply could not be done with straight lines and right angles. The discipline of the systematic grid was thus avoided, as was the dominant statement of a simply repetitive structure. Even better, the structural forces in themselves were supplying a new logic, in much the same way that Pier Luigi Nervi had harnessed the compressive forces of a complex vault with his aircraft hangars in the 1930s (Blundell Jones 2002, Ch. 9). Hugo Häring had also been interested in self-shaping structures with his barn at Garkau (Blundell Jones 2002, Ch. 2) which he saw in 1931 as evidence of a general move towards a more flexible and organic attitude in architecture:

Modern technology tends entirely towards elastic constructions. It considers building as a living body, it favours materials of the greatest tensile performance, it turns from stone to wood and steel, it interests itself in materials that can be moulded, and in those of the most enduring elasticity. [16]

8. (top opposite) Within the sports hall.

9. (middle opposite) The cable net roofs near the entrance seen from above and below.

10. (bottom opposite) The cable net roofs with their acrylic covering reflecting the evening light.

11. (opposite top right) Main stadium inhabited.

12. (top) Main stadium during the Olympic procession, 1972.

13. (right) The Olympic flame, set on the east side of the main stadium.

Architecture as landscape

Ever since the completion and obvious success of the Olympic complex, it has been noted among architects mainly for its cable roofs, while the groundscape around and beneath has been rather taken for granted, if not ignored. The clever sections which allow hidden servicing and separate people from vehicles are for the most part so well contrived that they go unnoticed, and the possibility of the place being cluttered up by ancillary facilities is well enough avoided to be forgotten. But gardens and groundworks also more generally go unremarked because trees and grass are regarded as 'nature' that has always been there, even more so lakes and mountains that have become part of the earth. Yet few landscapes are truly natural, and most are highly contrived, this one completely so. It takes imagination and skill to design a garden with real sense of place, and surprisingly few were produced during the twentieth century. To have made a park in Munich that competes with historic examples like Schloss Nymphenburg and the Englischer Garten is thus quite an achievement. As with the roofs, Behnisch and Partners did not manage this landscape alone, but worked with the office of landscape architect Günter Grzimek. The design had to consider the long term, but mostly it had to appear at its best by the opening of the Olympics, involving the implantation of 60-year-old trees and a planting programme that would mature quickly,[17] flowering at the right moment. The lake could not simply be dug and allowed to fill but needed lining, with careful control of its levels and planting.

A key requirement of the competition had been short direct routes, which had to flow efficiently across from the underground station and the peripheral car parks, but there were also long walks roaming over hill and dale, visiting areas of contrasted character treated as lawn or meadows or water gardens, and opening up chosen vistas. Lime trees were the primary material for lining paths and creating shade, often set out on a 7.5 metre grid to contrast with the swinging contours and curving paths: the organic against the geometric. Native white willows, mountain pines and Norway maples were used in certain places, with solitary oaks or pines as 'character trees'. The paths and steps were paved in varying ways with strong contrasts of texture. One difficult problem was the provision of emergency escape routes, some of which needed to be as much as 40 metres wide, but rather than sterilising large areas permanently with tarmac, these were contrived as areas of lawn on specially hardened ground. The large car parking areas, especially on the western periphery, were also softened by trees, with forms that followed the swinging curves of the general layout. The contrived land forms and lake effectively divided up the territory into different major spaces, but there was also a need for intimate corners, for places to sit and rest, areas to be alone away from the crowd. In certain seasons breathtaking drifts of flowers would appear, while in the winter certain slopes lent themselves to sledging runs and the lake could be used for skating. When unfrozen, the water's edge became a popular feeding place for ducks and swans.

14. (above) View of landscape from within sports hall.

15. (below) Lake and park with swimming hall behind.

16. (opposite) Visitors relaxing during the Olympics.

17. (near opposite) Landscape in spring with drifts of salvias. The trees behind are ginkgo bilobas.

18. (far opposite) Landscape and lake in the depths of winter.

Preparation for an informal architecture

The unprecedentedly free forms of the tent roof disguise just how far the Behnisch architecture still had to go to reach its mature state in the 1980s. The warm-up hall on the west side of the complex is in many ways more indicative of the stage they had reached. Here the main inspiration was to design the great steel trusses for the 100 metre span in triangular form so that they could also be glazed as rooflights, but the structure was repetitive and conventionally rectangular. The architectural innovation was to make the glass skin independent, using it to shape the rounded ends, and to dramatise the passage of steel members through the glass. Here was the beginning of a radical interplay of layers and ambiguity of space that was to become essential to the Behnisch armoury, but development of responsive and irregular planning was gradual.

Most of the buildings designed during the 1970s were orthogonal, though radial schools began with that at Oppelsbohm of 1969, and a polygonal first version of the Bonn Parliament dates from 1976. Confidently angular plans appeared with the Reutlingen old people's home of 1976 and the Birkach seminary of 1980, but not until 1983 and the competition project for the German National Library in Frankfurt did Behnisch's collage-like free-planning equal the interactive sophistication of late Scharoun. Their work became irregular enough by the late 1980s to earn the tag deconstructivist, but it was seldom wilful.[18] As postmodernism arose, Behnisch's architecture maintained the late modern alternative, and he also eschewed the new urbanism, denied all jobs in Berlin until he won the competition for the rebuilding of the Akademie der Künste on its original site, Pariser Platz. In this last great building, just complete at the time of writing, he fought the imposed conformity of the city planners who wanted stone facades with regular window holes.[19] His arguments for the glazed facade were twofold: on the one hand it is a public building that should open itself invitingly to the street; on the other, the identity of the city must grow from the bottom up, out of the conversations between individual buildings, not be imposed from the top down by decree.

Developing this architectural language was evidently a long exploratory process, though it was always geared to the experience of the user. The spatial experiments went hand in hand with technical studies intent on discovering how such

complex and irregular buildings might be achieved without inflated costs, and one of the main legacies of the Behnisch *modus operandi* is to show how spatial layering and constructional sequence can with great advantage be combined. Unfortunately the visual experience of layers, which increases the experience of depth in real life thanks to binocular vision, has a rather negative effect in photographs, all the more so in black and white ones. This is architecture that you have to visit.

Such developments in the firm's design vocabulary were accompanied by refinement of a working method which grew in relation to the Olympics project. The many interests and powerful personalities involved could have been overwhelming, leading to dilution or compromise of the concept, but Behnisch guided it through, persuading all to pull in the same direction. It proved the worth of acting as critic and manager rather than making designs more directly, a method which if successful allows greater creative range. Many architects fail to manage such transition of scale and lose their way, the work becoming dull and bureaucratic. The key to Behnisch's success is his gift to harness and bring to a focus the creativity of others, whether they be fellow professionals or young assistants: team work was essential. Grzimek reported Behnisch's advice to 'assemble a young team',[20] which was evidently what he was

19. (opposite top) Warm-up Hall on the Olympic site, 1972.

20. (opposite middle) Warm-up Hall, rounded end where the trusses pass through the glass. This became the hallmark of Behnisch work in the 1970s.

21. (opposite bottom) Seminary at Birkach, 1979. The angled plan, sloping glazing and highly articulated facade all signal the new 'organic' direction of this period.

22. (above) Akademie der Künste, Berlin, 2005, members' room on top floor with coloured glass roof, looking out across Pariser Platz and towards the Reichstag.

23. (below) Akademie der Künste, Berlin, the controversial glass facade which proclaims the building's public role.

doing himself and continued to do, for the Behnisch office consistently took on young architects fresh out of university for their first few years, giving them great freedom. In the later years at least, Behnisch himself seldom took up a pencil: he would steer projects through by advice and criticism, encouraging one idea and discouraging another, till they reached a level to bring first prize in the competitions that were the primary source of work. The partners helped, and some were excellent designers, but the commanding presence of Günter Behnisch himself seems to have been regarded by all as essential,[21] and it is telling that none of the splinter offices started by former partners has shown quite the same creative breadth.[22]

Once a commission was won, Behnisch also proved skilful in relations with clients and bureaucrats, protecting the burgeoning building from compromise and keeping the spark of inspiration aglow through a sometimes extended period of development and execution. By running jobs on site, controlling the budget, and organising subcontracts, he and his partners also managed to create the conditions under which a design could be developed and improved in detail during the construction period, even allowing some limited improvisation on site.[23] This extended the normally compressed design period and permitted an open dialogue with constructors and manufacturers, increasing the feedback between building and design. It also demonstrated that for Behnisch and those who shared his ethos, process was as important as product, and no perfect finished design inhabited the drawings. Architecture was a kind of endless quest, always changing, always subject to conflicting forces, always open to reinterpretation. Unfinishedness, open-endedness, and imperfection were of critical importance to him.

Human beings are not perfect: why should architecture be? It's the same with literature: when someone tells a story pedantically filling in every detail the joy goes out of it, but if the narrative remains incomplete, room is left for the reader's imagination…. And in the variety of materials and forms there exists for me a kind of freedom, a freedom in which things can discover their own identity. When there is an accidental hole in a sheet of metal or some other element revealing the nature of practical work, even if it is carelessly done, I hesitate to correct it. [24]

Notes

1. Günter Behnisch quoted in Behnisch 1992, p. 71: my translation.
2. According to Heinrich Klotz the first office in West Germany to take up this theme, Klotz 1977, pp. 33-35. Behnisch, in the interview with Klotz, claims that there was no other prefabricated system as advanced in 1962.
3. A memorable early project in this vein was Gropius's pair of Weissenhof houses, see Blundell Jones 2002, pp. 16-17.
4. From 'Das Neue ist nicht das Alte', signed article by Günter Behnisch, *Deutsche Bauzeitung* September 1987, pp. 32-39.
5. Initially Günter Behnisch and Bruno Lambart, since 1966 Behnisch & Partners (Günter Behnisch, Fritz Auer, Winfried Büxel, Manfred Sabatke, Erhard Tränkner, Carlo Weber).
6. Hugo Häring *Remarks concerning the craving for standardisation*, 1948, my translation. For Häring's design philosophy see Blundell Jones 2002, Ch. 2.
7. Blundell Jones 2002, Ch. 13.
8. Behnisch in *Planning of the Buildings and Facilities for the Olympic Games Munich 1972: progress of planning and consultation,* published by Karl Krämer Verlag, Stuttgart 1970.
9. Ibid.
10. 'It was a matter of creating an atmosphere of openness, transparency and visibility. If one takes such demands seriously this means that one should have neither axes nor monumental squares, but buildings of a scale and order given by the task: the framing for a festival of youth.' Behnisch, in catalogue of Maximilianstrasse Gallery, Munich 1978: my translation.
11. Since Otto had produced both the initial inspiration and some crucial decisions in the design development, and since it was the largest such structure of his career, it is regarded as an important part of his oeuvre (see Otto 2005, pp. 260-69) but the Behnisch team felt that their work was unfairly overshadowed when, on the basis of the highly visible roofs, it was primarily attributed to him. For Otto's account five years after the event see Klotz 1977 pp. 219-25 (German text).
12. See Carl Mertz in the volume cited under no. 8 above.
13. See monograph by Holgate 1997.
14. Carl Mertz op. cit.
15. Three are shown in the special supplement 'der mensch und die technik', *Süddeutsche Zeitung* 29 December 1971.
16. Hugo Häring, extract from 'Problems of art and structure in building', my translation, published in full in *9H* no.7, 1985, pp. 73-82.
17. Some mature trees came from Landshuter Allee which was being widened for the Olympic traffic: information from Christian Kandzia.
18. The favourite work for inclusion in the deconstructivist canon was the Hysolar Institute Stuttgart of 1987, whose job architect had in fact worked for Coop Himmelblau. Behnisch freely admitted to me that this experiment was somewhat 'wilful'.
19. My critique is in *The Architectural Review*, November 2005.
20. See Günter Grzimek's essay in Behnisch 1992, p. 33.
21. Karlheinz Weber is eloquent about Behnisch's role in the interview with Heinrich Klotz of 1977, and Behnisch identifies the specific roles of his various partners in the Olympics complex: Klotz 1977, pp. 57-59.
22. The best known is Auer + Weber, formed by two partners from the Munich phase. Also well known in Germany and later in origin is Kauffmann Theilig. Günter Behnisch's practice has now largely been taken over by his son Stefan, who seems to have a similar talent for leadership and is working internationally. It is called Behnisch, Behnisch & Partner (Günter Behnisch, Stefan Behnisch, Günther Schaller).
23. Two long-running projects, the Frankfurt Post Museum and Bonn Parliament, ended up different in style from the competition proposal, for young executive architects added to the older designs. In the Post Museum the main stair was widened after the architects observed on site that it seemed too mean.
24. Extracts from an interview with Behnisch by Hanno Rauterberg in *Die Zeit* of 12 February 2004: my translation.

Chapter 9. Carlo Scarpa: Castelvecchio Museum, Verona, 1957-74

If Le Corbusier's Plan Voisin of 1925, proposing the erasure of central Paris, represents the Modern Movement's attitude to historic urban contexts, we see how little value was ascribed to them. Everything was to be created anew, without reference to what had gone before, based only on a supposed objective rational analysis of function and building process. At the Bauhaus Gropius expressly excluded the teaching of history. Where art-historical examples were used, for example in Johannes Itten's Preliminary Course, they were treated only as formal products, to be analysed in terms of geometry, form, colour, composition, or balance, but not in relation to their art-historical or cultural contexts.[1] An overreaction to nineteenth-century academicism was combined with a current of progressive utopianism that placed value only on the new. Seen from our own disenchanted age, such wholesale dismissal of an entire cultural heritage seems hardly credible. Since the Enlightenment at least, we have been faced with an ideological divide between those who believe in progress, and those who perceive it as an illusion.

In the period of post-war reconstruction the progressives were in the ascendant, but they were challenged by a few individuals determined to reinvest historic context with value and meaning. Carlo Scarpa's interventions for the museum at the Castelvecchio in Verona present an outstanding example of this, though his work ostensibly took place at the scale of the intimate detail. He attempted to revive the continuity of history without resort to historical pastiche, by pursuit of craftsmanship which mixed traditional materials and forms with contemporary ones.

Cultural context

The architectural scene in Italy after the Second World War mirrored the political factions locked into an uneasy coexistence. Although the overt rhetoric associated with the public works of Fascism had been proved a hollow delusion, architects who had been closely identified with the regime continued to thrive. The most influential, Marcello Piacentini (1881-1960), completed the Via della Conciliazione in Rome for the Holy Year of 1950, and collaborated

1. Castelvecchio Museum: drawing of ground floor museum space showing layering of new frames in front of old openings.

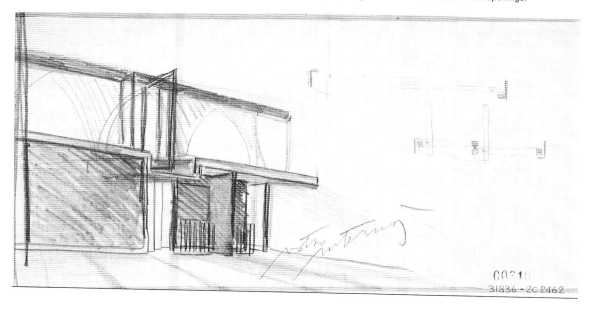

2. Side of the old fortress where an old drawbridge has been replaced by a modern bridge and a doorway in a glass panel.

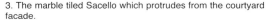
3. The marble tiled Sacello which protrudes from the courtyard facade.

with engineer Pier Luigi Nervi (Blundell Jones 2002, Ch. 9) on the Palazzo dello Sport for the Rome Olympics of 1960. His austere but eclectic historicism attracted few followers, so the work of the younger generation was largely divided between two other groups: one interested in historical repair and quasi-vernacular forms, the other in a highly engineered aesthetic of modernity representative of the 'economic miracle' and the age of *La Dolce Vita*. The latter was epitomised by Gio Ponti's Pirelli Tower in Milan, also engineered by Nervi.

Avoiding both poles, which tended to be associated with political patronage from the main parties, Carlo Scarpa (1906-1978) struck an independent pose. This was partly due to his education which distinguished him from his contemporaries. He did not attend architectural school, but the Academy of Fine Arts in Venice, where he studied sculpture and painting. He then developed an interest in architecture, and worked while still a student for various architectural offices. Later he was even a site manager on construction sites. In such experiences, before the commencement of his own architectural work, we see the grounding of Scarpa's unique language: a lack of rigid compositional orthodoxy, a delight in the variation of planar surfaces and textures, and a famously lively relationship with the craftsman. He was not excessively precious about his drawings, indeed alterations were made to them right up to the moment of construction; but those that survive show a constantly inventive and exploratory sculptural and spatial sense.

As a young man maturing under Fascism, Scarpa had dared to criticise the work of Piacentini in an open letter of 1931, thus exposing himself as an individual voice at a time when conformity to the regime ensured a trouble-free existence.[2] It was a plea for a more flexible framework of officially approved techniques. At this stage his professional work consisted mainly of small-scale interior and exhibition jobs, supplemented by teaching. Though associated with the Resistance during the war, he was reluctant to fall in with the immediate concerns of left-wing colleagues in the arena of social housing following the Liberation. Bruno Zevi recorded the stunned response of a group of architects meeting in Venice, where Scarpa declared his own position:

It is 1945, immediately after the Liberation. As an antifascist, Scarpa is invited to take part in a

4. General view of the courtyard showing the lawn and (to the right) the hedges which guide the route to the principal entrance in the angle of the two wings.

demonstration of left-wing architects. He listens to populist speeches calling for trade-union struggle, team planning and collective work. All at once he asks to be allowed to speak, stands up, and says, 'my sole aspiration is to find a Pharaoh who will allow me to build a pyramid'. General frigidity. He leaves the room. [3]

He was later in the field of funerary architecture to find his 'pharaoh' in the form of Giuseppe Brion, for whom he constructed the Brion chapel at San Vito d' Altivole near Treviso from 1969 onwards. Works such as this, where Scarpa was responsible for the entire complex, feature an eclectic mix of forms unlike anything that could be derived directly from historic precedent. Influenced by Frank Lloyd Wright and the traditional architecture of Japan, Scarpa's forms also owed much to the abstraction of contemporary art and the artisan techniques of craftsmen with whom he collaborated. The richness and variety that he created in such new projects went far beyond the norm for the period, but the refurbishment of existing structures placed more restraint on his fertile and inventive imagination. Here, instead of pursuing the exoticism of his preferred forms, his imagination turned towards

a creative juxtaposition of old and new, and to the creation of an architectural language which revealed both the process of construction and the historical layering of the original structure.

While awaiting the arrival of his pharaoh, the theme which emerged in Scarpa's work immediately after the war was the staging of temporary exhibitions and the permanent adaptation of museum spaces, commencing with the rearrangement of the Galleria dell' Accademia in Venice between 1945 and 1959. This was followed by the refurbishment of the Palazzo Abatellis in Palermo (1953-54) after war damage. The extension to the Canova plaster-cast gallery at Possagno in the Veneto followed between 1955 and 1957. In all these projects, display of the paintings and sculptures on specifically designed screens and stands showed a painter's eye for the framing and placing of a work. In the process Scarpa developed a language of display furniture for easels and plinths, which was combined with attention to wall openings in new surfaces and reconstructed areas, and related the exhibit to its context. He developed a vocabulary which could be reused to great effect in his series of interventions at the great fortress of the Castelvecchio in Verona between 1957 and 1974.

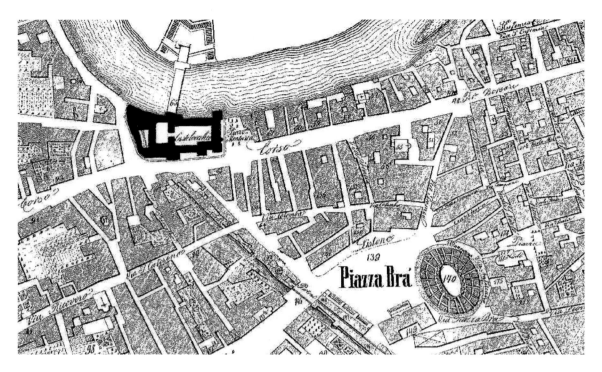

Castelvecchio, the context

The urban form of Verona is marked out by the grid of the Roman settlement bounded by the graceful arc of the river Adige. The clarity of this arrangement, with its emblematic combination of natural and ordered, of local and universal, exerted a subtle influence on Scarpa's work. The tightness of the original grid was relieved by circumstantial expanses of space around its boundary, best illustrated in the relationship between Piazza Bra and the surviving Roman Arena. The urban rhythm of tight versus open was supplemented by a layering of historical fragments exemplified by the present Piazza delle Erbe, once the centre of the Roman castrum, where the rectangular precinct of the Roman forum has been encroached upon to produce a lozenge shape, rendering its historical sedimentation apparent. Scarpa sought to expose layering similarly at the Castelvecchio. His method was to excavate the accumulation of material, a process of physical removal which made the past conceptually present.

Standing to the west of the Roman city, the Castelvecchio is a medieval fortress. It commanded both the important river crossing of the Ponte Scaglieri which passes through it, and the major cross axis of the castrum, the present Corso

Cavour which engages the surviving Roman gate, the Porta dei Borsari. Because of Verona's geographical position, the city was long a contested territory, and the Castelvecchio repeatedly served a defensive role. It was used during the Guelph and Ghibelline Wars, in those between Venice and the Duchy of Milan, in the Napoleonic wars between French, Italian and Austrian powers, in the Wars of Italian Unification and in the First World War. It held strategic military significance through seven centuries. After the Treaty of Versailles in 1919, northward expansion of the Kingdom of Italy at the expense of Austria to include Trento and Bolzano reduced the military importance of such fortresses, and the Castelvecchio was converted to a museum in 1924. Subsequent damage to the structure occurred during the Second World War, when it was used as a prison by the German army. Adding to this dark phase of its history, Galeazzo Ciano, Mussolini's foreign minister and son-in-law, was tried for treason there in 1944 by the puppet Fascist state prior to his execution by firing squad.

As the cultural values of Italian art were recast following the fall of Fascism, Scarpa's transformations would be subtle but significant, excising many nineteenth- and early twentieth-century elements. The last transformation before

5. (opposite) The Castelvecchio in a map of 1849 showing its strategic position on the river Adige and its relationship to Piazza Bra and the ancient amphitheatre (the Arena) on the edge of the Roman settlement.

6. (right) Ground floor plan, and (top) upper level gallery plan.
Key:
1. Passage to Reggia wing;
2. Torre del Mastio;
3. River Adige; 4. Cangrande della Scala statue;
5. gallery wing; 6. exit stair;
7. Sala Avena; 8. north-east tower; 9. Sala Boggian;
10. Porta del Morbio;
11. old entrance; 12. gallery;
13. Sacello; 14. new entrance;
15. library; 16. fountain;
17. pond; 18. main entrance to court; 19. bridge over moat;
20. moat; 21. commune wall;
22. road to Scaglieri bridge;
23 Scaglieri bridge.

7. Ground floor plan showing treatment of the courtyard with the paired hedges separating the lawn and the archaeological remains of an early Christian church (marked chiesa).

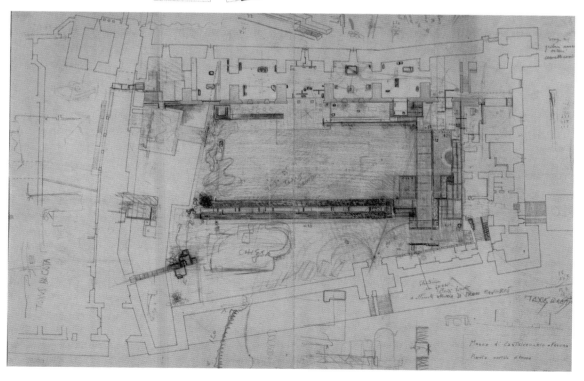

8. Detail of the treatment of the hard landscape which leads past a fountain towards the entrance to the museum.
9. (below) The Can Grande space, with the statue mounted on its cantilevering base and sheltered by its oversailing canopy.
10. (opposite) The entry landscape with its series of sculptural fragments.

he arrived, following the demilitarisation of the mid-1920s, had involved the decoration of the interiors with imitation Renaissance murals. This aesthetic had been acceptable in museum design at the beginning of Fascism, but by the mid-1950s such rhetorically historicist gestures were deemed inappropriate. Indeed, rather than applying a false history, Scarpa's work reflected the museum authorities' desire to redefine the building's past, to make the history tangible if not quite to lay it bare archaeologically. This determined many elements of his architectural language, including his use of materials and his preferred methods of bringing them together in an explicit way.

Visit to the building

The massive exterior of the fortress, bound on one side by the river, and bisected by the route to the Ponte Scaglieri through the Porta del Morbio, remained largely untouched by Scarpa. At first he concentrated on the renovation of interiors, then on the remodelling of the courtyard. Work began with the renovation of the Reggia, the palace wing beyond the route to the bridge, for the exhibition of paintings *From Altichiero to Pisanello* held in late 1958. The lower level of this exhibition was, in relation to the complex as a whole, on an upper floor. It therefore involved the introduction of an access route from the principal courtyard level via a staircase in the Torre del Mastio, which was adjacent to but separate from the bridge. The gallery spaces were dealt with simply. Fragments of medieval fresco were revealed, and a new steel and timber staircase connected the two levels of exhibition. These arrangements were initially intended to stand alone but became the catalyst for numerous interventions at the Castelvecchio which continued until the mid-1970s.[4]

For clarity it is best to begin our description where the visitor's circuit also begins, in the great courtyard. The strategies which animate the experience of the interior are introduced here, both in its overall arrangement and through detailed gestures. Scarpa subdivided the space with hedges to demarcate the archaeological remains of an early medieval church. The demarcation provided by the hedges is followed by a complex arrangement of paving and screens which define the entrance areas, for the library, for temporary events in the Sala Boggian – an existing upstair room used for exhibitions and concerts – and for the museum proper in the angle of the two wings.

11. Interior of the last room of the ground floor sculpture galleries showing an ironwork screen across the exit, and the balustrading around an archaeological fragment revealed below floor level.

12. (below left) Central room of the ground floor sequence showing the screen proposed in Fig. 1. The direction of the new paving contrasts with the emphatic directionality of the new steel beam supporting the upper floor.

13. (below right) The fourth ground floor room, demonstrating the individual treatment of the mounts for the exhibited sculptural group.

14. Upper floor gallery showing the variety of hanging techniques, on walls, on free-standing screens and on easels.

Essentially a paved carpet is created along the frontage of the two, with pools and sculptural fragments helping to arrest the direct movement of the visitor. The screen walls indicate the relative level of invitation, as a barrier to be negotiated for the subsidiary entrances, and a divider between ingress and egress. One of them runs through the glazed Gothic doorway designated as the museum entrance, parallel to that of the nearby Sacello and thereby defining the entrance threshold. Paving of various widths, textures, and levels creates a subtle diagonal path from the gravel area by the courtyard entrances. Misalignments and a picturesque placing of elements are unified by a complex arrangement which playfully delays the visitor with a composition free of didactic purpose, but evoking an atmosphere of contemplation.

This courtyard landscape is dominated by the elevation containing the principal exhibition spaces which are accommodated on two floors: sculpture on the ground and picture gallery above. Containing this new arrangement are the entrance room on the right-hand side and a great void space on the left, where the route through to the Reggia is revealed. The courtyard facade had been reworked by successive occupiers to present a more symmetrical and classical regularity. Scarpa demolished the monumental staircase on the left side of the elevation, creating in the resulting void the display space for the museum's prize exhibit, the equestrian statue of Can Grande della Scala, the medieval Veronese warlord. This dramatic object

is used to communicate between the two parts of the museum and the two principal floor levels, and is revealed to the visitor from different angles to provide an orientation point in the prescribed circuit. To set up this element within the composition, Scarpa preferred to accentuate the membrane quality of the wall to the courtyard by emphasising the individuality of the incidents. So the wall is treated as a series of alternating major and minor accents. Starting from the right, the entrance in a minor zone, then in a major one comes the so-called Sacello (a name meaning votive chapel) presented as a solid cubic mass protruding from the wall surface, with a glass roof and tripartite window above. Another minor zone follows, then comes the major central loggia, another minor zone, then a zone equivalent to the Sacello. Finally we reach the delamination of the wall that occurs at the 'Can Grande space'. Uniting these disparate elements is an abstracted fenestration system which gives an illusion of continuity behind the outermost layer of the facade.

Internally the treatment of the main wing of the museum is as deceptively laconic as it is externally, extending the language employed in the Reggia. However, the same attitudes to materials and construction produce an undecorated set of spaces where the objects on display and the sensitive detailing of their mounts impart an austere atmosphere to the room, which is further enhanced by the handling of the architectonic elements. For example, in the ground floor sculpture galleries,

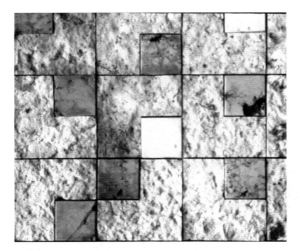

15. Detail of the Prun marble facing of the Sacello.
16. (opposite) The positioning of the equestrian statue of Can Grande della Scala, silhouetted against the medieval wall.

against the rhythm of the five roughly square rooms arranged in a traditional enfilade, new paving was inserted with a rhythm counter to the route, while that route itself was reiterated by the direction of the steel beams introduced to support the floors above. The beams are composite elements, the nature of which is fully expressed, and which expose some allowance for differential movement.

The two most characteristic elements, the solid of the Sacello and the void of the 'Can Grande space', make contrasting demonstrations about the possibilities of display. The Sacello is a small rectangular room built onto the facade, whose windowless walls carry a decorative pattern in small marble squares of the local Prun stone, a pattern related to the paintings of Piet Mondrian and other abstract painters.[5] The variation in colour, and in the rough versus smooth texture, bear witness in their emphasis on planar surface to Scarpa's training as a painter. Internally, the top light dramatises the display of sculptures and reliquaries, creating an aura for these relatively small objects. As Rafael Moneo has observed:

The way we look at a work by Scarpa, the unique way in which we 'set ourselves before it', which it forces us to adopt, reveals the painterly method followed by the architect in his work. When Scarpa tackled a project, he acted and worked like a painter: he was attracted by the effect produced on the painting by every last brush stroke, attentive to the effect on himself of a new tone of colour;

he was always alert to sieze that fluid polarization imposed by the work on his own evolution.[6]

However, this is not to undervalue Scarpa's spatial sense, which is more than adequately demonstrated by the treatment of the 'Can Grande space'. The statue of the nobleman originally crowned the roof of his Gothic tomb in the centre of the city, but in the interests of conservation it has been replaced with a modern copy. After various proposals, Scarpa chose to exhibit the original as the key element of the museum, both visible from the courtyard and intercepted by the visitor's route. Placed at first-floor level to echo its original elevated position, it was set on a huge cantilevered pedestal and as a result achieves a high degree of conceptual animation. Small bridges and balconies on either side allow for more intimate exploration of the sculpture, as Scarpa indicated in a sketch. But the treatment of the statue is only one element, for the great vertical space he occupies is as much on display as the warrior himself. The walls and roof of the block are successively delaminated: stucco is removed to reveal stonework and brick, tiles are removed to reveal copper, and the twin roof beams are exposed to span onto the adjacent wall. This space, with its highly articulated roof akin to a medieval baldachino, announces the unity of exhibit and architecture which Scarpa sought for all the museum spaces. That the visitor's route should seem always to pivot around this void is a testimony to Scarpa's skill in creating value by removing and revealing elements. It is the architect as surgeon, as Licisco Magagnato describes in his account of the project:

Too much attention has been given to Scarpa as a refined miniaturist engaged in designing splendid formalistic detail. In reality, the Castelvecchio Museum, with its linked sequence of precise almost surgical operations affecting the great walled enclosure... was an urban achievement of remarkable scope... We can see the firmly architectural quality of Scarpa's work, animated by a seemingly inexhaustible sequence of formal inventions articulating the skeleton, the framework partly accepted as historically pre-existing, partly explored through that surgical operation (intended to lay bare all the genuine survivals), and partly built anew, to bind together the scattered limbs, to fill in the gaps without concealing the wounds of time, suturing the links and revealing the joints.[7]

The circuit of the galleries passes through this space from the ground floor suite of sculpture rooms, across to the sequence of rooms in the Reggia beyond the line of the bridge. From the upper floor the path then returns at high level to the picture galleries in the upper floor of the main block, giving plenty of opportunity to observe the statue from many angles, as John Ruskin had when he remarked on its smile.

However, the Castelvecchio deals, above and beyond the careful housing of exhibits, in a larger order of architectural and urban expression. It attempts nothing less than the revelation of the structure of a historic phenomenon, peeling back the onion-skin layers one by one. This is its true subject, but the story is told without being too didactic, accepting the necessity of seducing the visitor into a comprehension of that phenomenon.

Much reliance is placed on intimate and exquisite detailing, but this sensitivity is not only self-serving, not just pursued for its own obvious delight. Rafael Moneo has asserted that:

...though it may often seem that the contrary is the case, Scarpa's work has little to do with the exploitation of the work of the craftsman collaborating with him, for what emerges from his work is not so much the skill of the worker as the wisdom of the mind that designed. [8]

Moneo addresses the scale of the detail, but his suggestion that the ensemble is of more value than the sum of its parts might also be applied at the urban scale. The autonomous nature of the detail finds its most comprehensive motif in the area of composition, and it is this compositional skill that enhances the work's effect. The fundamental method of composition is that of collage, the quintessential twentieth-century artistic device.

Architectural collage

First exploited by the Cubists, collage stands at the root of both abstract and figurative traditions in the visual arts. Its ability to produce ambiguous compositional effects has recommended it to architects obliged to deal with existing material. The collaged element can be read both as intrinsically woven into a composition and simultaneously independent of it. So in a Cubist collage, the wood graining is at once the surface of the depicted guitar and the rectangular piece of wallpaper it is in actuality, *'simultaneously innocent and devious'*.[9] In Scarpa's reinterpretation, the statue of Can Grande della Scala becomes as much a part of the representational fabric of the Castelvecchio as an independent object on display. The other property of collage, which endeared it to the Surrealists, was that of juxtaposition, as in the memorable phrase *'the juxtaposition of an umbrella and a sewing machine on an operating table'*.[10] The power to set up dialectical relationships by juxtaposing distinct and seemingly unrelated elements is seen in Scarpa's

17. (opposite top) One of the galleries with a medieval window and translucent glazing onto the walk above. Paintings are hung on walls, on a free-standing screen and on an easel.
18. (above) Upper floor gallery, again showing a varitey of display techniques.
19. (below) Shop by the corner entrance on the ground floor.
20. Stair leading to the upper galleries: the tapering plan does not read.

work even at the level of placing sculptures on their stands, or placing new iron screens against existing openings, each element brought further into relief by the presence of something that contradicts it. Collage allows intervention in history without parodying the historical fragment or denying the contemporary. It permits the confident, assertive gesture to assume the role not of the destroyer of context, but of its sensitive and willing servant.

It was to be expected that adherents of progress should condemn Scarpa's work for its supposed idiosyncrasy and lack of universal applicability. But this is to ignore the cause of his supposed retreat into subjectivity and formalism. It was surely a reaction to the unholy alliance between contemporary architectural ideologues, suppliers of building systems and components, paternalistic and often corrupt public authorities, and philistine private developers: all those who had continuously impoverished the European urban experience since the Second World War. It is against this dire context that attempts like Scarpa's to re-establish some sense of historical continuity should be judged, and in that context it is inevitable that the past itself in the form of its artefacts and contexts should play the fundamental role, since the artefacts aimed at the future had proved so unsuccessful.

The technique of collage which Scarpa employed, both as evocative form and as synthetic history, led Manfredo Tafuri to compare him with Piranesi, citing particularly the fictive history of the Campus Martius plan.[11] Such comparisons are relatively rare however, for the tendency in publications since Scarpa's death has been to focus on his skill in the articulation of detail. This was essential for the realisation of his projects and is well supported by the evidence of the drawings, but its overemphasis has resulted in Scarpa being compartmentalised as a kind of exemplary genius of the detail.[12] Such a reading, based on an essentially autonomous view of architecture, ignores both the tumultuous political context of Scarpa's career and the conflict between tradition and modernity that characterised the history of Italian twentieth-century architecture. The very ambiguity of Scarpa's architectural language subverted the received wisdom that context and modernity were opposed, presenting instead a series of meditative demonstrations on the potential unity of the functional, the aesthetic and the contextual. Scarpa's attitude to context as displayed at the Castelvecchio is an exemplary one because of the stealth with which he creates

his achievement. His work is often busy in the expression of its elements, yet at the same time it is always deferential to the spare display of exhibits, allowing them to command the visitors' attention, often literally. Despite working within a prescribed environment with a display of pre-determined items, Scarpa managed to produce what was probably the definitive masterpiece of twentieth-century museum design. His aesthetic could be idiosyncratic and so personal as to defy definition, but its gestures should not be confused with the essentially ameliorative intention which animated the proponents of 'townscape' in the same period.[13] Scarpa's intention was to create a memorable experience from the conjunction of past and present without resort to historicism, while respecting the integrity of the objects, buildings and spaces with which he dealt. That is why his own contribution, always richer when reciprocally tied to its context, developed its own integrity through the continuance of a material tradition.

EC

Notes

1. For examples of Itten's method in the Preliminary Course see Bayer, Gropius and Gropius 1938, pp. 30-35.
2. The letter signed by the Venetian Rationalists including Carletto Scarpa (sic) dated 13 May 1931 = IX (the number of the year of the Fascist era) was published in *Il Lavoro Fascista* on 19 May 1931. It is reproduced in Dal Co and Mazzariol 1985, pp. 279-80. The letter included a plea for the officially sanctioned taste in Italian architecture to be influenced by contemporary developments in Germany and Austria.
3. Bruno Zevi *'Beneath or Beyond Architecture'* in Dal Co and Mazzoriol 1985, p. 271.
4. For the 'Reggia' see Beltramini, Forster and Marini 2000 pp.164-71.
5. For a discussion of the intellectual origins of the Sacello see Marisa Dalai Emiliani *'Il progetto di allestimento tra eddimero e durata: una traccia per le fonti visisve di Carlo Scarpa'* in Beltramini, Forster and Marini 2000, pp. 41-52.
6. Rafael Moneo *'Representation and the Eye'* in Dal Co and Mazzariol 1985, p. 236.
7. Llcisco Magagnato *'The Castelvecchio Museum'* in Dal Co and Mazzariol 1985, p. 159.
8. Moneo op.cit.
9. Rowe and Koetter 1978.
10. The phrase was adopted by the Surrealists as a definition of the beauty they sought, from the Comte de Lautréamont (Isidore Ducasse) collection *Les Chants de Maldoror* 1868-9.
11. Tafuri 1980, p. 111.
12. See Murphy 1990, also Kenneth Frampton's explicit homage *'Carlo Scarpa and the Adoration of the Joint'* as Chapter 9 in Frampton 1995, p. 299 onwards.
13. Represented for the English-speaking world particularly by Gordon Cullen in the 1950s and 1960s pages of *The Architectural Review*. Tafuri commented *'There is nothing of this kind in Scarpa: neither chronophilia nor chronophobia appears in his works; rather there is an almost "natural" relationship with the multiplicity of historical time.'* Manfredo Tafuri *'Carlo Scarpa and Italian Architecture'* in Dal Co and Mazzariol 1985, p. 79.

Chapter 10. Lucien Kroll: Maison Médicale, Brussels, 1969-72

Thirty-three years on it is hard to describe the sheer impact of the Mémé. It sprang upon a world in which the dull certainties of an ordinary modern architecture still reigned, and it suddenly gave participation a dramatic new image. Just to see its anarchic presence in contrast with the monolithic hospital next door was to register the essential difference between bottom-up planning and top down. Giancarlo De Carlo (see Chapter 13) had already made radical experiments in participatory housing with considerable success in Terni in 1968, but the results had been clothed in a conventional clean concrete architect's architecture.[1] Lucien Kroll further loosened the reins, ceding all such convention and cleanliness in favour of a self generating architecture. It was allowed to look as untidy and unpredictable as it needed to be, and seemed quite scandalous: *'There are twenty-seven windows in the catalogue,'* Kroll claimed: *'Most architects choose two or three. Why not use all twenty-seven?'* [2]

We would never have thought of it, for it went quite against the conventional wisdom that repetition cheapens and is therefore compulsory. Even worse, it went against the assumptions of architectural good taste and a prevailing belief in the supposedly universal benefits of simplicity and proportion. With typically naughty wit, Kroll was challenging both the technological argument and the aesthetic one, as he has continued to do in books and articles, and in a string of similarly anarchic projects, ever since.[3]

1. Side of the Maison Médicale in all its complexity, social facilities below, residences above.

128

Lucien Kroll was born in Brussels in 1927 and studied architecture at the Ecole Nationale Supérieure de la Cambre in Brussels, completing in 1951. After an intial partnership with Charles Vandenhove he set up his own office in 1957, and worked for the next twelve years on a steady stream of social and domestic projects which were sensitively planned, well-built, and politely modest in appearance – a mild neo-vernacular, as Francis Strauven called it.[4] His interest in participation began with his very first independent project, a gradual conversion of the Abbey of Maredsous for Benedictine monks which started in 1957, continuing in stages until 1972. He explored techniques of participation further in 1962 when building the block of apartments where he still lives and has his office:

It appeared suitable to make a couple of plans, then interview the tenants so that decisions could be reached unanimously with regard to the desires of each individual. I discovered that each one was different, and that attraction and aversion create a cityscape truer than any created on paper.[5]

Kroll's projects for the Benedictines led on to the construction in the late 1960s of a monastery in Rwanda, Africa. It was followed by other projects there, including a new town, which was to be formed by providing a framework in which people could build for themselves:

We suggested to the President that we take the shanty towns of Kigali as our models… We not only wanted to leave the Ruandans to build what they would have built for themselves elsewhere but also to motivate them through model projects.[6]

The political implications of this development in the context of liberation from colonialism perhaps sharpened Kroll's perception, but this moment of Utopian optimism remained largely unfulfilled.

The Maison Médicale

The Mémé and surrounding buildings were a delayed product of 1968, the year of revolution and protest. The Catholic University of Louvain decided to leave its old city for Louvain la Neuve,

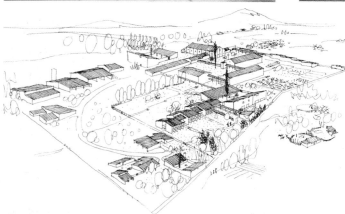

2. (above left) Housing for nuns at Ottignies 1974.
3. (above) Shared housing where Kroll has his home and office 1962-65.
4. (left) Gihindamuyaga Monastery, Rwanda, 1968.
5. (below) The monster hospital that provoked the rebellion of the Mémé, Woluwé St Lambert, Brussels.

6. Children's playground outside the school at the base of the Mémé: Kroll always sought integration rather than the division of zoning.

7. The restaurants at one end of the development, grouped by the bureaucratic demand for a common kitchen, not to be avoided.

8. Elevation of a building group. Floors run through on a constant horizontal level but the meeting of the building with the ground varies throughout, accommodating many social facilities, and the residences are allowed to grow to different heights with varied roof treatments.

9. (left) The polystyrene model in Kroll's office which served as the main coordinating instrument in planning the whole development. The architects were allowed to change and add things but not to take them away.

10. (opposite) Isometric projection of the whole development as it was intended to end up.

rebuilding its enormous medical faculty in Woluwé St Lambert on the outskirts of Brussels. A huge monolithic hospital was planned, and next to it a social centre, with accomodation for medical students, restaurants, shops, social facilities, and an underground station. This large development had been planned according to the usual bureaucratic principles, but following reforms induced by the 1968 rebellions, the master-plan was put to the students for approval. They rejected it, requesting specific changes that were considered but could not be met. To break the deadlock, the authorities suggested that they be permitted to choose an architect from the university's list. Unimpressed by those included, the medical students consulted colleagues in architecture who recommended Kroll, popular as a teacher and for his interest in participation. He was handed the commission in December 1969, and the project was at first allowed some freedom, since the authorities were more exercised by the hospital which was late on site and exceeding its budget.[7] Kroll had his chance to develop an alternative kind of planning:

This was the time in which modern architecture had become academic: it had authority but had lost its merits. Fundamentally, it had become restricted by an artificial and autistic technology. There was a new fascination with the copious variety with which a network of social groups could make an imprint on the environment. The question was: do the architects and technological possibilities support them, or do they disrupt everything? [8]

The crucial recognition was the negative effect of master-planning due to its inherent homogeneity and oversimplification. It all too easily represents dictatorship, or at least the centralised political power that imposes it, and it can equally represent the single-mindedness of a purely technical approach, as in prefabricated mass-housing blocks which say everything about the system and almost nothing about community. In contrast, old towns and villages have a complexity and irregularity that has resulted from the accumulation of a thousand gestures, each part built and rebuilt according to people's needs and wishes, therefore representing not only the presence but also the memory of their interrelationships. When people built for themselves, there was a fairly automatic process of feedback, of discovering how space conditioned life and then adjusting or reinterpreting

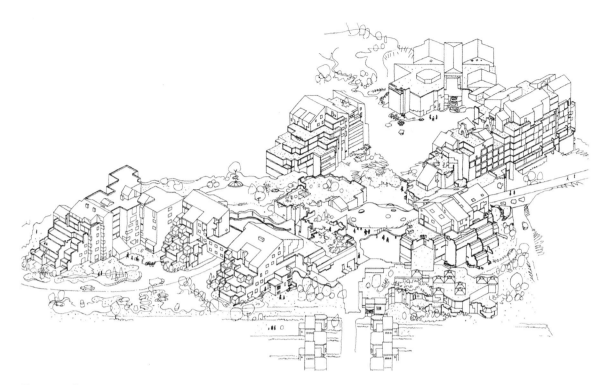

it appropriately. But as architects increasingly took over the design of residential neighbourhoods it became a somewhat blind imposition; they would, as Kroll puts it:

absorb themselves in fashioning the architectural object without imagining what behaviour this will impose upon its inhabitants and without experiencing, even through study groups, the unanimities, the contradictions, the incompat-ibilities, from which a complex milieu is woven. [9]

So how could one regain the responsive complexity of a real urban environment? Kroll set out to make what he called a 'soft zone' with a 'spongy urban tissue'. He had to conform in some ways to a master-plan that had already been predetermined, and he had been provided with a long and elaborate brief enumerated in square metres, including apartments of many sizes, restaurants, cinema and theatre, chapel, sports hall, crèche, kindergarten, post office, shops, and even a metro station. The important thing was to avoid quickly 'solving' the general organisation by disposing functions in zones according to the Athens Charter, by imposing a formal structure like

a great square, or by letting the communications and services dominate – the street or sewer network. Any gesture of this kind would establish a hierarchy prioritising some activities over others, in consequence ignoring completely those at the bottom end. But as Kroll put it: *'there are no neutral everyday activities'.*[10] Instead, he brought together student representatives, friends, assistants and colleagues for a series of brainstorming sessions to imagine how the life of the new quarter might be conducted:

I get up, wash, it's cold, the neighbour's radio annoys me, I go to get bread, we make coffee, the latest news, I inspect the planting I did yesterday in the park, we pay our rent, I take the neighbour's baby to the crèche floor, I read, we go to work at the faculties, I return with rice and vegetables for this evening's guests.... [11]

With a whole group of people imagining routines such as this, everyone became passionately interested in the projected life, and it became possible to make lists of activities and interactions, seeing how the various functions in the campus might need to relate both horizontally and vertically.

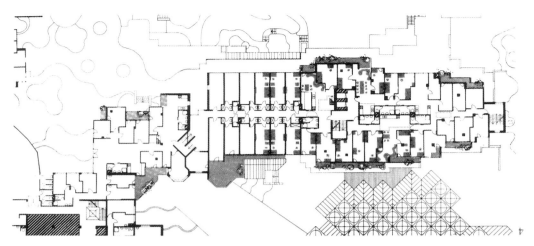

11. Plan of the Mémé, based on an orthogonal grid despite the irregularity.

12,13. (opposite top) Modular organisation of the facade.
14. (opposite middle) The SAR plan module and Kroll's variant.

The next stage was to develop an interactive method for the planning process of disposing the parts. Kroll began by dividing his staff into six groups and giving each responsibility for particular elements: restaurant, flats, shops, administration, culture, and open space. Each knew how many square metres were allotted by the brief, and these could be represented by squares of plastic foam one storey thick placed on a large site model and colour-coded according to use. Pieces of string represented communications. Someone started to place material – a restaurant at a central point – then others joined in, each arguing for the particular needs of the parts for which they were responsible, so the foam model grew along with its string linkages. Kroll made a rule that there was to be no major replanning, only adjustment – *'you have to keep your mistakes, nature does!'* – so that the history of the cumulative process would be preserved. Despite the fact that each team leader had been made second in command within another team to maintain connections, Kroll soon noticed that the teams were becoming too attached to the areas assigned to them, too much the authors. He broke them up and reassigned them, dividing the site next into physical sectors or plots, each the responsibility of one group. They were obliged to retain the general arrangement established by the model, again correcting and adjusting. As more work was done, the teams again became possessive about their working areas – *'resembling private property of peasant type'* – so Kroll reassigned them again, dividing

the accommodation vertically by storeys. The team responsible for open space were prompted to run some of their string along the contours to get the best connections, so exerted as much influence as those in charge of blocks of building. Throughout this process team members got to know better and better the relationships and territories that they were creating, and there was scope for corrective criticism of things that did not work, but the cumulative ordering process rolled on. The medical students were consulted whenever possible and made some key decisions, like the central placing of the Mémé (Maison Médicale), besides confirming decisions already made and helping to enrich the development. They were more specifically involved later on in the detailed planning, where personal preferences were allowed to determine even the size and shape of particular rooms. Some peculiar rooms arose and Kroll was later criticised for allowing this, since the students would soon move on, leaving someone else to inherit their folly. He found, though, that there was competition to own one of the most impractical rooms of all, which had been made narrow and seven metres high. He points out that many of us live quite happily in houses built earlier for others, that we easily adapt them to our needs or adapt ourselves to accept their idiosyncrasies. The critical point is that they are individual and different, reflecting a complex social landscape full of memories. They are no mere bleak repetition of a 'machine for living in' designed for an 'average man', nor simply a direct consequence of the quickest and cheapest building technology.

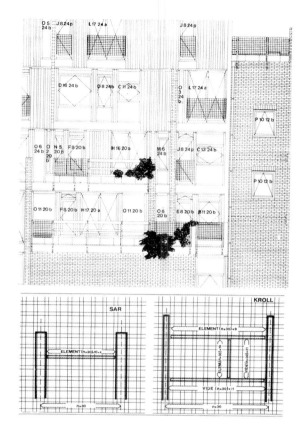

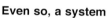

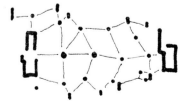

Even so, a system

Given Kroll's love of irregularity and belief in the unpredictable, it comes as a surprise to learn that the Mémé and adjacent buildings were built on an orthogonal grid and to a strict module. This was based on a modified version of the SAR[12] module developed by the Dutch theorist N.J. Habraken as part of his theory of supports, with a basic dimension of 30cm.[13] Part of the reason for this was the incorporation in many places of variable partitioning to allow for future changes, most radically in the 'attics' of the residential buildings where the students could negotiate not only their own room volumes, but also the shared social space. But the very adoption of a module implied acceptance of industrialised building technology, which seemed inevitable in the 1960s and had been allowed in many cases wholly to dictate the form and organisation of buildings. The fact that architects as sensitive to issues of place and habitation as Aldo van Eyck (Chapter 3) and Günter Behnisch (Chapter 8) had become deeply involved

with prefabricated systems shows how dominant such thinking was, and Kroll was absorbed in it too.[14] But though he accepted industrial production as inevitable, he was deeply critical of the way it was going, and had been exploring how a systematic approach might be played for maximum diversity instead of the usual numbing repetition.

One assumed but unwritten rule was the regular placing of columns, which was meant to be both rational and economical but tended to leave an insistent rhythm. Retaining the grid system, Kroll decided to vary the intervals, creating his 'wandering columns' which upset the engineers but was easily achieved by thickening the slabs.[15]

15. Kroll's 'wandering columns'

16. Hard landscaping where the bricklayers were encouraged to improvise, adding a craft dimension. This area was an external playground for the school.

Another possibility was to vary the number of storeys of different parts of the building and to vary the treatment of the roof, where convenient adding balconies or open decks. Although planning based on strictly orthogonal axes was a basic assumption, this did not necessitate precisely rectangular profiles, so corners could be stepped both in plan and section, fragmenting the building and increasing views out. Most importantly, facades could be varied, with every possible cladding material in every possible colour. Since all was planned by modular coordination, all was effectively interchangeable, but Kroll wanted it as random as possible, even in places resorting to the use of playing cards as a form of random generator.[16] Timber windows in the end proved cheaper as obtained from local workshops than from large factories, and other kinds of handcraft were included where possible.

Masons and bricklayers were invited to participate and given considerable freedom with some of the groundworks. They were even encouraged to make a couple of giant brick figures in one of the entrance halls. The landscaping was given over to Louis Le Roy, an ecologically-minded Dutch landscape architect who worked with the students with all kinds of found materials and heaps of demolition spoil. A thousand trees were planted and plants were given by neighbours, weeds were encouraged, climbers placed next to buildings and planting boxes added to roofs. Thus the wild garden intended to soften the buildings and to humanise the spaces between was well on its way to fruition by the time the authorities angrily intervened and brought in their bulldozers. For them, it had all gone too far.

How much participation?

Democratic politicians and public officials often pay lip-service to the idea of participation, pursuing manoeuvres to 'consult' the population and to gain nominal approval when a project has largely been determined, but real participation is rare since it requires a transfer of power normally unthinkable to those in possession of it.[17] The university undoubtedly commissioned Kroll to placate the students, expecting some discussion and perhaps some minor adjustment to the residential quarter, but not a major rethink. However, Kroll had long been experimenting with forms of group self-determination, and recognised the invitation from the authorities as an opportunity: *'a fissure generated by the inner contradictions of the system, into which one should throw oneself, act, and flee before it closes up again'.*[18] Though invited to the discussions, the academic authorities refused to engage, but Kroll did manage to involve the students in many design decisions normally reserved for the architect, not least the partitioning of their own rooms for many individuals. Students were in fact involved at every stage, but most effectively via the committee of elected designates from the Mémé, which was the constant discussion partner. They helped determine things like the horizontal and vertical linking of functions, the use of flexible partitions, the centralised provision of wash-places, the making of vegetable gardens on terraces, and the creation of links with neighbouring suburbs. Many important issues must also have been decided along the way by Kroll's assistants, despite his tactics in moving them on from task to task to prevent too much individual identification. All the same, neither he nor his co-workers retained design control in the usual sense, for the outcome depended on the process and was therefore unpredictable. Rather than imposing order, their main aim was to prevent the domination of any single ordering system, allowing the complexity of multiple decision-making to erupt by itself. The image clearly caused consternation: before the development was even finished, Kroll's office was suspended from supervision and Le Roy's landscape was torn out. Then for several years there was a lack of maintenance which left the buildings dirty and unloved, but Kroll was engaged once again in the late 1970s to complete the underground station, which has healed the rift and added a new sense of centre. Gradually the quarter has developed a more comfortable identity, but it is of course also a media celebrity.

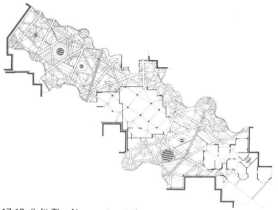

17,18. (left) The Alma metro station.
19. (above) Plan of concrete roof canopy.
20. (below) Cross-section of central part.
21. (bottom) Edge of the station with residential buildings behind.

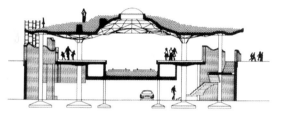

Later projects

In his early years Kroll built single houses for people as a sympathetic and congenial friend, and he could have continued the small-scale local career of a peaceful barefoot architect helping people realise their personal dreams. But the Mémé placed him on a world stage, and he was henceforth sought out by clients because of his progressive views, not locally in Brussels, but rather from France, Holland and Germany. He had always been interested in the larger issues and always took a critical stance, first concerning the ideological errors and arrogance of the Modern Movement, second concerning authoritarian, totalitarian, or economically obsessed politics. These are common targets in his scathing critiques of large-scale post-war housing schemes, several of which he has been commissioned to study and ameliorate. The founding model for this process was a social housing area at Alençon with relentless ranks of five-storey prefabricated slab blocks. Kroll was invited to humanise it in 1978, and he suggested a dual strategy. The existing slab blocks could be modified by adding and sub-tracting flats, conversion, recladding, changing roofs, and so on. A sample block was converted as catalyst in the hope that the residents would later take the initiative for themselves. The other recommendation was to colonise the empty and sterile spaces left between the blocks. A school, further houses, and social facilities were added by a local architect.

The intention of these projects was to overcome the oppressive simplicity by making them more like traditional towns and villages, simply by generating complexity and interaction. Kroll believes that lining people up in identical flats is like putting them in uniform, and his language adopts the military metaphor as the essence of oppression and colonial paternalism. It takes an act of courage even to paint one's door a different colour, he claims, whereas if the doors are already different colours there is a possibility for individual identification. Complexity and difference is important, therefore, in itself, and even before the individual starts to engage with the building. But thereafter it is the process of use, of give and take between life and fabric, that bestows meaning on the building.

Many other Kroll projects have opposed modernist zoning and the habit of mind that divides things into rigid categories. When consulted about new premises for an Academy of Dance in Utrecht in 1987, he advised them not to move out of the

22, 23. (top) Social housing at Alençon as existing and as converted by Kroll in 1978.
24, 25. (above) Kroll's diagramatic projections showing ways to add to and reclad residential buildings.
26. (below) Plan of central Utrecht showing the two separate existing buildings refurbished by Kroll as a dance school.

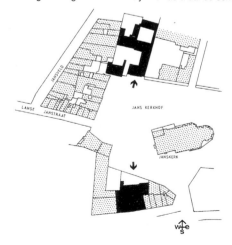

27. Kroll's ecological centre at Belfort, 1995, view of interior with glazed rooflights.

titles of his books: *Bio Psycho Socio 1: Ecologies Urbaines* 1997 and *Tout est Paysage* (*All is Landscape*) 2001. In the mid-1990s he designed an eco-centre in Belfort to promote education about the natural world and our responsibilities towards it.[22] Ecology has also been a constant theme in relation to energy use and pollution. In 1999, collaborating with a contractor, Kroll won a competition for a secondary school in Caudry, eastern France, intended to provide a realistic example of sustainability. Very high standards had to be met in terms both of operating and embodied energy, and daylight had to be provided to a usable level in all classrooms, which meant introducing it from both sides on both storeys. Water consumption had to be minimised and rain run-off absorbed. Transport energy in bringing materials had to be calculated and also the cost of removing waste materials from the site. Targets not met in any of these aspects would have resulted in heavy financial penalties, but all were achieved. The project was a valuable demonstration of how many normal processes and activities are wasteful and polluting, and what kind of constraints architects would face if they were expected genuinely to build sustainably.[23]

A critique and a way forward

The Mémé and many subsequent Kroll projects provide both a critique of current practice and an image of how things might be: what they might become. The critique is on several levels, both explicit and implicit. His constant mixing of functions and pursuit of complexity *per se* challenge zoned masterplans, and his constant concern to make links with the context challenges the glorious isolation of buildings which are imposed as solitary objects – buildings to which he gives the name 'autistic'. His rationale of construction challenges widespread assumptions behind structural and technical determinism in building. A parallel area in which he has been very active – though it is not discussed here – is the effect of the computer. Kroll got into CAD very early, partly from the fear that it would add yet another layer of technical discipline to alienate architecture from the user, partly because he saw that it could aid the management of complexity.[24]

old city but to find buildings there that could be reused, and as a result it was split between two places on adjacent streets, with a three-minute walk in between. Rather than being exiled to an educational ghetto on the outskirts, the students therefore take part in the life of the town.[19] An even more extreme example, unbuilt, was a brewery for the town of Sélestat. The owners naturally assumed a common territory for their operations behind a single fence, but Kroll thought it would suit the town better to divide it into separate departments and spread them around, reinforcing the town rather than setting up in competition.[20] With the Technical College at Belfort he sought the reverse – to bring the life of the locality into the college – by making its central square fully public and connecting it into the network of the neighbourhood. The college's departments were designed as separate institutions around the square, each with its own entrance. A few private houses were dispersed between them, and Kroll intended to heal the isolation of nearby tower blocks by building up to their doors, but the invisible lines by which bureaucratic institutions define their territories this time proved too strong.[21]

Kroll's work has also from the beginning been concerned with the idea of the inhabited landscape as a kind of ecology, and this is reflected in the

As his reinterpretation of techniques undermines ideas of building practice, so Kroll's unrestricted mix of styles and materials implicitly undermines architects' assumptions about good taste and professionalism and their right to impose it on

138

others. He scorns Gropius's too easy dismissal of the problem of mechanisation: *'the repetition of the same thing for the same purpose exercises a settling and civilising influence on men's minds'*.[25] He also denies the pervasive illusion of universal good taste that allowed modernist architects to turn their backs on the local and the specific. Perhaps most threatening to architects in the image of the Mémé, though, is the creation of a process whose outcome is unpredictable, which therefore appears to be out of artistic control. This denies what many consider to be the very essence of the designer's task: to shape and order things. But it also reminds us that the village, the town, the city, is necessarily the product of many hands and many minds: it has to be a shared thing.

The tower blocks and slabs of mid-twentieth century social housing were evidently not shared enough, and were treated too much like a technical packaging problem, with too little thought about community. People felt powerless to make themselves 'at home'. However, these environments were merely extreme cases of a more general phenomenon that has swept the modern world: people are no longer able or allowed to build for themselves. Even given the site, the money, and some carpentry skills, you cannot simply start building your own house without meeting the needs of many bureaucracies, whose demands are met only by having everything drawn up by a specialist in advance. Most people in most cases are much more limited by finance, and in rented accommodation one is not usually allowed to make significant alterations. Giancarlo De Carlo reported that people in Milan no longer bother to look at a flat before renting it: they only count up the number of square metres. All this amounts to an expropriation of people from control of their habitat, and a consequent loss of the expression of use from building, but we know from studies of pre-industrial societies how intensely and automatically buildings can reflect beliefs and values, and how they contribute to a shared reality (see discussion in Chapter 3). When the feedback loop between building and using is broken, people feel powerless, alienated, and finally indifferent.

With the Mémé Kroll produced the most powerful image of participation in the late twentieth century. Although it was in many ways compromised – an opportunity that opened only to close again – it provided the rest of the world with a hint of Another Architecture, of a new path of development.

It reminded us how very political architecture always is, how much it is a battle between vested interests. Crucially, it showed us the possibility of reconnecting a built world with its inhabitants, which is perhaps the only effective way to escape the alienation and expropriation brought about by modern technology and bureaucracy. In various projects Kroll and other pioneers have shown that participation produces differentiated and varied buildings in response to purpose, that it initiates a feedback loop between building and using, permitting a dialogue to develop and helping to root people in a place. It also regenerates almost forgotten building rituals which engage users to identify even before completion, and the sense of 'belonging' so engendered encourages actions of care and maintenance so that life can continue to unfold.

PBJ

Notes

1. See Zucchi 1992, pp. 106-16.
2. Interview with the author, 1986.
3. Kroll 1986, 1987, 2001.
4. Francis Strauven 'The Anarchitecture of Lucien Kroll', *Architectural Association Quarterly* Vol. 8, No. 2, 1976, pp. 40-44.
5. Kroll 1987, p. 32.
6. Ibid, p. 26.
7. Ibid, p. 36.
8. Ibid, p. 40.
9. Kroll 'The Soft Zone', *Architectural Association Quarterly* Vol. 7, No. 4, 1975, p. 52. (The most detailed description of the design process published in English).
10. Ibid, p. 52.
11. Ibid, p. 52.
12. Stichting Architectural Research 1965.
13. Habraken was already considering the difference between permanent supporting structure and cladding or dividing elements of shorter life which could be changed by the tenants: see Kroll 1986, pp. 56-60, 115-121.
14. Including detailed discussions with precast concrete manufacturers, see Kroll 1986, p. 33.
15. Kroll 1986, pp. 42-45.
16. Ibid, p. 56.
17. For detailed discussion and many instances see Blundell Jones, Petrescu and Till 2005.
18. Strauven op. cit., p. 42.
19. Blundell Jones 'Kroll Drama' *The Architectural Review* November 1989, pp. 55-58.
20. Kroll 1987, pp. 98-101.
21. Blundell Jones 'Kroll's open school' *The Architectural Review* March 1987, pp. 63-68.
22. Blundell Jones 'Green guage' *The Architectural Review* November 1996, pp.71-73.
23. Blundell Jones 'Sustainable School' *The Architectural Review* January 2002, pp. 69-73.
24. So much of Kroll's book *Composants* (*The Architecture of Complexity*, Kroll 1986) was about CAD that the German edition was entitled *CAD Architektur*.
25. Gropius 1935.

Chapter 11. Ralph Erskine: Byker Housing, Newcastle, 1969-75

Born into an English family in 1914, Ralph Erskine studied architecture at the Regent Street Poly-technic in London before emigrating to Sweden in 1939, where he lived on until 2005 and became the leading architect of his generation. As a member of CIAM and subsequently of Team Ten, he also played an international role, and from the 1960s he started to design projects in the UK, of which the huge Byker housing development was probably the most important.[1] Nationally regarded as a key work of the 1970s, it both consolidated Erskine's international reputation and seemed to point to a new and enlightened direction for housing through user participation. It was innovative both socially and architecturally, and no mere coincidence that the architect had come from a country with one of the most advanced welfare states and the best social housing standards in Europe. But just as it began to make the face of new council housing acceptable, privatisation was taking root.[2] The

1. Part of the Byker Wall seen from the inside.

last parts of Byker were still under construction when Margaret Thatcher came to power in 1979. She turned over housing to the private market and ordered a widepread sell-off of council housing stock, making it almost a stigma to be a council tenant. These political changes, still unreversed at the time of writing despite the return of the Labour Party, make it difficult fairly to assess the somewhat run-down Byker that we see today.[3]

Erskine was attracted to Sweden for its progressiveness both in politics and in architecture. Brought up and schooled as a Quaker, he identified with the honest thriftiness of the Swedish character and the egalitarian nature of the social democracy that had been established in 1932. These political values had found expression in the new so-called 'functionalist' architecture which was established with the Stockholm Exhibition of 1930 designed by Erik Gunnar Asplund, and which spread from there across Scandinavia.[4] Swedish modernism had grown from strong roots in the neo-classical revival called 'Swedish Grace' of the 1920s and in earlier National Romanticism, and architects like Asplund, Sigurd Lewerentz and Sven Markelius developed their work on a foundation provided by gifted architectural predecessors, including Ragnar Östberg, Carl Westman and Lars Israel Wahlman.[5] This small architectural world had enlightened clients willing to invest heavily in buildings of high standard while accepting changes that modernity was bringing.[6] By contrast in the England of the 1930s an imperial conservatism stagnated, reaching its peak in the work of Lutyens, so Erskine's excite-ment is understandable.[7] Having gained a place in the office of Weiike and Odeen, he invited his fiancée Ruth to come over and marry him, and they were there when the war broke out. As a Quaker, Eskine was a committed pacifist, but he offered his services to the Ambulance Brigade only to find his route home cut off. Sweden remained neutral, but with the economy badly affected and building work reduced, the Erskines had to eke out a living finding design work when possible. Trapped in Sweden until 1945, they had become so established that they decided to stay permanently.

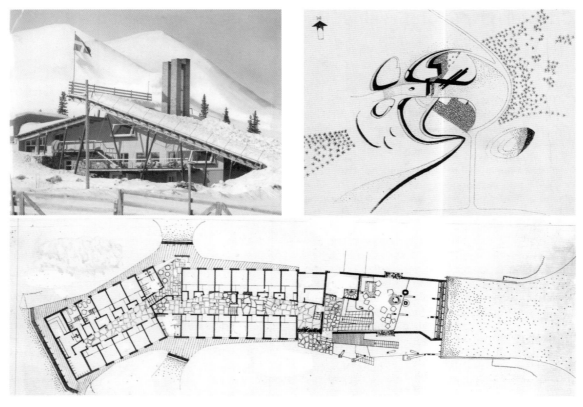

2, 3, 4. Ski hotel in Borgafiäll, 1948, main front, site plan and ground floor plan.

Just how much of Erskine's architectural manner is due to his British background and innate character, how much due to his adopted Sweden is hard to say, but by the time he designed a ski hotel in Borgafiäll in 1948 much of his characteristic architectural vocabulary had already emerged. It followed the continental organic tradition in its articulation of parts to make up separate wings and in the specific planning of rooms according to function,[8] and it was very un-English (though similar to the work of Asplund and Aalto) in its frequent departure from the right angle in plan. However, the overwhelming virtue of Erskine's hotel lies in its response to the climate with its great sheltering and overhanging pitched roofs, the largest of them serving as a nursery ski slope. It was characteristically sensitive in its transitions between inside and out: projecting balconies and windows on the south side created a soft and layered threshold, while a free-standing hearth and chimney in the double-height social space made a clear inner focus. Here was a building that not only took its rightful place in the beautiful mountainous landscape, but even adopted snowdrifts as part of its formal vocabulary. Canted structural columns and exposed steel ties dramatised the way the snow load was carried.

In the 1950s Erskine quickly built up a flourishing practice in Stockholm, producing many houses and housing schemes, and also some large industrial complexes. The style was varied and inventive, following what became known as 'The New Empiricism' and his range of architectural interests grew.[9] As his reputation increased, he gained larger projects in a wider range of places including district master-plans. In response to a job in the extreme north at Kiruna he also developed a special interest in Arctic architecture, perhaps because the extreme conditions intensified the extent to which buildings had to be shaped by climate. At CIAM in Otterlo in 1959 he presented a scheme for an Arctic city to his Team Ten friends, explaining in detail the different

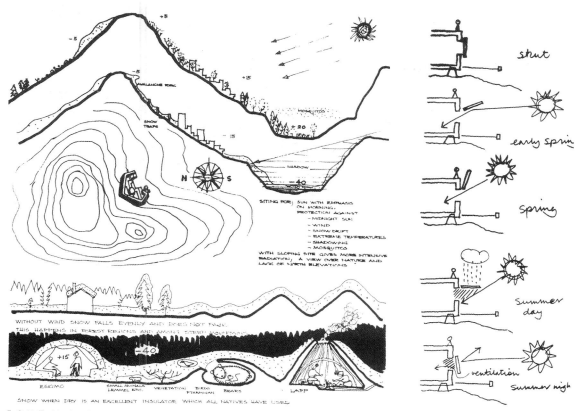

5, 6, 7. Erskine's reflections on coping with the northern climate as presented to CIAM and Team Ten. Top left: plan for an Arctic city with protective wall against the north. Above: comparative houses. Right: an Arctic window for climatic adjustment.

conditions of life in the north with its short summer and midnight sun, its desperately cold dark winter and drifting snows. He explained the variations of temperature and light, the importance of orientation and wind, the need to insulate well, to minimise exposed surfaces and to avoid cold bridges, adding that *'possibly one could get some sort of expression of the special conditions that exist there, and it seems to me that there are considerable plastic possibilities in this enclosed winter-cell and open summer-cell.'*[10] He went on to address the need to allow for individuality and for *'the irrational funny things that people do'*,[11] noting that modern affluence had been achieved at the cost of some neurosis, so that though the 'old physical slum' had been eliminated, it had been replaced by a new 'emotional psychological slum'.[12] This he identified as a major problem, evidently inviting some discussion, but his Team Ten colleagues failed to pick up on it, instead criticising his work stylistically. Peter Smithson

dismissed his 'Mickey Mouse styling' with puritanical zeal, because of the varied materials and colours, and because of a tendency to exaggerate. Aldo van Eyck also called for simplification, but added a note of envy: *'Your work is beautifully done, there is no question of it. You could, I believe, probably design anything'.*[13]

The design for Byker began nearly ten years later, in 1968. Erskine had already built several successful housing projects in Sweden, where social housing was a political priority and the rate of construction the highest in the world.[14] He had begun to work also in England, planning Clare College, Cambridge from 1966, and housing developments at Killingworth and Newmarket. When the Conservatives gained Newcastle City Council in 1968 and decided to hand over Byker to a private planning consultant, his international reputation and housing experience made him an ideal candidate.

Old Byker

Byker lies on the north side of the Tyne a mile east of the centre of Newcastle. It had begun as a village, but was built up in the late nineteenth century with terrace houses on a grid plan to house the industrial workers from the shipyards and engineering works. It was not back-to-backs as in the Midlands but 'Tyneside flats': two floors with one entered directly and the other up a flight of stairs. Sanitation was poor, overcrowding common, and poverty rampant, so it is hardly surprising that clearance and redevelopment was mooted in Newcastle's City Development Plan of 1951, and that nearly 1200 dwellings were condemned by the Medical Officer of Health in 1953 as unfit. But with other slum areas to be considered, redevelopment was slow, priority driven largely by the relative urgency of sanitary conditions. Compulsory purchase orders were not made until a decade later, and demolition did not actually start until 1966.[15] Meanwhile it had been noticed that the area had a strong character, retaining a remarkably close-knit community despite the degradation of living in the shadow of the bulldozer for nearly twenty years.[16]

Neighbours were always ready to help each other, particularly in times of difficulty. Money, or rather the lack of it, helped cement the friendly spirit. The low and uncertain wages and long hours of hard manual labour forced people to support each other. This feeling of belonging was engendered not only by helpful neighbours but also by having one's family nearby. Children played together in the back lanes and went to school together. Young men married the girls they had sat next to in school and went to work with those they had played football with in the street. Young married couples set up home near parents and the cycle began again. [17]

When in 1966 the council finally announced its intention to demolish and replace every house, this projected violence naturally raised the anxiety of the residents, who made it clear that they wanted to remain in the area retaining their roots and relationships, and to have some say in the planning process. Public participation was a new and progressive concept which the council were prepared to embrace, committing themselves to 'Byker for Byker people'.[18] All the same, the decisive large-scale gesture in the development plan of 1963 had been the provision of a motorway around the north edge of the site, and the initial demolitions, pushing no less than 3000 people out of the area, were made simply to free the ground where it was intended to run. Two years before Erskine was engaged, the making of a barrier against motorway noise was already the top design priority.

Initiating a dialogue

At first Erskine considered rehabilitating the existing houses, but they were in poor physical condition and posed problems of space, aspect, daylighting, traffic safety, lack of open space, and steep streets which were hazardous in winter. Decisive, however, was the tenants' own preference for new housing and the wish of 80 per cent of them to remain in Byker. This would require a rolling programme of partial demolition and replacement, so that people could be moved over as new houses were completed, and an early adjustment was made to curb the rapacious demolition programme.

Such acceptance of process, involving careful sequencing and constant readjustment rather than laying down of plans as hard and fast, was a crucial virtue of Erskine's approach. He did not impose a master-plan: his 'Plan of Intent', accepted by the City Council in 1970, was couched in rather general terms. It promised an 'integrated environment for living' in collaboration with the residents, including social facilities. It would maintain the character-istics of the neighbourhood, rehouse the residents without breaking family ties, respond to the site, and provide through its form a local identity for each group of houses.

Contact with the area and its inhabitants was a high priority, and during the initial planning phase Erskine's architect-daughter Jane and his assistant Arne Nilsson lived in Newcastle, while Erskine made frequent visits. Once the commission was awarded, they set up a permanent office in an

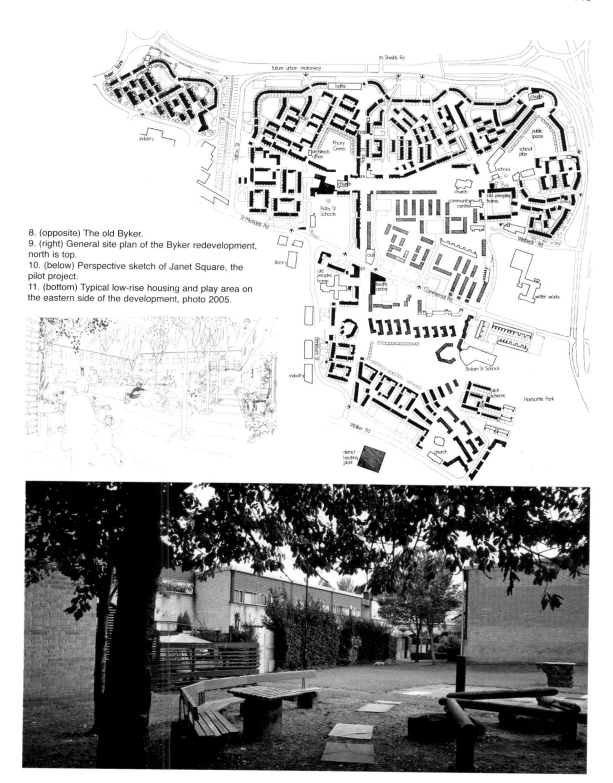

8. (opposite) The old Byker.
9. (right) General site plan of the Byker redevelopment, north is top.
10. (below) Perspective sketch of Janet Square, the pilot project.
11. (bottom) Typical low-rise housing and play area on the eastern side of the development, photo 2005.

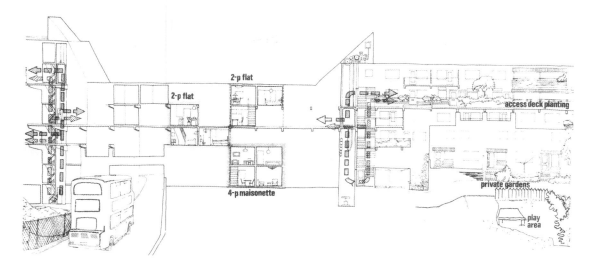

Second floor plan, two-person.

5m

Third floor plan.

12,13,14. (opposite and previous page) Inside and outside different parts of the Byker Wall photographed in 2005.
15. (top) Section through the Wall showing distribution of flats.
16. (above) Typical flat plans.
17. (below) South side of the Wall

old funeral parlour at the centre of Byker, and the executive architect Vernon Gracie lived in a flat above. Extra fees were allowed for this public front, and local people were invited to drop in at any time of day to discuss their problems, to allay their fears, and eventually to see the drawings for the flat or house they were being allocated. Much time was spent on matters quite unconnected with the new architecture, and the architects found themselves in the front line for every kind of complaint,[19] but social contacts were made, the people came to trust the architects, and the architects learned about their problems and their way of life.

A parallel 'community development project' was set up by the council in 1971 funded by the Calouste Gulbenkian Foundation. It had its own 'Action Centre' on the site, and helped to organise Tenants' Associations. Through these joint initiatives a dialogue was started for the first time on a human level and on their patch as opposed to having to deal with faceless bureaucrats at town hall. Even if the extent of real participation was later exaggerated, a critical sociological report of 1978 was obliged to admit: *'although the architects inherited a situation where council credibility was at a low ebb because of delays and uncertainties… they have established close and sensitive links with the community'.* [20]

Another aspect of participation was the early organisation of a pilot project on the southern part of the site involving 46 dwellings. This experiment hit more snags than expected, but unforeseen shortcomings were remedied in the main design.

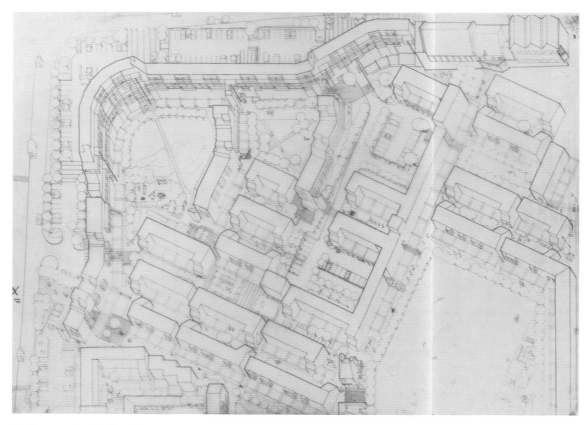

18. Axonometric projection of the north-west corner showing the relationship between the Wall, public spaces and low-rise housing.

Avoiding repetition

Erskine's considerable experience of housing in Sweden had made him well aware of cost limits and building regulations. He therefore knew both where to spend the limited money to greatest effect and how to plan for maximum variety, and he had developed a series of strategies that could be reapplied fairly directly to Byker.[21] He was acutely aware of the dangers of repetition which invariably come with large schemes. The temptation is to design one or two flats or houses offering efficient use of space and straightforward construction, then to repeat them endlessly, choosing optimum orientation and spacing to get the best use of land. This kind of 'rationalism' geared to efficient mass production was advocated by Walter Gropius in the 1920s (Blundell Jones 2002, p. 17), who lightly dismissed the problem of repetition.[22] But his friend Ludwig Hilberseimer had already un-

blinkingly drawn in 1927 the serried ranks of blocks that this process would inevitably produce, lacking all sense of place and scale, and treating dwelling like packaging.[23] Sweden's pioneer Modernist Erik Gunnar Asplund had early understood this danger, and even in his first housing scheme for Stockholm of 1917, he showed how the simple repetition of houses could be mitigated by a layout responding to the local topography. In the modernist manifesto *Acceptera* of 1931, written with a group of friends, he contributed a section on 'the individual and the mass' with pictures of soldiers and dancing girls moving in unison to underline the dangers of uniformity,[24] and in his own modernist work he consistently sought to exploit the particularities of the site and to articulate elements of the programme so that they developed individual identities. Precisely this organic side of the Swedish inheritance was taken up by Erskine.

19. Many low-rise houses have gardens and courts which tenants can develop as they wish, as seen in 2005.
20. (below) Existing buildings were incorporated.

The layout at Byker

The need for a motorway screen around the northern edge of the site was readily accepted, for it fulfilled the consistent desire throughout Erskine's housing work to create clear edges, relating not only to earlier protective walls bounding housing schemes but also to his plans for Arctic cities where the wall functioned as a climatic shield. It resulted in the dramatic and famous Byker Wall with which the whole development has become identified. A mere one or two rooms thick, it rose in places to a height of 8 stories, but could be played against the changing ground levels to get endless variations. Balconies and access galleries on the sunny south side contrasted with solid brickwork on the north, broken only by small windows and vents. It was punctuated with projecting triangular roofs over the lift shafts which accentuate the Newcastle skyline. The access galleries were made wider than the balconies to differentiate them.

Only 20 per cent of the accommodation was placed in the Wall, the other 80 per cent being in low rise houses within the protected enclave. To avoid too stark a differentiation between the two, a number of short tails were added to the inside of the wall, dropping away from it and enfolding spaces next to it. In the general plan the earlier grid of streets was abandoned to avoid the steep slopes, the new arrangement being made more nearly to follow the contours, but existing buildings including churches, schools, industrial works and the old bath house were retained, becoming anchor points for the new street network and helping determine its geometry. They housed community facilities, and in addition the new development included a post office, a chemist, a butcher and a greengrocer in the local centre of the south part. Premises for a medical practice were also included.

The widespread post-war policy to separate cars from pedestrians resulted in priority being given to a network of major pedestrian streets along primary access routes connecting with the outside

world, while minor alleys allowed local connections. The relatively simple two-storey terrace house types, nearly always rectangular and necessarily restricted to Parker-Morris space standards, were grouped around small courts, often with a different house type defining an end or corner. At a larger scale, the grouped courts and streets became named neighbourhoods clearly divided by the main pedestrian streets, which identified the phased stages of the redevelopment, social groups being moved across in turn with neighbourly relations intact. Shops, hobby rooms and other social facilities were included, and existing trees were retained where possible. External benches and picnic tables, plants on pergolas, children's playgrounds and a great variety of paving types contributed to a richly varied local landscape of varying scale which made each part of the development unique and created a strong sense of place. Many houses had walled back courts which could be used as small yards or gardens, motorcycle parks or outdoor workshops according to the tenant's wishes. Houses onto pedestrian streets were given door steps and overhanging porches to mark an extension into the public realm, and window boxes were designed into the access galleries and balconies of the Wall, again at the intersection of public and private. The new

Byker contained many different kinds and scale of threshold, with a consequent sense of progressive enclosure and ownership.

The buildings were constructed with relatively cheap and banal materials like brick, timber and concrete, with shallow pitched roofs in corrugated sheets, but including a wide range of colours. Brick banding on the south side of the Wall helped differentiate storeys while a large scale patterning in several different types of brick made abstract decoration on the sheer unbroken wall to the north. Some houses were timber clad, with horizontal or vertical boarding, and timber everywhere was treated with strongly coloured stains. Windows were mostly conventional, but continuous horizontal openings served in places to stabilise a complex composition, and triangular lights in special positions added necessary accents. Roofs were nearly always made apparent, giving a sense of shelter and protection. The great sloping planes on the Wall provide a landmark across the city, but even the low-pitched house roofs show a crinkly edge, and small steeply raked porches add greatly to the effect. All these things helped assure a visually complex and varied environment with plenty of local landmarks, somewhat like an old town which has grown up piecemeal over the years.

Participation and its limits

The Byker development was widely regarded as a great architectural success, and much of this was attributed to the participation process both by the architects and by the council. All the same, later studies concluded that two main aims had not been fulfilled. Firstly 'Byker for Byker people' was not achieved because only a minority of the original inhabitants ended up living there, most of the original 12,000 population having moved out for one reason or another.[25] To be fair to Erskine, the worst haemorrhage was the 3000 people displaced before he arrived for the sake of the intended motorway that was in the end never built. The other charge was that the people had not really had much say in the design, and here again the planning of the motorway was a blatant example of violence imposed from above, but the new street pattern was also hardly a matter open to negotiation. Also imposed, if in the name of good sense and current practice, were the rules and regulations, yardsticks and codes taken for granted in the definition of public housing. Some tenants

First floor.

First floor.

First floor.

4500

Ground floor, two-person.

Ground floor, three-person.

Ground floor, four-person.

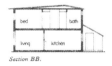

Section BB.

21. (opposite) Main pedestrian routes give way to narrow alleys along the contours, sometimes as here with a portal.
22. (top) Row houses with small front gardens and rear entrances.
23. (left) Typical two-storey house and flat plans as presented in *Architects Journal*.
24. (above) Section of a two-storey house.

expected to assist in the design of their own homes, but this occurred only to a limited extent in the pilot project.[26] The sociological report commissioned by the council reported, however, that a road had been moved back 2 metres after tenant requests, and that a playground was relocated, so changes at this scale were real.[27] The architects' open shop and the Council's Community Project were jointly successful, too, in allaying fears and generating the community solidarity that assured social connections after the move. The transfer of communities as coherent groups of neighbours from old areas to new also assured social continuity, and the allocation of dwellings in advance (with right of refusal) allowed people to prepare for new lives and new neighbourly relations before the crisis came

upon them. All these things undoubtedly made good sense, but some tenants expressed regrets after the move about aspects of their former lives that they had lost. Some missed the streets as places of community and gathering and as arenas of personal expression. They were at a loss about where to organise Jubilee celebrations,[28] and regretted the disappearance of the clear threshold, the ritually washed doorstep leading to the front room with its symmetrical mantel display and net curtains.[29] One informant expressed worry about what would happen when someone died in the Wall, how they would be laid out, and the coffin be got in and out.[30] Birth had also taken place in the old houses, accompanied by ritual observances. A mother had to remain in bed for two weeks and could not step outside the house for six; she was not allowed to comb her hair, handle flour, or place her hands in cold water.[31] Such rituals were an integral part of the old life, helping to promote a dignified and ordered existence despite the hard physical and economic circumstances, but they obviously could not persist. The streets, had they been kept as they were, would now simply be choked with cars. Birth and death take place in hospital as they now do everywhere else, regardless of the erosion to the concept of home. Redevelopment with its concurrent violence certainly accelerated change of all kinds, but change was inevitable.

Given that it had to happen, Erskine found ways to mitigate the violence, by allowing continuity, preserving memory, and providing good soil in which the new community could grow. His architectural elaboration, criticised by Smithson as 'Mickey Mouse' and by Colin Amery as 'Folksey detailing'[32] was often construction-based and has stood the test of time, allowing Byker to accept the *bricolage* of inhabitants and the changes of doors and windows that lets them render the place their own.[33] Despite Amery's fears, the Wall has not become a vandalised embarrassment like other high-rise schemes of the period, but remains popular. Like Lucien Kroll (see Chapter 10), Erskine understood the need for sheer complexity of form to encourage user-identification, and he avoided the usual dominance by technical and economic issues. Through imaginative exploitation of the givens, he succeeded in recreating a strong sense of place: in sowing strong hints of what a community might be; how it could be planned and nurtured; and how dwellings might relate to places of communal togetherness. Despite all shortcomings this was surely more enlightened than recent private housing developments in the UK, which sell themselves on promises of homeliness that they cannot keep, negate the landscape in their automatic sprawl, attempt no definition of community, regard boundaries not as neighbourly connections but as potential points of dispute, and sentence people to a car-bound existence. Erskine did not solve all the problems, and the participation he initiated was limited, but he provided a worthy and enlightened example for others to follow and to develop.

PBJ

Notes

1. The main competitor would be Clare Hall, Cambridge, 1966-69, a radical attempt to redefine the Cambridge College.
2. It was a form of privatisation, in that the local authority's architectural office had been displaced by Erskine's private firm.
3. The accompanying photographs taken by the author in August 2005 show some gentle material degradation. Byker has remained council housing but was found still mostly occupied, with street furniture intact, and a surprising lack of graffiti.
4. See my monograph on Asplund, Blundell Jones 2006.
5. Ibid.
6. It is extraordinary that Asplund's two greatest projects, the Woodland Cemetery and Gothenburg Law Courts, both ran for 25 years and through several design versions, yet ended up better as a result. Normally long-running architectural projects are reduced and compromised, as well as becoming stale. Asplund's clients and their advisers seem to have understood well what was at stake.
7. 'I first came to Sweden at the end of the thirties to escape from English conservatism. I found in Sweden, at the time, the forms and technology of the modern architectural movement we, rather superficially perhaps, called "internationalism".' Erskine at CIAM 1959, quoted in Newman 1961, p. 151.
8. The principle is explained in relation to the work of Hugo Häring and Hans Scharoun in Blundell Jones 2002, Ch. 2.
9. For a concise summary of this phase of Erskine's career see the special issue of *Architectural Design* on Erskine by Mats Egelius, vol. 47, no. 11-12, 1977.
10. Newman 1961, p 167.
11. Ibid, p.167.
12. Ibid, p.168.
13. Ibid, p.169.
14. Egelius in *Architectural Design*, p. 810.
15. These facts and more from a pamphlet *The Byker Redevlopment* published by the City of Newcastle upon Tyne in 1981.
16. A moving visual and written portrait of the place is given by the Finnish photographer Sirkka-Liisa Konttinen in her book *Byker* (1985). She lived there to record life in 1970.
17. From the pamphlet *The Byker Redevlopment*, see n. 15.
18. This trend followed a recommendation of participation in the Town and Country Planning Act of 1968, backed up by the Skeffington and Seebohm reports, see Hampton and Walkland 1980, p.10.
19. They kept a daybook which recorded all kinds of contacts, including children engaged in hide and seek: see *Architects Journal*, 14 April 1976, p. 341.
20. Zutshi 1978, p. 40.
21. These are coherently listed by Egelius in his chapter 'Housing for People' in *Architectural Design*, pp. 809-822.
22. See Gropius 1935.
23. See Hilberseimer's book *Gross-Stadt Architektur*, Verlag Julius Hoffmann, Stuttgart, 1927.
24. See Blundell Jones 2006.
25. See Peter Malpass 'A reappraisal of Byker', *Architects Journal*, 9 May 1979, pp. 961-989, and Part 2, 14 April 1979, pp. 731-744.
26. Zutshi 1978, p. 51.
27. Ibid, p. 23.
28. Ibid, p. 23.
29. See photographs in Konttinen 1985, also the description of the cleaning ritual on p. 38.
30. Ibid, p. 113.
31. Ibid.
32. *The Architectural Review*, December 1974.
33. At my visit in August 2005 it was evident that nearly all the original doors had been replaced by off-the-peg panelled hardwood types, and some windows by other styles such as leaded lights, but Byker is robust enough to take it. These things may be reversed with listing at Grade 2.

Chapter 12. Norman Foster: Willis Faber & Dumas, Ipswich, 1975

Norman Foster was born in Manchester in 1935. Following National Service in the Royal Air Force he studied at Manchester University School of Architecture and at Yale University in the United States. There he met a fellow British student, Richard Rogers, with whom he formed the partnership that founded British high-tech.[1] Foster's headquarters for insurance company Willis Faber & Dumas in Ipswich, finished in 1975, can be considered the first mature and complex work of this school, for it was completed before his former partner's larger Pompidou Centre, the subject of Chapter 14. The guiding principle of high-tech was a universalising rational exploitation of technology,[2] but this was subject to the individual cultural conditioning of the architect. A brief excursion into the influences of Manchester and Yale on Foster's early work is therefore helpful to reveal some elements behind the design of the Ipswich building.

Manchester presented a cityscape of large scale nineteenth-century industrial structures, but it was a pioneering work of mid-twentieth-century modernism that exerted the most lasting influence on Foster. The engineer Sir Owen Williams's Daily Express building on Great Ancoats Street of 1939 was an awe-inspiring behemoth, especially when lit up at night as the presses rolled. By day its rounded black glass forms concealed the concrete frame of the printing hall. Eschewing conventional architectural languages, it was to this native engineering tradition that Foster returned in developing his own architectural forms. Reflecting on the buildings that had influenced him, Foster also remarked on the impact of such nineteenth-century glass structures as Barton Arcade (1871) and Lancaster Avenue (c.1873, demolished) as inspirations for the social possibilities of new constructional technologies.[3] At Barton Arcade, glass and cast-iron vaults and domes light floors of offices above a retail passageway, creating a back-street world more radical in its architectural language than the conventional street facade to Deansgate. Lancaster Avenue had a section stepped back to maximise light to lower levels,

1. Willis Faber & Dumas's black form as it presents itself to the streets of Ipswich.

2. (top) Owen Williams' Daily Express, Manchester, 1939.
3. (above) Norman Foster, Fred Olsen building, London, 1969.
4. (below) Willis Faber & Dumas, central well with escalator.
5. (opposite top) Entrance seen from escalator.
6. (opposite bottom) Office floor at the perimeter.

though its construction was a hybrid of cast-iron and timber. Foster cited all these structures as sources for Willis Faber & Dumas in his initial presentations.[4]

The other seminal influence on Foster was his study at Yale, which proved far more stimulating than his earlier studies at Manchester. By the time he arrived in 196I, the school at New Haven had superseded its Ivy League rival Harvard as the foremost American architectural academy under the leadership of Paul Rudolph. In this intense and competitive environment, Foster was exposed to figures such as Louis Kahn, Vincent Scully, James Stirling and Serge Chermayeff, all contributing in different capacities to the intellectual life of the school. Kahn's ideas about served and serving spaces (see Blundell Jones 2002, Ch. 16) were directly apparent in the graduate studio occupying the top floor of his Yale University Art Gallery of 1953. Stirling was developing the use of patent glazing in Leicester University's Engineering Building (Chapter 6), while Chermayeff's emphasis on the analytical approach to design, as expounded in the book *Community and Privacy,* laid foundations for Foster's design method in both architecture and urban design.[5] Following their return to Britain from Yale, Foster and Rogers, though not yet professionally qualified, set up in practice together with their respective wives Wendy and Su as Team 4. This name announced the arrival of a younger generation on an architectural scene already dominated intellectually by the proponents of Team Ten. The major achievement of the practice was the Reliance Controls factory in Swindon of 1965-66, a 30,000 square feet industrial shed which prefigured aesthetic choices in subsequent projects by both architects.[6] However, commissions were scarce, and following the disbandment of Team 4, Foster set up independently in 1967. He collaborated with Buckminster Fuller on an abortive underground theatre project in Oxford, then successfully completed a building for IBM at Cosham in 1971, associating himself with the burgeoning world of information technology by placing a sleek rectangle of mirror glass in a green suburban context.[7]

It was Willis Faber & Dumas that established the reputation of the practice as radically innovative in both technical and social thinking. The design originated in 1971 as a project to relocate and consolidate the insurance company from different sites in Southend and the City of London, where it

7. (opposite) View from top of central well towards entrance.
8. (opposite bottom) Daytime view from street.
9. (above) The swimming pool on the ground floor.
10. (below) Glass screen between swimming pool and entrance hall.
11. (right) Series of projections showing the floor plates from bottom to top.

had come to feel somewhat cramped. The firm chose Ipswich for its relative proximity and fast travel time. With its ground floor swimming pool and roof garden, the building as completed displayed a particularly benign form of work environment, the white-collar worker's leisure time being accommodated on the premises. Depending on political perspective this could be interpreted either as a symbol of employer benevolence or as a foretaste of the appropriation of free-time by work. Advanced technology seemed to promise that mechanisation and computerisation of work processes would lead to increased leisure time, and the cost of energy was not yet in question.[8] Both the technological expression and the architectural development of the white-collar workplace can be traced back to early examples like Peter Ellis's Oriel Chambers in Liverpool (1864) with its pioneering glass facade. Although this building was not widely known, it represented an elegant aestheticisation of industrial building principles which had developed in Britain in the mid-nineteenth century, but which were usually

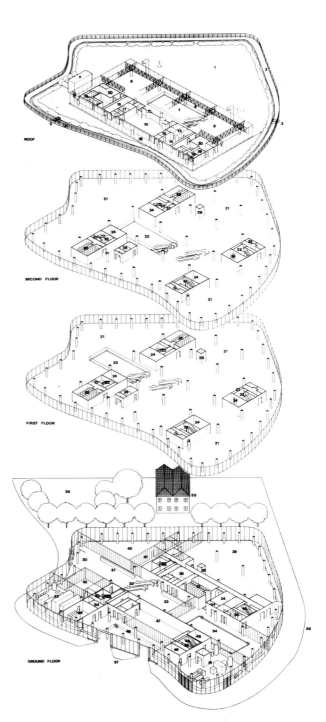

12. (top left) Glass wall as an insubstantial membrane from within,
13. (above) and as an impenetrable barrier on the street.
14. (left) The innovative glazing detail for which the building became world famous.
15. (below) The restaurant on the roof within its black box, and the quilt of green lawn that turns it into a garden.

16. (opposite) Section showing the edge of the building, the tapered floors, and the glass fins supporting the external envelope.

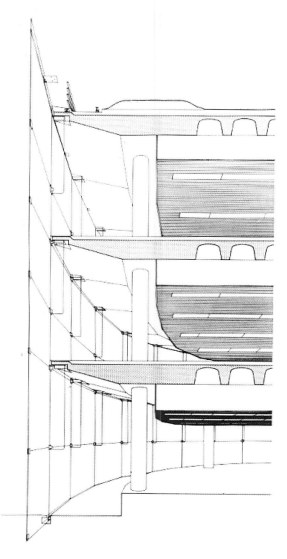

the triumph of a totalising aesthetic combined with transparency (Blundell Jones 2002, Ch. 14) which, despite the claims of open-ended flexibility, induced a coercive order both in furnishing and use of space. Deep plan forms and uniform artificial lighting ensured the completeness of the vision, but also provided the bureaucratic image for a type of corporate environment that came increasingly into question during the 1960s.[10] Material prosperity brought disillusionment with such working practices, while computerisation promised a less regimented form of employment. As Reyner Banham pointed out, this was fundamentally an issue of style with a certain *flamboyance de rigueur* to distance the new environment from the herd.[11] The worker could have it all: secure job, pension and a lunchtime swim, relief from the struggle of commuting and the amenities of a rural location. Willis Faber & Dumas's move from Central London to Ipswich demonstrated that the world of work in the financial service sector had clear benefits, just at the time when traditional manufacturing was poised for a precipitous decline. For this vision of an idyllic work environment developed against the background of political strife that characterised British industry in the 1970s. Initiatives by successive governments encouraged employer/employee cooperation, as in the successful competitor economies of Japan and West Germany, but the energy crisis of 1973 undermined this optimistic view of social and technological progress. Growing unemployment and the decline of manufacturing did not immediately affect the office environment, but it did mean that innovative constructional experiments such as Willis Faber & Dumas failed to spawn direct and immediate progeny. But within Foster's *oeuvre*, the projects of the Frankfurt Commerzbank (1991-97), the company's own headquarters (1986-1990) and the Swiss Re tower (1997-2004), all show its influence.

The curved perimeter
The visual impact of the Willis Faber & Dumas building was compared at the time with the recently completed but urbanistically more disconnected Greyfriars Centre opposite.[12] This suffered the familiar problems of brutalist buildings, failing both in social and material terms. In contrast, the company needed to present a less aggressive image, and this came only after a lengthy process of internal consultation, site acquisition and tailoring of the design to specific requirements. The site was

hidden behind elaborate historicist facades. The young James Stirling had firewatched from the building in the early part of the Second World War, and had later developed an architectural interest in its qualities,[9] which he perhaps communicated to Foster. Ideas about the development of the modern workplace were disseminated through examples like the Larkin Building (1904) and Johnson Wax Building (1939) by Frank Lloyd Wright, which demonstrated the architectural potential of the top-lit atrium and of paring away conventional ornament. Later examples by Mies, especially the prismatic Seagram Building in New York of 1958, presented

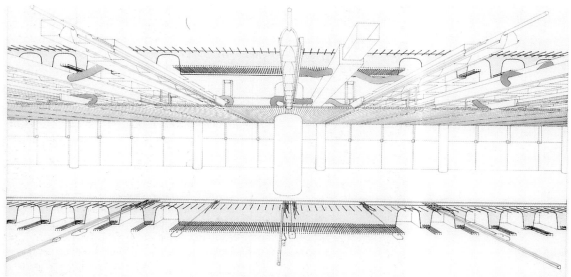

17. Section drawing showing the floor and ceiling voids and the services provided through them.

an accumulation of small plots lying between the medieval core and the new ring road, and it had an irregular curving boundary. It was the decision to follow this line with the building's glass perimeter that proved the making of the project, but the idea came relatively late.

The formal coherence of the finished building masks much more complex origins. Early on in the design process the building was imagined as a series of independent shelves sitting within the glazed envelope of a space-frame, a homage to the influence of Buckminster Fuller. Only the difficulties of realising that vision prompted the final design, for in a lengthy process of transformation the initial concept was modified, the environmental aspects translating into a grass roof and low-rise form. The initial independence of floor and envelope gave way to a tentative gesture of attachment, and the social ambition was transferred to the central atrium. The final arrangement is beguilingly simple. A bank of three revolving doors placed in a shallow concave angle on the perimeter leads to a spine formed by six escalators which rise through the central atrium with a view of the swimming pool beyond. In a 'sandwich' section, two layers of open plan offices are caught between a ground floor slice of entrance, pool and service areas, and a rooftop crust of restaurant and lawn-covered roof. All is supported by a grid of columns at 14-metre centres in both directions, which carry concrete waffle slabs. A subsidiary 'necklace' of columns

carries the cantilevered edges of the slabs, where the thickness of the floor is reduced to allow a taller edge zone. Here the suspended glass perimeter wall provides dramatic 360° views for the whole office floor. Four vertical cores arranged symmetrically around the spine provide an even distribution of services, feeding into floor voids for easy redeployment of cables. It was already predicted that telephone-based communication would be replaced by electronic and digital media. This servicing strategy was intended both for the initial occupant and to allow for future subdivision, should the building require division between different departments or tenants.

The *parti*[13] of the building fulfills the Corbusian principles of the Domino frame, indeed Malcolm Quantrill relates it specifically to the Five Points.[14] The free-form floor plate is supported on regularly spaced columns, and animated by the vertical circulation (staircases and ramps in the original model, escalators in the later interpretation). The free facade, as envisaged by Le Corbusier, was realised in Ipswich to a degree almost unimaginable fifty years earlier, despite the precedent of metal-framed glazing on Owen Williams's buildings. Familiar as we now are with computer-generated fluid facades, it is hard to imagine just how revolutionary Foster's curving envelope was, for British architecture of the 1950s and 1960s had been rigidly rectangular, any curves and odd angles being condemned as 'irrational'.[15] Buildings were

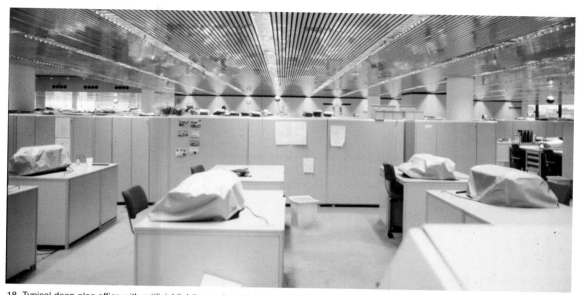

18. Typical deep-plan office with artificial lighting and ventilation in the ceiling, cabling under the floor, allowing flexibility of office layout.

conceived as objects and constructed to their own rectangular discipline within irregular sites, leaving pools of residual (and wasted) space around the edges.[16] Foster could successfully 'rationalise' his swinging perimeter on the basis of efficient land use, but he still had to deal with the irregularities of the difficult relationship between the skin and the grid, and to devise technological means to deal with these variations within a vocabulary of standard parts as his high-tech philosophy demanded. It was his genial innovation to demonstrate that the apparent rigidity of the building components was adaptable to atypical forms, and that paradoxically, the serial anonymity of the elements was capable of producing a highly specific *genius loci*. His rejection of the standard modernist solution of the office tower (as promoted at the Economist only a decade earlier – see Chapter 5), in favour of a lower building height which respected the profile and irregularities of its context, produced a startling but ambiguous urban presence. And the clarity of the internal arrangement, almost Beaux-Arts in its hierarchical disposition of elements, presented a democratic image of office life. The visual impression of solidity in daylight and transparency at night added to the building's urban ambiguity, and the dynamism of its external skin distracted attention from the medieval origin of its footprint, while the traditional urban scale was overturned by the horizontality of its stacked floor plates. It could even finally be regarded as a conventional perimeter

block around a central courtyard, the honorific space – complete with axial symmetry – embodied by pairs of escalators. This type of central space soon became commonplace in deep plan office design.

A technical revolution
The curtain of glass was suspended from the topmost edges and linked into a continuous fabric by corner plates and neoprene seals. This technological advance was a prototype for a new kind of curtain wall developed with glass manufacturers Pilkington, and athough their solution had many imitators, few managed the dramatic elegance of the original. A description of its physical properties in no way prepares one for the extraordinary visual effect. The final omission of all the frames and mullions seen on Helmut Jacoby's preliminary design perspectives reduces the legibility of the single glass sheets, one piece blending effortlessly into the next around the building's perimeter. This effect is enhanced by the tinting of the glass, since by day it enhances reflection, creating a visual distraction, while at night, with the building illuminated, the substance of the glazing dematerialises almost completely. Deceptively simple in its modest lack of presence, the glazed skin belies the sophistication with which this marvel was achieved. Each floor is enclosed in a skin of two vertical sheets, the consistency of the module broken only at the ground where greater height was needed.

19. Sainsbury Centre, University of East Anglia, the glazed end.

20. Sainsbury Centre and its pedestrian bridge.

Apparent continuity of surface is subdivided into separate patterns for each floor internally, for the upper sheet is restrained by a flange of glass perpendicular to the skin, suspended from a notch in the tapered perimeter of the slab. The exception to this uniformity is the roof-top restaurant where the glazing system is simply suspended from the space-frame roof. The lawn on the roof, with its strange echo of a village green, was perhaps the most seductive feature of the entire building, but Foster described it in a typically deadpan way:

...in capital terms a landscaped roof is more expensive than asphalt. However, we beefed it up a little and it provided such a good insulating quilt that we were able to eliminate expansion joints – with their attendant, costly, double rows of columns and piles – across the entire building. Allied to that are considerable long-term energy savings. [17]

While the building's technological narrative involved innovation and risk-taking, the radicalism of the social agenda in its office floors – as opposed to its restaurant and swimming pool – is harder to discern. The argument was that a conventional hierarchy between honorific reception and boardroom areas, and more modest accommodation for the mass of the workforce, had been abandoned. In its place was a democratic office environment free of internal obstruction, sharing horizontal views out through the glazed perimeter, or vertical and diagonal views into and across the atrium. All the same, some sense of hierarchy reappeared in the status-ranked furniture and in a layout which allowed senior officers more surveillance.[18]

The simplicity of the 'open plan' strategy, has also been contrasted with the articulation of office environment achieved at Herman Hertzberger's

Centraal Beheer in Apeldoorn, another insurance company office completed in the same period. The Dutch architect developed the place-making ethos of Aldo van Eyck (see Chapter 3) into a dense matrix of office spaces on several levels, where individual occupants see each other across shared internal public spaces. The repetitive gridded construction of Centraal Beheer is countered by this visibility, while at Willis Faber & Dumas the visual association of person and place is obscured by the exaggerated depth of the floor plate and confused by the reflective surface of the ceiling and glare from the exterior.

The undeniable glamour of Willis Faber & Dumas's sleek image has proved highly compatible with the commercial identity of a financial corporation, as the phenomenon of the brand image has come to the fore. Its less explicit social agenda has meanwhile been overlooked. Reticence about the formation of a new social pattern produced during a period of industrial and political turmoil exploits the supposed neutrality of technology as a mask which might be mistaken for the substance. The limits of this strategy were connected with the building's function. As an office headquarters, its consistency of corporate image is tolerable even with the unusual inclusion of a swimming pool at ground floor.[19] But unity of space and uniformity of use would hinder transformation to more diverse purposes. Subdivision would be problematic, and individualisation would run counter to the collective nature of the building. The limits of adaptability and individuality have therefore been very much set by the architect. Environmentally too, the building has proved somewhat dictatorial: Foster ignored the specific differences of orientation in favour of his uniform facade treatment, which leads us back to the universalising claims of high-tech.

High-tech in a classical mode?

With both of its leaders first knighted then admitted to the House of Lords, high-tech has become an establishment architectural language, but the movement's apparent uniformity in the 1970s and 1980s can now be seen as having divided into two overlapping aspects: 'image' and 'objectivity'. 'Image' suggests an optimistic and technology-based future for architecture, involving dramatic juxtapositions of people, their environments, and the machine. 'Objectivity' developed out of *Sachlichkeit*, part of the Utopian mythology of the 1920s. It was in contrast cooler, deliberately reticent, underplaying the changes that new engineering forms would bring, and explaining them in non-threatening matter-of-fact terms. To describe this divide as between fantasy and reality would be to oversimplify, though the environments achieved often bordered on the fantastic. Rather, the divide lay between an aggressive expression of technology (represented by Centre Pompidou: Chapter 14) and a sleek representation of an effortless future enjoyed by somewhat passive inhabitants. The contemporary technological parallel was the space race between the United States and the Soviet Union, where feats of engineering became overshadowed by the bathos of playing golf on the Moon. The question arose as to whether the achievement was worth the effort, especially once the limits of energy resources were understood.

Willis Faber & Dumas's highly polished form expressed one particular strand of optimism left over from the 1960s. Eschewing the overt trappings of counterculture visible in Centre Pompidou, it represented by its sheer neutrality the probity of the corporate environment, a narcotic combination of lack of differentiation and absence of stimulating incident. But despite its achievement of the status of a *Gesamtkunstwerk*, the direct legacy of the building is a curious one, as might be expected with a structure whose principal aesthetic motif is to dematerialise, to dissolve into fragmentary reflections and transparent surfaces. The same shock value could be witnessed in the next East Anglian building completed by Foster in 1977, the Sainsbury Centre for the Visual Arts at the University of East Anglia at Norwich (Fig. 19). Here, gallery and teaching functions were combined in an uninterrupted shed in a campus setting. The technological breakthrough was again important, for not only was the structural frame continuous between wall and roof: the gasketed cladding system

21. Richard Rogers, Lloyd's Building, London, dominated by service towers on the perimeter.

was also devised to work equally well vertically and horizontally, for the first time in architectural history completely denying the distinction between wall and roof.[20] The beguiling modesty of scale of the Ipswich and Norwich buildings is lost to Foster's later works, no longer discernible in the Hong Kong and Shanghai Bank or Swiss Re headquarters, although the organic form of the latter, and its tendency to disintegrate in close views, could be seen as fulfilling a tradition in optical illusionism started by Mies van der Rohe's Glass Skyscraper project of 1922.

A more interesting contrast can be drawn with a building on a larger scale that succeeded Willis Faber & Dumas as a flagship of British hi-tech in the next decade, Lloyd's of London by Richard Rogers (1986). Both buildings occupy highly irregular plots, and the central atrium space in each case provides a stabilising motif. Both atria are animated by the constant movement of the escalators. But there the similarities end, since the floor plates are treated so differently. Rogers disperses service cores to the perimeter, where they occupy space between the irregular plot and the rectangular office floor. This move, eulogised as essentially 'gothic',[21] provides the exterior with a muscular expression which Willis Faber & Dumas completely avoided through absorbing its cores within its plan. Though the comparison might seem forced, the two buildings illustrate polarised 'classical' and 'gothic' tendencies within high-tech, between a regularising tendency and an elaborating tendency, almost between Burkean and Ruskinian views of beauty. Though always contained by a perceptual frame of utility, the classical or Burkean beauty tends toward perfection and smoothness of form, while the Ruskinian rejoices in the animating concepts of growth and decay: almost a difference between expression of product and expression of process. Thus a crucial difference within early modernism, between the dominant rationalist orthodoxy and the organic 'other tradition' can be seen to produce its own branches within the apparently homogenous high-tech school.[22] It continues with a slightly younger generation of already knighted architects, in the contrast between works by Michael Hopkins and Nicholas Grimshaw, though their mature work has been modified by the more conservative architectural atmosphere of the 1980s and 1990s. Foster's Willis Faber & Dumas, with its ambiguous form, seems also to prefigure several British architectural debates of that period: the retrieval of urban coherence, the interest in local context, the growing concern with energy issues and the search for innovative materialisations. Buildings like Ipswich's Greyfriars Centre prompted a general perception by the 1980s that British towns were under threat from unsympathetic redevelopment, and the influence of 'townscape' attitudes and the growth of the conservation movement were exerting a strong influence on planning authorities. Intent on appearing good citizens, a prestigious company like Willis Faber & Dumas could have been content with a polite but conventional structure. Instead, by commissioning Norman Foster, they gained an enigmatic building which seemed capable of satisfying both poles of the debate, the modern expression of function and the preservation of historical context. The question remains, however, as to whether the building's visual gift to the street in daytime – a ribbon of reflections and a neutrally expressed entrance – was adequate for such a large structure. The conventional defence is that the shifting reflections of surrounding architectural features dissolve the impression of bulk, thereby eroding the building's apparent substance. But the subtle faceting of the edges of the individual panes also serves to emphasize their crystalline presence, hard, brittle and impenetrable.

EC

Notes

1. The Foster and Rogers couples were in partnership as Team 4 between 1963 and 1967. Norman and Wendy Foster went on to set up Foster Associates which has continued with minor adjustments of the name until the present.
2. The term high-tech seems to have developed as a label to describe work which reacted against the aggressive aspects of new brutalism through an optimism about technological solutions and the adoption of an engineering aesthetic.
3. For the Barton Arcade and Lancaster Avenue see the Catalogue in Geist 1983, pp. 351-359.
4. See Norman Foster 'Royal Gold Medal Address 1983' in Jenkins 2000, p. 485.
5. See Chermayeff and Alexander 1963. For a brief account of the scene at the Yale Architecture School see Alan Powers, *Serge Chermayeff, Designer Architect Teacher,* RIBA Publications, London 2001, pp. 208-12.
6. For Reliance Controls see *The Architectural Review,* July 1967, pp 18-21.
7. For a snapshot of these years see Reyner Banham 'LL/LF/LE v Foster' (1972) in Jenkins 2000, pp. 27-32.
8. The oil crisis of 1973 was provoked by Arab oil producers restricting supply to countries which had supported Israel in the brief Yom Kippur War of that year. The quadrupling of oil prices led to a period of economic recession in most industrialised countries which lasted until the early 1980s. A by-product of the crisis was the first widespread realisation of the dependency on finite energy sources and a growth of interest in alternative energy sources.
9. For Stirling's connection to Oriel Chambers see Girouard 1998, pp. 38, 97 and 112.
10. The effects of the technological optimism of the workplace was satirised amusingly in Jacques Tati's film *Playtime* (1967).
11. See Reyner Banham 'Grass Above, Glass Around' (1977) in Jenkins 2000, pp. 43-7.
12. For the Greyfriars Centre designed by Edward Skipper & Associates, 1964-66, see Nikolaus Pevsner (revised by Enid Sutcliffe), *The Buildings of England: Suffolk,* Penguin, Harmondsworth, 1974 (2nd Edition), pp. 307-8. Given its brutalist aspirations it is a matter of some irony that it should be derided by the chief propagandist of that school, Reyner Banham (1977) op. cit. p. 43.
13. Norman Foster uses this quintessentially Beaux-Arts term in 'Social Ends, Technical Means' (1977) in Jenkins 2000, p. 463.
14. Quantrill 1999, p. 79.
15. Nikolaus Pevsner *Pioneers of Modern Design*, Pelican, Harmondsworth, 1960, p. 217.
16. The potential problem had been appreciated early during the period of post-war reconstruction as shown by 'Space left over: Making the best of the odd corner' in *The Architectural Review,* October 1951, pp. 233-41. The phenomenon later became identified by the acronym SLOAP (Space left over after planning).
17. Foster 'Social Ends, Technical Means' (1977) op. cit., p.468.
18. Evident and admitted by staff on a visit by Cambridge School of Architecture in 1979, PBJ.
19. The swimming pool has subsequently been spanned over to accommodate more office space, a move which did not compromise its listed status. See Harwood 2003, p. 324.
20. This was the forerunner of the flat glass roof, another Foster innovation that has now become standard practice.
21. Peter Davey, 'Renault Centre', *The Architectural Review*, July 1983, pp. 31-2.
22. See Wilson 1995.

Chapter 13. Giancarlo De Carlo: The Magistero at Urbino, 1968-76

Giancarlo De Carlo was an extraordinary intellectual presence in Italian architecture, famous as a teacher and writer as well as an architect and town planner. Born in 1919, he completed his education on the eve of the Second World War then fought as a partisan against the Fascists. He did not build until the 1950s, but by then he was already known as a writer, having produced books and articles on Frank Lloyd Wright, Le Corbusier and William Morris, and having served as editor on *Casabella Continuità*.[1] In 1951 he had organised the exhibition 'Spontaneous architecture', an early attempt by a modernist to draw attention to the virtues of the vernacular.[2] As a protégé of Ernesto Rogers and a lively young figure in the Italian architectural debate, he was soon invited to the CIAM conferences, where he became one of the leading members of Team Ten (see Chapter 3, p. 60). This was an influential meeting of minds, generating lifelong friendships between De Carlo and Aldo van Eyck (Chapter 3), Alison and Peter Smithson (Chapter 5) and Ralph Erskine (Chapter 11) among others.[3]

This group produced some of the earliest and most penetrating critiques of modernist architectural theory: of narrow functionalism, zoned planning, of playing into the hands of entrepreneurs and bureaucrats; but at the same time they advocated a deeper understanding of the city, of the changes wrought by modern life, of the sense of place and the possibilities of participation.

From the beginning De Carlo was interested in the city as well as individual buildings, and he denied as artificial the disciplinary gap between architecture and town planning. In the late 1950s he had the good fortune to be invited to undertake a master-plan for the little city of Urbino instigated by an extraordinarily visionary client, Carlo Bo, head of the university.[4] This prolonged study laid the foundations for De Carlo's practice and teaching of 'reading the territory' as the critical initial act of research for any architectural design. Urbino had a long and noble history as the seat of the Dukes of Montefeltro, patrons of artists such as Pierro dell Francesca and Paolo Uccello.

1. Arrival at Urbino in the Mercatale, looking up at the twin turrets of the Palazzo Ducale and the fortification bastion with the Rampa.

2, 3. The Collegio del Colle of 1962-66, first and best of De Carlo's new colleges outside the town.

4. Aerial viw of Urbino identifying four of De Carlo's conversions: (1) Faculty of Economics, (2) Magistero (3) Rampa and stables, (4) Faculty of Law.

Its skyline is dominated by the famous Palazzo Ducale, built for Duke Federigo by the Renaissance architect Francesco di Giorgio in the fifteenth century. Situated away from the coast, the city had long profited from being on the Rome-Rimini road and from strong local agriculture, but after Italy's unification in 1860 and the consequent changes in economy and communications, its population dwindled and it was reduced to the role of local market town with some tourism. The walled city had remained remarkably intact, but much of the old fabric was in a poor state, and such money as was spent on new building was not spent on the centre, but instead on the outskirts in a sporadic and chaotic way. The development of the university offered an injection of new life, but it would also double the town's population. The question was how to balance the interventions needed against the preservation of historic fabric. This issue faced De

Carlo at precisely the time when the hearts of cities were being thoughtlessly ripped out across Europe to make way for 'comprehensive redevelopments'.

Between 1958 and 1964, De Carlo made a thorough study of Urbino and the state of its fabric, identifying wall structures and street networks, noting buildings of historic value and also those ripe for demolition, and trying to arrive at an understanding of how the city had worked socially, and where it had lost coherence. He found that *'the pattern of urban activities has progressively slipped out of its original morphological mould, dissolving people's originally sharp awareness that urban forms are where they are because they clearly fulfil a given role'*.[5] In the process of investigation he made some remarkable discoveries, like the great spiral ramp in a fortification bastion that had allowed the dukes to ride on horseback up into the town, but which had been filled with rubble when reused as

5. Main entrance of the Magistero on Via Saffi, Urbino's spinal street seen in the centre of the aerial photo opposite.

6. (below) New-build rear of the Magistero seen from the upper street. The round window belongs to the top floor café.

the foundation for a nineteenth-century theatre. Eventually he was able to restore and reinterpret both. But only a few buidings in such cities can be preserved and renovated as museums. In most cases they have, rather, to earn their living and the price of their renovation by accepting new roles. This is where the expanding university came in. The dominant fashion of the period was for new out-of-town campuses, and De Carlo did indeed plan a series of new colleges on the outskirts. They were built separately but within walking distance on adjacent hillsides, in a brick and concrete architecture that speaks uncompromisingly of its time: the Collegio del Colle of 1962-66 is perhaps De Carlo's best ever new-build project.[6] But the university also needed a presence within the old city, to bring students and staff to its bars, cafés and bookshops, and to help animate its streets. Several ancient building complexes that had housed monasteries and convents were proving difficult to convert for housing or commerce without destroying their integrity. These might lend themselves well to new social uses at a similar scale by institutions like university faculties, and were so identified in the master-plan. De Carlo started modestly with a conversion for university offices around an old court, where only the staircase stood out as a new-build element, but there followed over the next thirty years three huge conversions for the Faculties of Law, Education and Economics. All involved subtle reinterpretation, it being necessary in each case to find an ordering that made sense of the new while preserving some respect for the old. The Faculty of Education, the Magistero of 1968-76, is chosen for detailed study here because it involved the most radical reinterpretation.

The old walled city grew up defensively on its steep hillside to a form largely dictated by the contours. The road from Rome arrived from the west into a hollow outside the walls that long served as a market place (Mercatale) and remains today the arrival point for tourists. Directly behind and above it are the symmetrical turrets of the Palazzo Ducale, the city's climax and focal point. Behind the Palazzo runs the longest spinal street, Via Saffi, traversing the town from north-west to south. It is off this street, towards the southern end, that the three Faculties converted by De Carlo lie, the Magistero being in the middle on the east side. It took over a whole city block set between a pair of streets that run eastward from Via Saffi following the contours, accepting the definition of the existing

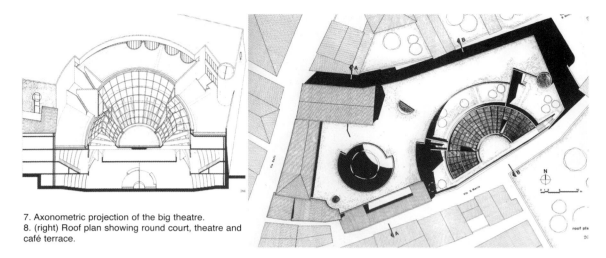

7. Axonometric projection of the big theatre.
8. (right) Roof plan showing round court, theatre and café terrace.

brick perimeter wall. In the eighteenth century this block had been a convent and in the nineteenth an orphanage, but by the time of De Carlo's survey, the houses to the west were in poor condition and the east end a neglected garden. Only the corner church had an interior worth preserving: it was reused on the ground floor for an experimental cinema, and on the first and second floors for a library. Former house facades complete with windows on Via Saffi and Via Santa Maria were preserved to maintain the streets, used to front rooms of small scale such as offices and seminar rooms.

Theatre as focus

De Carlo obliged himself to work within the given irregular volume, yet he needed greatly to increase the accommodation. Advantage could be taken of the changes in level by digging out the site to a lower level than the bottom street, but only if the problem of daylight provision was solved. It was also desirable to resurrect the garden terrace in some form, to retain some sense of the chain of green spaces across the city. The brilliant plan solution was to introduce two circular bodies within the irregular perimeter: a big semicircle like a great classical theatre, and a smaller fully circular court. The half-circle is the archetypal form for gathering to share some great communal event in which the few address the many, as beautifully illustrated in De Carlo's friend Aldo van Eyck's diagrams of inward and outward looking groups (see p. 45). Van Eyck also noted the use of circles as choreography with photographs of tribal dances published in *Forum*, and the circle was a recurring theme in

both men's works. At a small scale it was used to define local foci: to make a space for a sculpture or to define a playhouse in van Eyck's orphanage, (see p. 42) or by De Carlo to make the sitting bays on the top floor of the Magistero. But the Magistero's theatre worked at quite another scale and embraced contemporary notions of flexibility. By equipping the two lower levels with folding and sliding partitions, one great theatre for celebratory lectures or degree ceremonies could be turned into six separate rooms, two on the lower level and four on the gallery. Further lecture halls follow the same form at upper levels, a semicircular one in the centre and four segmental ones in the galleries. The whole great complex is lit from above by a conical rooflight which reveals in the roof the presence of the theatre beneath, like a glass replica of an antique theatre set in its hillside. The great void, which transmits reflected daylight some 15 metres deep into the heart of the building, retains for all a connection with the sky, but it also makes users aware of each other's existence. To attend any lecture is to participate in the great ritual circle, and to be reminded of those special times when the main vessel overflows with the life of 1500 persons as a single community.[7]

The second circle is not half but full, and much smaller. It serves as courtyard and lightwell for the western half of the plan, penetrating to natural ground level to set a reassuring datum, and providing a glimpse of an outside world with paving and a tree. Staff offices take part of its perimeter, but gaps in various places occur at every level to provide light and view for the foyers.

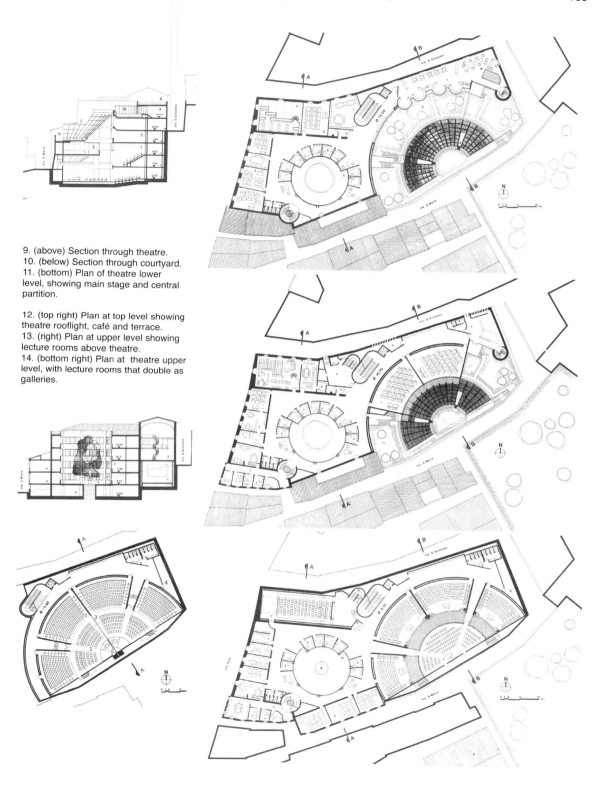

9. (above) Section through theatre.
10. (below) Section through courtyard.
11. (bottom) Plan of theatre lower level, showing main stage and central partition.

12. (top right) Plan at top level showing theatre rooflight, café and terrace.
13. (right) Plan at upper level showing lecture rooms above theatre.
14. (bottom right) Plan at theatre upper level, with lecture rooms that double as galleries.

15. Interior of rooftop café, with views across valley. 16. (opposite) Café terrace and theatre rooflight. 17,18. (opposite below) The great theatre and its rooflight from within.

A cunning plan adjustment in meeting the shape of the given figure was the inward projection of the northern third of the court to a smaller radius. This conveniently prevents it from seeming directionless for those entering or looking in, which a pure circle would have been. The positive forms of the two contrasting circles make both identifiable to the user, and set them in an inevitable contrast: full and empty, inside and outside, large and small. Together they seem to fill the plan most conveniently, taking precisely the area available, while leaving between a series of circulation halls as irregular residual spaces, street-like rather than corridor-like, and of fluid indefinite form. The value of such irregular spaces had already been understood and exploited by such masters as Hans Scharoun (Blundell Jones 2002, p. 59 and 195-201) and Alvar Aalto, but the norm in the 1970s was to let circulation spaces be dictated by the same grid as everything else, reducing the perceptible difference. One navigates through the Magistero by recognising the convex forms against the irregularity of the perimeter. A key element in the spatial sequence, well positioned, is the main stair or semi-ramp. Conveniently taking up a slack corner between the great theatre and the old church, it is cleverly placed, aligning itself with one quadrant of the theatre, but reconciling the geometry of the two plan circles by linking their radii with a right angle.

Strolling around the town, you could be forgiven for not even noticing the presence of the building. Its modest main entrance is a simple stone-framed traditional doorway in Via Saffi, asymmetrically placed towards the uphill end of an anonymous three storey facade. The subordinate entrances, equally holes in the wall, are even more modest. The top northern corner on Via San Girolamo is a totally new construction but in solid plain brickwork with some high-placed window slots and a service door. Only a large round window high on the east end gives a clue of anything special. The whole block, in fact, presents itself like a city set behind its defensive wall and gates, for you enter to find streets, houses, market place and theatre. Since the site perimeter was pre-shaped by a thousand years of anonymous occupation, the reworking took place inside out, almost a reversal of the expected figure-ground pattern for new building,

19, 20. (opposite) The great rooflight and valley view. 21. The building seen from outside the town.

and only having seen the inside can the visitor gain any sense of what it is about.

An alternative view thus far unmentioned is of the building seen from beyond the town across the valley. The Magistero takes its place in Urbino's skyline: old and new roofs present themselves along with a brick stair turret, and the upper part of the great glass cone stands in for the theatre. All this speaks of a major institution and a modern intervention, of a city that lives on adapting itself to new circumstances. The street-level experience and rooftop view are linked within the building as a drama that gradually unfolds. At first the Magistero seems a world within itself, but as one rises from level to level, one encounters an increasing range of glimpses out, first of the surrounding streets, and then of the roofscape of the city. The full drama of the panorama is not discovered until reaching the rooftop café, an appropriate social climax. Here at the top level the outer wall of the great theatre gives way to a horizontal slot of window, over which a roof is cantilevered. A great concrete plate sweeps around in an arc to crown the building, securing a horizontal datum among the jostling levels, its effect exaggerated by shadow and by the depth of its parapet. This is paralleled by a second parapet securing the top edge of the glass cone, and between the two is a roof terrace with grass and trees, an outdoor extension to the café. Views of houses and an adjacent church allow the illusion that one is still on the ground, and remembering the earlier garden terrace on the site. Yet turn around and the south-east opens to a breathtaking view of

landscape and sky, ranges of mountains stretching far into the distance. From city centre one is suddenly transported to the country. At either end of the arc of garden are lower terraces accessible by stairs. These lead down to a further semicircular terrace at the focus, orchestra of the ghost theatre that one clambers over as if among the ruins of an antique hillside. The panorama backdrop, reminiscent of sites like Epidaurus and Taormina, makes it all the more compelling.

Despite careful preservation of old brick facades, of the corner church's plaster ceiling, of old carved stone door frames and window cases, this was not a restoration project. It involved great violence. Almost the whole site had to be gutted and then dug out, cleared of its archaeology. The rebuilding would have been quite unthinkable without modern technology, without reinforced concrete for the huge retaining walls and for wide-span floor plates which carry soil and trees. It would also have been unthinkable without the electric light and artificial ventilation that make habitation of the deeper spaces possible. Yet the usual effects of a deep plan systematically structured building were completely avoided: no grid of columns, no regular ceiling studded with rhythmic flourescents in a dominant if supposedly flexible order. The opposite is the case: De Carlo made every effort to make every part specific, differentiating one floor from another and excising voids to let daylight penetrate to the deepest parts, as a visible presence if not as sole source of illumination. Apart from the circular court and the theatre rooflight, skylights were also

174

22-25. The meandering circulation spaces and upper lecture halls.

added over all three main stairs, and floor voids cut in the foyers to allow glimpses from level to level and to share the keyhole-shaped windows of the southern facade. All this involved ingenious plan/ section thinking to get everything to work together harmoniously. To achieve this it was vital that the existing fabric was understood in all its complexity, so accurate surveys had to be made in advance just to see what was possible, a primary act of 'reading the territory'. Then an arrangement of the accommodation had to be devised that would somehow mesh with the old context, accepting its offers of space, light and relative position. With the majority of conventional conversions, old fabric is treated as neutral 'available space', and the new programme is forced in without respect for the old or permitting the new to develop an identity of its own. The great imaginative skill of De Carlo's conversions lay in finding an arrangement that marries the two, so that the new programme is bolstered by the memories of the site, and the two become deeply fused. This is equally the case with his two nearby conversions for the Faculties of Law and Economics, both of which retained more of the existing internal fabric, as it was better preserved and of greater value.[8]

26. The small circular court with low winter sun.

Participation

By the time the Magistero was finished, De Carlo had been working in Urbino for twenty years, so he had intimate knowledge of the city fabric, and also of its officials and local people. Friends and assistants reported how, on visits to the city, he would be accosted by citizens in search of advice about how to extend or adjust their properties, and after discussion at a café he would quickly draw solutions on scrap paper that they could take away with them.[9] Long collaborations with the university, which retained an unusual autonomy for Italy,[10] allowed much discussion of how its needs might be met, and the local bureaucracy was small scale, retaining some flexibility. This was important, as De Carlo admitted in an interview of 1979 that:

Bureaucracy is our main enemy today... bureaucracy has a tendency to forget, simplify, run after problems of quantity and efficiency... My patron therefore is the people. That is possible here because it is a small town; I know everyone at least by sight, and so am able to discuss things with them. Then they support me by pushing their council. Sometimes people get frightened, particularly at the beginning of building, as when I was excavating the inside of the Magistero. Nevertheless they now feel that these buildings 'belong' and are proud of them, telling vistors about them and selling postcards of them. That stems from the long-term communciation between us. [11]

27. Housing at Mazzorbo in the Venetian lagoon, 1987. De Carlo reinterpreted the local vernacular housing in scale and form, even readopting the bright colours used in nearby Burano..

Such sentiments are a reminder that De Carlo was an early pioneer in the theory and practice of participation in architecture. He criticised the way that new buildings are presented in naked perfection as if use could only despoil them,[12] and in his own work he made every attempt to involve users. A decade earlier he had built a housing scheme for steel workers at Terni that was the fruit of long discussion and negotiation with the inhabitants, and he was to repeat the process in modified form in the 1980s with his housing at Mazzorbo in the Venetian lagoon.[13] In an outspoken and well-argued lecture of 1969, he had urged that *'all barriers between builders and users must be abolished, so that building and using become two different parts of the same planning process'.*[14] He argued not only for consultation with users, but for feedback into the design from the stage of use – for him a crucial but often forgotten aspect of the architectural process. With such feedback the design would no longer be a blind prescription aggressively imposed on the helpless user, but would instead emerge from a creative dialogue. De Carlo had discovered early on in his career that people do not necessarily use buildings in the way that architects intend,[15] and in describing the Magistero, he even went so far as to declare that *'the way use corrupts is the most interesting part of architecture'.*[16] He meant of course the deviations from the predictions of the functionalist method proposed by the Modern Movement, and indeed the whole narrow programmatic way of thinking that it represented. It was not that the functionalist intention had been wrong, but that it had been far too limited, failing to take into account the choices that people might make. The 'corruption' was a sign that a dialogue with users was beginning.

Participation could also apply to the construction process. The planning and building of the Magistero took eight years, leaving plenty of time for contemplation and careful development. It was built by local contractors with whom De Carlo already had established relationships of mutual respect:

More and more there is a tendency to forget that craftsmanship is important. It is not enough to think about architecture; you must make it too... Craftsmanship is very important indeed, and in Urbino you can find and train people who not only work well but with passion – a matter of quality rather than quantity. It's more than a matter of production to them, and it has meaning. For example, the man who lays reinforcing bars for the concrete wants to show me how beautiful his work is, even though he knows it is going to be hidden – it's a matter of pride. It is therefore possible to use poor simple materials like bricks and poured concrete because they are worked perfectly… In some cases I have worked with the same person for 20 years, so it's a developing relationship and the work is a matter of discussion between us… Here in Urbino it happens naturally, probably because the construction industry has not yet been industrialised. [17]

The Magistero is unique, unthinkable without the strong response to context, and it would make no sense repeated on another site. As a 'conservation project' it is radical, and in no sense slowed down by a museum mentality. Embedding it in the old city block has given it a powerful sense of place, and the contrast between new and old adds a sense of the passing of history, revealed in its chronological layers like fossils in geological strata. Its hybrid character excuses the building from having to make a definitive and utopian statement about its institutions's intentions, which most new buildings are obliged to do for better or for worse, and which they are then very often stuck with, perhaps too unambiguously. Another duty excused the Magistero was the need to have a 'style', and it seems as a result rather less dated than De Carlo's new-build additions of around the same time. The new body within an old skin is instead rather mysterious, but once discovered, the Magistero presents a resonant and fascinating dialogue between modern university and ancient city. It makes a place by mixing social interaction with inscribed memories, and the process of accretion is not complete, for there is an implication that more layers are yet to come. The solution of functional problems, particularly structure and daylight provision, was bold and ingenious, but more important still was the discovery of a new and coherent order of things poised serendipitously within the order of the old.

PBJ

Notes

1. *Le Corbusier, antologia critica degli scritti,* Rosa e Ballo, Milan, 1945; *William Morris,* Il Balcone, Milan, 1947; 'L'insegnamento di F.L.Wright', *Domus,* no. 207, 1946. For further material on these early years see Giorgio Ciucci, *'Then perhaps, and even by different paths, art will come',* in Samassa and Tonicello 2004, pp. 289-317.
2. At the IXth Milan Triennale 1951: it predated Bernard Rudofsky's *Architecture without Architects* (MOMA, New York, 1964) by more than ten years.
3. For an account of Team Ten based on De Carlo's version see Zucchi 1992, pp. 26-35.
4. *'The university of Urbino is under the guidance of an outstanding person, the writer and literary critic Carlo Bo, who has been its Dean continuously for more than thirty years. He has made almost as deep an impression on the town as Federigo de Montefeltro did in the 15th century.'* De Carlo in Lasdun 1984, p. 52.
5. Zucchi 1992, p.46, quoted from De Carlo, *The History of a city and plans for its development,* Cambridge, Mass, 1970.
6. These colleges are described by De Carlo in *'The University Centre, Urbino',* a chapter in Lasdun 1984, pp. 50-71.
7. Similar use of a great theatre as the focal point and symbol of a university is found at Alvar Aalto's Technical University of Otaniemi, Finland 1955-64.
8. For a critique of the more recent Faculty of Economics see Peter Blundell Jones 'Long game at Urbino', *The Architectural Review,* October 2002, pp. 69-72.
9. Paolo Ceccarelli in Samassa and Tonicello 2004, p. 241.
10. Explained by De Carlo in Lasdun 1984, p. 54.
11. De Carlo in an interview with Judi Loach, *The Architectural Review,* April 1979, p. 213.
12. *'There is hardly a magazine or newspaper column that illustrates architecture taking the user into account; that furnishes news about how architecture really functions in its daily existence; that publishes images, photographs or articles in which the people who use, transform, and recompose the three dimensional physical organism which they have been given are actually present. It is as if architecture were merely a potential space and not an actual place, concrete, made of real materials, and inhabited by people in a permanent and continually changing relationship.'* De Carlo, 'Architecture's Public', first published in *Parametro* no. 5, 1970, reprinted in Zucchi 1992 and in Blundell Jones, Petrescu and Till 2005, pp. 3-22.
13. See Peter Blundell Jones 'Lagoon grouping', *The Architectural Review* July 1987, pp. 21-27.
14. From De Carlo 'Architecture's Public', see n. 12.
15. Rykwert 1982, p. 22.
16. De Carlo in an interview with Judi Loach, *The Architectural Review,* April 1979, p. 214.
17. Ibid.

Chapter 14. Renzo Piano and Richard Rogers: Centre Pompidou, Paris, 1969-77

From the late nineteenth century the image of the Parisian avant-garde was projected against the backdrop of the traditional city and its imperial improvements under Haussmann.[1] The cityscape of boulevards and arcades had been unconsciously appropriated by the bourgeoisie, but it also lent itself to an anthropomorphic reading by the avant-garde. For the Surrealists, Paris was a great body in which the dreamer could lose himself or herself.[2] After the Occupation and Liberation, the Situationists took a more strident tone, decrying the Americanisation of the city by consumerist spectacle and the destruction of its bohemian environment for commercial developments.[3] One quarter at risk was the Marais, the atmosphere of which the Situationists sought to preserve because of its juxtapositions of industry and dwelling, of leisure and markets, and its opportunities for the fortuitous occurrences and chance encounters that they prized.[4] When the events of May 1968 burst forth, the Situationists were quick to claim them as evidence of their desires reaching fulfilment. The explosive combination of Maoism, anti-Americanism and youthful hedonism

was eventually suppressed, but the new President of the Republic, Georges Pompidou, was quick to realise that culture could play a valuable role in representing the values of the state. His cultural policy was also a reaction to his predecessor de Gaulle's rule, and to the severe divisions it had exposed in French society. Pompidou even commissioned new interiors for the Elysée Palace in womb-like and op-art forms from contemporary artists and designers.[5] At the urban scale, the representational demands of corporations were satisfied by the development of La Défense as a business district. Then on 11 December 1969, in a traditional act of high cultural patronage, Pompidou decreed that a new type of cultural centre should be built in the heart of Paris. This provided a chance to appropriate the apparel of contemporary culture for public patronage, while the choice of site in the Marais would neutralise a troublesome working-class quarter. An architectural competition was organised to create a public facility at the centre of urban life, generating and framing that life rather than being a mere product of it, but this

1. Centre Pompidou, ground floor of entrance hall a year or two after the opening.

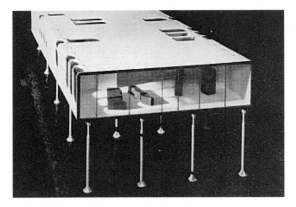

2. (left) Richard Rogers, Zip-up Enclosure, 1970: remarkably similar in concept to Foster's Sainsbury Centre, see page 162.

3. (above) Team 4, elevation of Reliance Controls Factory 1965 (now demolished). This shows the architects' early interest in making a vocabulary entirely from assembled components.

4. (opposite left) Archigram, 'Arcade' 1969, a forerunner of Pompidou on paper.

benign intention concealed a subtly conservative agenda, revealed by one of the administrators after the opening: Beaubourg (as the project was known at this stage after the name of the district): *'is the meeting of the tastes and preoccupations of a president and the aspirations, still latent, of the French people'.* [6]

The competition brief demanded easy accessibility for all elements of the programme: a new library, temporary exhibition facilities, a new National Museum of Modern Art, a centre of industrial design, a cinema and performance spaces, and IRCAM (the institute for Research and Coordination in Acoustics and Music). The assessors, who included Jean Prouvé, Philip Johnson and Oscar Niemeyer, awarded first prize in 1971 to architects Renzo Piano and Richard Rogers. Their scheme was chosen not only for its internal merits, but also for the radical decision to devote half the site to a public open square.

The architects

Richard Rogers was born in Florence in 1933, the nephew of the leading Italian architect and critic Ernesto Rogers (1909-69). He was educated at the Architectural Association in London before undertaking graduate study at Yale University, where he met Norman Foster. Returning to London, Rogers and Foster formed the practice Team 4 Architects with their then wives (see Chapter 12). Following the disbandment of that practice, Rogers teamed up with a younger architect who had designed the Italian Pavilion at the Osaka Expo in 1970, Renzo Piano. Born in Genoa in 1937, the son of a building contractor, Piano had been educated at the Politecnico di Milano under Ernesto Rogers before brief periods working for Franco Albini in Genoa and Louis Kahn in Philadelphia. Both architects, in their independent careers and in their initial work together, were interested in exploring the possibilities of new lightweight materials, their production and assembly, and the creation of more flexible forms of building.[7]

A flexible framework

Piano and Rogers' design for the Pompidou Centre extended the interest of both architects in the open and flexible use of technology. The site was a north-south orientated urban block, and the architects' first radical decision was to divide it in half, leaving the west part as an open square for public activities. The Pompidou Centre building took up the other half, entered through its western façade from the square. This pushed to an extreme the idea of the flexible and fully convertible building that originated with Mies (Blundell Jones 2002, Ch. 14), providing a great neutral trellis structure into which the various changing parts of the programme could be temporarily inserted as required. For maximum flexibility of use the largest possible volumes were required, so the structure was achieved in a single cross span of 48 metres, while longitudinally the building was divided by thirteen transverse frames creating twelve bays of 12.9 metres. To allow flexibility of height, the five main levels were set at 6 metre intervals, which could be subdivided to twice 3 metres where there were small rooms. The rhythm of the structural frame was strongly reinforced visually by diagonal cross bracing right across the main facade. The structural design, by Peter Rice and Ted Happold of Ove Arup & Partners, involved cantilevered 'gerberettes' projecting beyond the main trusses, which provided a 5-metre zone outside the columns on the long sides of the building for circulation and services. This was occupied on the west side by walkways and escalators, and on the east

5. Cedric Price: Fun Palace Project for Joan Littlewood (unbuilt) 1960-65.

6. (below) Centre Pompidou: the competition project.

side by the huge servicing elements required to air-condition the deep plan, following and taking to an extreme Louis Kahn's idea of served and serving spaces (Blundell Jones 2002, Ch. 16): both architects had been influenced by Kahn, Rogers through study at Yale, Piano though working in his office. The servicing machinery remained on the outside for easy exchangeability and was painted in bright colours. The net result of all this was to monumentalise the structure and services at the expense of the content, which, being flexible, was permitted no permanent identity. The proliferation of tubes led to comparisons with oil refineries and the nickname 'Pompidolium'. Piano remarked in retrospect:

The reference to the world of industry was almost literary: it was Jules Verne's sea-going vessel, an ironical look at technology. A taste for the polemical prevailed, and form was used symbolically to destroy the typical image of a monument and replace it with that of a factory. The factory as a place for making and, therefore, also for making culture – that was the aim. [8]

Though this was the first time such a building had been executed at large scale, the general concept was not unprecedented. In pursuing a sense and effect of urban animation, Piano and Rogers found many of their sources in *Archigram*, the magazine and eponymous London based avant-garde group, whose technical and biomorphic urban proposals owed much to science fiction. With such a prestigious commission, however, they were faced with the awesome task of turning the spirit of those collages into an achievable reality. The design of the complex as a large open framework into which individual elements of the brief could later be inserted owes much to the work of the Architectural Association tutor Cedric Price, particularly his Fun Palace project of 1960-65.[9] Commissioned by the impresario Joan Littlewood, this unrealised project had been designed to accommodate spontaneous alteration to different theatrical and entertainment purposes, and the whole structure was intended to have a limited life of only ten years. Price's concept was even more open-ended, and he is reported to have expressed disappointment that the floors at Pompidou could not be moved.

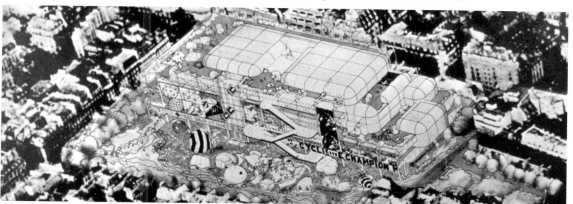

7. Corner of the face to the square.

8. Skidmore, Owings and Merrill, Lever House, New York, 1952.

Reinterpreting the urban

But to see the building merely as an object is to miss the intention of its lively content and of its interaction with the urban context, particularly through the square newly created by Piano and Rogers. This invited spontaneous street-life and has always been regarded as a great success, a breakthrough in urban thinking, though its originality is not fully evident without knowledge of the chronological context. The urbanism of the Modern Movement, virtually institutionalised after the Second World War, had by the early 1970s revealed itself as unsatisfactory, denying the individual, denying place, and denying history. It was overconditioned by the demands of motorised transport and its attendant engineering structures, which produced a conflict between human and mechanical needs. It was easiest merely to divide the two by separating vehicle and pedestrian routes, but this produced the phenomenon that Richard Sennett called 'dead public space'. In his book *The Fall of Public Man* he took as example Skidmore Owings and Merrill's New York skyscraper Lever House (1951-52), remarking:

The ground floor of Lever House is an open-air square, a courtyard with a tower rising on the north side, and one storey above the ground, a low structure surrounding the other three sides. But one passes from the street underneath this low horseshoe to penetrate to the courtyard; the street level itself is dead space. No diversity of activity takes place on the ground floor; it is only a means of passage to the interior. The form of this international-type skyscraper is at odds with its function, for a miniature public square revivified is declared in form, but the function destroys the nature of a public square, which is to intermix persons and diverse activities. [10]

Lever House stood among the most significant American examples of Modern Movement urbanism, but concentration on the creation of an object-in-space deprived the ground plane of any activity. The Centre Pompidou, as Piano and Rogers's building came to be known, attempted to overcome this problem of sterility, by increasing the technical logic in the design to create connections and relationships between building and space which were direct and visually stimulating. The facade to the square has always been the more important, and its principal motif soon became the logo for the institution, its commercial

9. The square, typically animated, and the west side of the building with its escalator run.
10. The Museum of Modern Art as first installed: the industrial impression was later quashed by a conventional conversion.

brand. Here the strong diagonal lines of the main public escalator signify one of the most visited viewing points in Paris, serving both the Centre Pompidou and the city as a whole. It suggests that the life of the plaza has been lifted up to form the public elevation and to signal the building's function as a cultural institution. The rationalisation of the circulation as a single diagonal and the decision not to erect projection screens as intended in early design versions (descendants of constructivist agitational devices) allowed the architecture to speak for itself, and the square, despite its lack of any permanent designed elements, has always served as a public gathering place, populated by entertainers as well as salespeople. This success was achieved regardless of the internal necessities assumed to be the primary focus according to the dictates of modernism. Instead, attention was concentrated on the escalator facade, which allowed the visitor to view the city of Paris and to become part of the cultural tourist spectacle visible from the square. Vertical circulation and the experience it offered became the sign of the building, but distracted from its cultural purpose. As Alan Colquhoun observed in *Architectural Design*:

11. The rear of the building with its prodigious display of servicing pipes earning the nickname 'Pompidolium'.
12. (below) Upward view of the cantilevering 'gerberettes' and the outboard circulation system.

13. (opposite top) Section showing building and square, and the wide span with circulation to right and servicing to left.
14. (opposite middle) Typical upper floor plan.
15. (opposite bottom) Ground floor plan including the public square.

What evidently appealed to the jury was the uncompromising way in which the building interpreted the centre as a supermarket of culture and gave no spatial or plastic form to the various departments exhaustively specified in the brief. The building was to be a symbol for the hoped-for ultimate fusion between cultural disciplines and the assimilation of culture in the market-place. If Baron Haussmann had asked for an umbrella to represent the market as a new type among the many existing types of public building, the jury of the Centre Pompidou chose an umbrella to symbolize the fact that culture as a whole was a market place and to incorporate this symbol in a unique and neutral building type into which, as into a box room, one could put the whole of that vague unclassifyable baggage called 'culture'. [11]

However, because of the necessity of coordination between the main frame and the infill, and the intention that the framing elements had a longer life, it was important that the construction of the two be compatible. This resulted in the paradox of a series of identical units serving a variety of functions. In the thirty years since the Centre's completion, this vision of flexibility has proved inadequate,

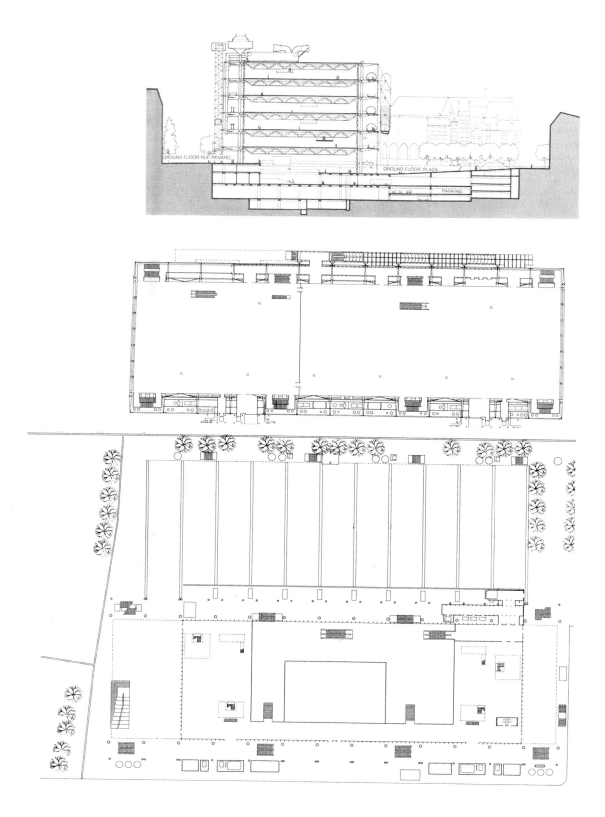

for the building has had to be completely closed during refurbishments. Reality thus contradicts the architects' generous vision of creating a responsive environment which could engage the changing needs of the public over time, and of the supposedly anti-monumental structural frame in which they are contained. Colquhoun pointed out that, in contrast to the ephemerality of the original intention:

In terms of the various activities which go on in the building, the architecture has nothing whatever to say. But it does not follow from this that the building is 'modest' or 'non-rhetorical' in other respects. Given the enormous size of the building, and given the decision to make it with a series of uninterrupted loft spaces, it was inevitable that, if it was not to be unbelievably boring (the oppression of non-rhetoric), that some large gestures would have to be made on the outside, and it is possible that as the design of the building progressed, it was realised that the scale of the structural members would be so vast that it would be impossible to maintain the delicate lightness of the original concept, and that something far more heroic would have to be asserted. [12]

It is these heroic gestures that have become the building's most recognisable features, the eastern facade with its servicing elements, and the western facade with its famous escalators. The eastern one provokes the question of whether service ducting was an appropriate architectural expression for the main street facade of a cultural institution. Perhaps this gesture lies within the tradition of *épater le bourgeois*, but there are also echoes of Russian constructivism in creating a form of dramatic signage for the huge building, but ordered without any strong compositional motif. What it does allow is a high degree of sculptural modelling of the cantilevered end bay, its double-height filigree of diagonal bracing contrasting with the densely packed and colour-coded ducting. And despite the intended transparency of the Centre Pompidou's technical operation, the building's accessibility remained a problem. Originally the ground floor was to remain unenclosed, allowing entry both from Rue du Renard and from the square, but fears about security brought on by international terrorism in the 1970s caused this optimistic gesture to be suppressed.

The museum and its contents

Another problem at Centre Pompidou was the overpowering impact of the building on the objects it was intended to house. Especially in the National Museum of Modern Art, the relentless presence of structural members, especially the 3-metre deep and 50-metre long main trusses, was particularly intrusive, distracting attention from the paintings and small sculptures on display. Dissatisfaction with this resulted in the commissioning of Italian architect Gae Aulenti in the mid-1980s to create a series of conventional rooms within the structure.[13] It seems ironic that this supposedly revolutionary museum had to resort to white plaster walls and concealed lighting like a traditional gallery space.

This irony is compounded when one considers the original intention to change the way that art was received. The cultural provocations of the early twentieth-century avant-garde took place, despite aspirations to the contrary, in conventional and often commercial gallery spaces, while state institutions and public galleries were yet more conventional in their taste. After the Second World War, former avant-gardists like Picasso, Braque, and Léger were considered, in their different ways, to represent the cultural values of a liberated France. The younger generation – Yves Klein, Alberto Giacometti, Jean Tinguely – sought a less structured arena in which to present their work, breaking traditional distinctions between painting, sculpture, and performance. The icy classicism of Paris's previous Museum of Modern Art with its peristyle, grand staircases and monumental sculpture, therefore no longer seemed appropriate.[14] The enhancement of cultural life by French film, made internationally popular by the Nouvelle Vague, helped shift the boundaries of significant production from permanent to more ephemeral arts. In the decade after 1958 André Malraux, de Gaulle's Minister of Cultural Affairs, increased state patronage for contemporary art, as France sought a non-partisan identity in the period of the Cold War grounded in its cultural fecundity. But while that period concentrated on cultural heritage and the heroes of modernity, Pompidou's cultural policy was more interested in the contemporary scene and in breaking barriers between disciplines.

But all the Centre Pompidou could do was to place different artistic disciplines in close proximity. The scale of ambition represented by the size of the institution, and its reliance on administrative bureaucracy, inevitably meant that its content

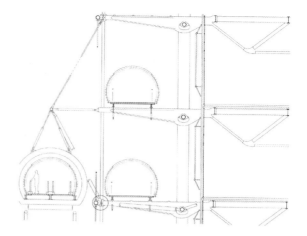

16. (opposite top) The roofs of Paris as seen from the top of the escalator.

17. (opposite bottom) Rooftop restaurant.

18. (above) Detail of the 'gerberettes' and suspended circulation system.

19. On the escalator.

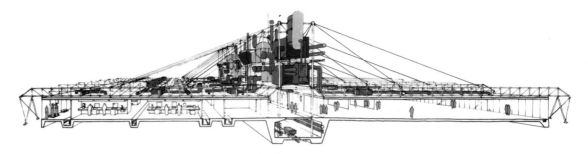

20. Richard Rogers, Inmos Microprocessor Factory, South Wales 1982, sectional perspective: again open flexible floorspace was provided by a long-span structure and an architectural rhetoric of exposed servicing. The factory produced computer chips: the appropriate high-tech client.

would represent a form of official taste, in contrast with the spontaneous creativity to which it had aspired. The separation of functions in horizontal layers, and the representational independence of the escalator circulation, made the technical compartmentalisation of the building perhaps a truer image of its public role than the rhetorically unifying gesture of the escalators. In its desire to display its collections to and with the city, it could only facilitate creative engagement in an entirely traditional manner. Within its own aesthetic terms Centre Pompidou could even be considered historicist, for

21. Richard Rogers, Lloyd's Building London 1979-84.

its exaggerated expression of industrial elements is reminiscent of Russian constructivism. This was strangely appropriate, since the programme of the building was similar to the constructivist idea of the social condenser, involving a mechanical encounter between cultural production and its audience in a great alembic. The mechanistic nature of this scene, and the emphasis placed on the undoubted technological achievement of the building's construction, distracted from the developing commodification of culture, as yet more consumer products, similarly valued and relatively interchangeable, became available to a larger audience. The Dadaist strategy of aesthetic appropriation of industrial products was also reflected in Pompidou, though the Dadaists' irony and anarchism was dissipated by the state patronage of the institution.

Classical links?

It is surprising to find, in a building whose functional rhetoric seems to deny the validity of formalist compositional devices, that some qualities of the Centre Pompidou's facades are associated with the conventions of classical architectural culture, especially the creation of a monumental representative facade in a public square. This completely inverts the avant-gardist gesture, for as Colquhoun has observed of the avant-garde:

On the one hand, it wished to abolish the academic (elitist) culture in the name of 'free creation' (the artistic equivalent of liberalism). On the other it proposed a severe functionalism and a pure formalism which were unacceptable to the 'average man' because they excluded all these conventions and habits of feeling to which he is attached (and to which the commercialism of the liberal state attaches him more and more firmly). [15]

If Centre Pompidou was an attempt to create a non-elitist cultural institution (albeit one created at the direct behest of a political elite) while offering a popular location and a space of public appearance (the traditional civic unity of public building and public space), it fails to offer an appropriate architectural articulation. The architects' desire for flexibility set tight limits on the functional framework required for the intended 'free creation', thus precluding innovative manipulation of the building form. That this form should be so rhetorically technical as to disallow popular identification with cultural prototypes, replacing them with the atmosphere of the fairground, is at best also merely ironic. Many visitors, for example, ascend the escalators to enjoy the magnificent view over Paris but fail to enter the gallery spaces. Sensation and effect take over from any true appreciation of the content, an effect replicated in numerous cultural landmarks that followed. This is seen also in the aesthetic ideal of transparency, which promised to allow communication between disciplines and, in characteristic modernist terms, between inside and out. Literally embodied in Centre Pompidou's extensive glazing, this superficial transparency became a symbol of the French state's self-renovation during the Mitterand presidency.[16] The technology of advanced glazing systems was employed, for example, by Jean Nouvel at the Institut du Monde Arabe (1987-89), showing a further aestheticisation of Centre Pompidou's strategy.

Meanwhile, Centre Pompidou's architects had moved on, both personally and architecturally. One can conveniently compare Centre Pompidou with Renzo Piano's subsequent work on the adjacent site for IRCAM (1988-89). Rather than being given a free-standing island site, Piano here had to deal with existing nineteenth century buildings, but he managed to produce a work both technically innovative and respectful of its surroundings, so brickwork is used, but as rain screen panels rather than load-bearing wall. It is a measure of his restless talent that Piano chose not to imitate his own earlier work, but concentrated instead on the context, an issue which had by then returned to the fore in architectural debates as an alternative to the optimism of high-tech.

Signatures and branding

The Centre Pompidou soon became an internationally identifiable landmark. It was the first example of a museum building being both a vehicle for economic regeneration and a piece of urban

22. Renzo Piano, IRCAM building 1988-89, built next door to the Centre Pompidou.

rebranding. In the decade after it was opened, the museum proliferated both as a civic adornment and as a focus of public life. Other French cities, and then German and Spanish cities, followed its lead, helping to promote a cadre of international architects. Fortuitously, museums provided briefs that were both monumental and open to personal interpretation, creating an opportunity for stylistic pluralism that architects exploited to the highest degree. But Pompidou's uniquely identifiable high-tech was not directly imitated, nor were its component systems reused elsewhere. Most influential was the image: an assemblage of industrial building components as an architectural language that could soon be exploited as an ironic signage of culture (along with Doric elements) by Stirling and Wilford's Staatsgalerie at Stuttgart (pages 84-87). The cultural experiment in Paris had perhaps been too successful to spawn serious imitations. A cooler expression characterised Piano's Menil Collection in Houston (1981-86), Norman Foster's Sainsbury Centre in Norwich of 1977 and his Mediatheque at Nîmes of 1984-93. Rogers returned to Pompidou's form of muscular architectural expression with the prestigious workplace in Lloyd's of London (1979-84). As the language of high-tech was transferred to other building types, the initial furore over Centre

Pompidou's architectural language subsided, and its urban virtues proved a more persistent legacy.

The flagship cultural monument has become a familiar strategy, and every city that formerly wanted its Pompidou now wants its Guggenheim, but Pompidou was not without advantages. Not only was a great area of the site given over for public use and a new feature added to the urban skyline: the building itself provided a new vantage point from which to appreciate the city. In its social beneficence it acted as a contextualising device, something other architects were seeking through more self-conscious architectural means. Despite the novelty of its architectural language, Centre Pompidou's urban plan was finally quite conservative, relying on a traditional relationship between public space and public building. The clarity of this arrangement, and the successful appropriation of both space and facade by the public, led to its citation as a counter model to the inhospitable urban spaces of modernism. This aspect has been repeated in Rogers' subsequent *oeuvre*, notably in the Channel 4 headquarters in London of 1994. It was also expressed in the work of the British government commission into urban regeneration that Rogers chaired, published as *Towards an Urban Renaissance* in 1999.[17]

Conclusion

If the boulevards of Haussmann's Paris with their aesthetic of modernisation were a bid to pacify the revolutionary arena of 1789, 1830, and 1848, perhaps Centre Pompidou bore the same relationship to the struggles of 1968. A spectacle of modernity as heroic as the Eiffel Tower was also a good way to satisfy the demands of intellectuals for a new cultural scenario. Yet it soon emerged that, despite the novelty of the building's dress, its contents met rather conventional needs for tourism and cultural validation. The building's relationship with its content was too easily ignorable, reducing the threat or at least the question posed by its interdisciplinary ethos. Its creation provoked a commercial redevelopment of the area, thanks to its effect on property values, but it failed in its own terms to achieve the promised flexibility both internally and in relationship to the wider urban environment. Ultimately its achievements lay in the technological and urban spheres rather than in the cultural or the aesthetic.

EC

Notes

1. See Giedion 1966, pp. 744-775.
2. For an example of the Surrealist interpretation of Parisian urbanity from 1926 see Aragon 1994. For a recent survey of the relationship between the city and artistic production see Wilson 2002.
3. Sadler 1998.
4. Elements of the Marais were frequently exploited in the typical Situationist production, the psychogeographic map. For a discussion of this and its connection to the eventual building of the Centre Pompidou see Sadler 1998, pp. 62-66.
5. For a positive assessment of Pompidou's cultural patronage see the catalogue of the exhibition held to commemorate the twenty-fifth anniversary of his death *Georges Pompidou et la Modernité,* Editions du Jeu de Paume / Centre Georges Pompidou, Paris 1999.
6. Claude Mollard, *L'Enjeu du Centre Pompidou* quoted in Alan Colquhoun, *Critique* in *Centre Pompidou,* AD Profiles No. 2, Architectural Design, London 1977 (unpaginated).
7. See Appleyard 1986, p. 310.
8. Renzo Piano quoted in Lampugnani 1995, p. 10.
9. For Fun Palace see Cedric Price, *Cedric Price*, Architectural Association, London, 1984.
10. Sennett 1986, p. 12.
11. Colquhoun (1977) op. cit., unpaginated.
12. Ibid.
13. Catherine Lawless 'The new fitting out of the National Museum of Modern Art in the Centre Georges Pompidou' in *Casabella,* Vol. 49, No. 515, July/August 1985, pp. 54-63.
14. The Palais de Tokyo built for the Paris Exhibition of 1937 and designed by architects Dondel, Aubert, Viard and Dastugue was adorned after the Second World War with a 9-metre high monumental bronze sculpture of 'France' by Emile Antoine Bourdelle that had first been exhibited in 1925.
15. Colquhoun (1977) op. cit., unpaginated.
16. See Fierro 2003.
17. Rogers et al. 1999.

Chapter 15. Aldo Rossi: New Cemetery of San Cataldo, Modena, 1971-78

A general disregard for urban context in post-war architecture led to a reaction in the 1970s, reopening the question of memory, both as physical presence and as poetic content. Nowhere was this stronger than in Italy, but it had also been the birthplace of Fascism, which cast a long shadow across Italian architecture for decades after the Liberation. The regime had appropriated both historic Italian forms and the mantle of modernity, provoking the reaction of a search for new directions after 1945. Working in Rome, Adalberto Libera concentrated on social needs through housing, drawing on interests in the vernacular and anonymous architecture. Luigi Moretti, more closely associated with the fallen regime, retreated into a concern for spatial values, which was evident both in his buildings and in his journal *Spazio*.[1] In Milan Ernesto Rogers, editor of *Casabella* and the foremost Italian member of CIAM, transformed the work of BBPR (Banfi, Belgiojoso, Peressuti and Rogers) from the cool abstraction of the open cube memorial to deportees in the Cimitero Monumentale in Milan (1945-55), to the super-medievalism of the Torre Velasca (1958), a controversial addition to the city skyline.[2] With its jettying upper storeys, this building suggested that BBPR had adopted a conservative stance towards urbanism, based on historical precedent. This mood also affected the circle of younger architects around Rogers and *Casabella* including Carlo Aymonino, Giorgio Grassi and Aldo Rossi who, like their predecessors Team Ten, were keen to expose the failings of modernist urbanism in developments like QT8 (Quartiere Triennale Ottava) built for the Eighth Architecture Triennale of 1947.[3] But unlike Team Ten, this group, which became known as 'La Tendenza', were disenchanted by modernism and, in reaction, their work became suffused with an atmosphere of nostalgia and memory.

Recovery of history

Milan's expansion under the economic miracle, and the consequent displacement of its inhabitants, exposed new problems in what had been a coherent city.[4] By the 1960s, historical architectural

1. Torre Velasca, Milan, 1958 by Banfi, Belgiojoso, Peressuti and Rogers.

2. Cemetery at Modena: the cubic sanctuary seen through one of Rossi's archetypal windows

3. Palazzo della Ragione in Padua, one of the buildings depicted in Rossi's *Architecture of the City*.

forms had escaped their abuse under Fascism and were opened to serious research. This concerned not only anonymous urban fabric and vernacular typologies, but also the compositional value of monumental structures such as medieval and Renaissance civic palaces. The ostensible political context was less a picturesque romanticisation of previous social conditions than a search for a type of authenticity that left-leaning intellectuals of the period often ascribed to working-class life. Aldo Rossi (born Milan, 1931) shared this general interest in 'realism', simultaneously reflected in the contemporary cultural and cinematic phenomenon of Neo-Realism. He emerged first as a significant theorist, and then as the creator of potent architectural images in drawn and built form.[5]

The Architecture of the City

Published in Italian in 1966 and translated into English in 1982, Rossi's principal theoretical work *The Architecture of the City* presented a tough critique of the modernist city, but took a Marxist line in arguing for an almost fatalistic adherence to the *zeitgeist*.[6] Rossi proposed that architecture stood outside the fluid tide of history, drawing its power from its geometry and the accumulation of patina through its survival over time. This emphasised the collective experience of the city, reduced the relative importance of the single monument, and led to a concentration on architectural typology. Examples cited, such as the Roman arena at Lucca, evoke the power of form to support different uses and interpretations over centuries, contradicting the simple functionalism advocated by orthodox modernists.[7] Rossi shared with modernist urbanists a concern for the significance of collective and typological fitness, but he also reached back beyond the development of industrial functionalism to the classificatory forms created by Durand.[8] Even so, the typology in Rossi's design work was a poetic rather than a scientific category, and in his own work he tended to reapply a handful of forms in different combinations and contexts, which paradoxically created a highly recognisable and individual architectural language. Rossi's early buildings like the Gallaratese housing block (1969-70) and the school at Fagnano Olona (1972) had a strong social basis, expressed through the hierarchical connection between individual and collective spaces, though symbolic and monumental qualities were already dominant, both through a deliberate exaggeration of scale and in the use of significant motifs such as the square window – often divided in four – the clock, the column and the chimney.

4. School at Fagnano Olona, 1972.

5. Gallaratese housing, north Milan, 1969-70.

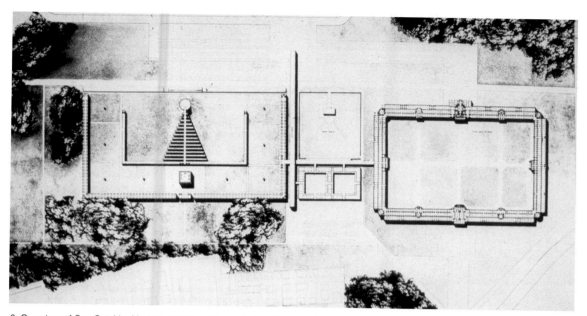

6. Cemetery of San Cataldo, Modena, site plan. The walled enclosure to right is the nineteenth century cemetery, the left part by Rossi.

There was some direct inspiration from the *Pittura Metafisica* of Giorgio de Chirico of half a century earlier, and from associated artists like Carlo Carra and Mario Sironi. While recovering the symmetry and formality of the classical tradition which had been cast aside by modernists, Rossi avoided the risk of appearing merely old-fashioned by pursuing an unornamented simplicity of construction and a strictness of form.

The Cemetery at Modena
The neo-classical cemetery of San Cataldo in Modena, created by Cesare Costa between 1858 and 1876, had gradually become overcrowded. Between 1967 and 1969 Carlo Scarpa attempted to address this problem, but his efforts came to nothing, so a competition to design an extension was organised, and it was won by Rossi in 1971. His suggestion for a large extension was taken up, and work began in the early 1980s. It is as yet incomplete, but extensive publicity has ensured that the haunting images in drawings and photographs nonetheless capture the quintessence of Rossi's work. In *A Scientific Autobiography* Rossi described the projects's genesis:

In April of 1971, on the road to Istanbul between Belgrade and Zagreb, I was involved in a serious auto accident. Perhaps as a result of this incident, the project for the

7. 'Some of my projects with a figure of a saint', 1972 – a Rossi drawing inspired by the *Pittura Metafisica* of Giorgio de Chirico.

8. Sanctuary seen from the central gateway.

cemetery was born in the little hospital of Slawonski Brod, and simultaneously, my youth reached its end. I lay in a small, ground-floor room near a window through which I looked at the sky and a little garden. Lying nearly immobile, I thought of the past, but sometimes I did not think: I merely gazed at the trees and the sky. This presence of things and of my separation from things – bound up also with the painful awareness of my own bones – brought me back to my childhood. During the following summer, in my study for the project, perhaps only this image and the pain in my bones remained with me: I saw the skeletal structure of the body as a series of fractures to be reassembled. At Slawonski Brod, I had identified death with the morphology of the skeleton and the alterations it could undergo. [9]

The figure of a human skeleton provides the structural image for the new cemetery. Taking his cue from the high-walled and colonnaded rectangular layout of the original nineteenth-century cemetery, Rossi proposed a new precinct of roughly equal dimensions. In the original, the graceful

stoas of columbaria provided continuous enclosure with chapels situated in the main ranges, the centre being left for burial. Rossi inverted this schema, occupying the centre with a monumental complex in which the meanings of the new cemetery are focused. He planned this central complex to consist of three parts: the communal grave, the ossuaries and the sanctuary, though only the last has been constructed, and in amended form. The intended communal grave took the form of a monumental cone, derived from the Enlightenment precedents of Boullée and Ledoux, as well as from more familiar industrial precedents.[10] Rossi wrote:

In the communal grave, the remains of the abandoned dead are found; dead whose links with the temporal world have dissipated, generally persons coming out of mad-houses, hospitals and jails – desperate or forgotten lives. To these oppressed ones, the city builds a monument higher than any other. [11]

The cone was intended as the head of the skeleton, while the rib-cage was formed by the ossuaries, a series of parallel rows of burial vaults describing a triangle in plan, and rising towards the cone. The last and lowest of these wings forms an open enclosure, but only one half of this final row has yet been constructed. Finally, in a reversal of the open cube of BBPR's memorial to the deportees in Milan, there is the sanctuary, a hollow cube open to the sky and punctured with regularly spaced square openings. It has the appearance of an abandoned building site, of unfinished business. As Peter Eisenman observed:

The Sanctuary of the Modena Cemetery takes as a model the city of the dead of the Enlightenment. Here it represents contemporary life (the collective housing unit). It also becomes the intersection of life and death, ruin and rebirth. This cemetery, in Rossi's words, is the 'architectural place where the rationality of the forms is an alternative to the senseless and disorganized growth of the modern city.' It is the collective monument which represents the relationship between the institution of the city and death. The Sanctuary itself... has the initial appearance of collective housing, an apartment block. But it has no floors, no window frames or panes. This is no romantic ruin, but rather an unfinished and abandoned building analogous to death. 'The empty house is the same as the house for the living. The windows maintain their formal condition on the wall, but without the elements, the

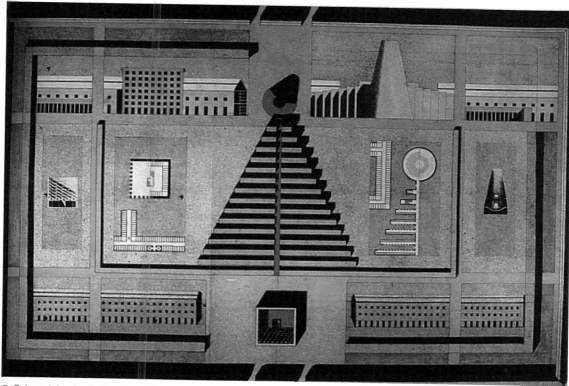

9. Coloured drawing by Rossi combining the various archetypal forms of the cemetery, mixing plan, section, and elevation.

frames, the mullions and the glass – which signify occupation.' The deserted work becomes in Rossi's terms a monument, more important than any other, to the abandoned dead and the abandoned living. The configuration, the empty house in the cemetery, is the space of memory of the living – it is occupied by the living as they remorselessly remember the dead. Closed to remorse, death becomes a sentiment which has no history. [12]

The abandoned house or the deserted factory are among the images exploited by Rossi for the elegaic qualities they evoke, yet there are other meanings and echoes, suggesting less personal connections, indicative of a broader historical perspective. The barracks-like quality of the columbaria of the new cemetery evoke the barracks of the camp at Fossoli, the site of deportation for all the victims of the Nazi occupation of Northern Italy which was built outside the nearby town of Carpi. The two places are less than 20 kilometres apart, and the same train line passes both. Given his sensitivity to the resonance of banal forms and their echo of

twentieth-century horrors, the ambiguities of Rossi's aesthetic choices are surely no coincidence. They express a context which is not only general and cultural but, in such proximity to a significant site, also local and historical.

An undertone of disquiet and threat, evident particularly in sombre drawings of the project, do not deter the bereaved when they visit the cemetery. Following a black-clad widow from the

10. Perimeter wall of Rossi's extension.

11. The court and stoa.
12. (below) The beach huts.

bus stop, through an underpass, through a break in the wall and past the flower seller, one emerges in the great neo-classical colonnade. Glimpsing the 'blue of the roof' through the portico, one is drawn to a view from the top of a rickety cemetery ladder of the new columbaria behind a high enclosing wall. Entering through a small doorway, one is set adrift in an immense stoa, shadowed and featureless. Nearby marble beach huts contain families in their final leisure. Upstairs flowers slowly wither by the innumerable square containers, enamelled photographs gazing out without a blink or tremor (or a smile). Crossing the barren lawn, one enters the abandoned house. In its shadows a square of sky is framed and an old woman sweeps up dead leaves. As Rossi writes:

Besides the municipal exigencies, bureaucratic practices, the face of the orphan, the remorse of the private relationship, tenderness and indifference, this project for a cemetery complies with the image of cemetery that each one of us possesses.[13]

In this cemetery the presence of the crowds of the dead constitute the ground in which the architecture is rooted. Identified and compartmentalised, the individual can be distinguished from the mass to remind the visitor that we are all bereaved.

A universal statement

The resonances identified in Rossi's work by critics went beyond the urban and architectural sphere to stand for a more general cultural condition:

...since the Second World War man's condition has radically altered: the events of 1945, the full comprehension of the meaning of the Holocaust and atomic destruction, have changed the bases on which life can be lived. For man faced with a choice between imminent or eventual mass death, heroism, whether individual or collective, is untenable: only survival remains possible. The problem is now of choosing between an anachronistic continuance of hope and an acceptance of the bare conditions of survival. And when the hero can be only a survivor, there is no choice. The condition of man which formerly contained this alternative has ended, and the continuous 'narrative' of the progress of Western civilization has been broken.[14]

13. The neo-classical colonnade.

14. The new colonnade.

Eisenman's formal criticism overcomes the millenn-ialist tone of the intellectual context he describes. His analysis resonates in the work of architects like Rossi, who ignored the attractions of commerce and the distractions of technology to produce work of disquieting power, embodying the uncertainties of contemporary life. In an era when nostalgia appears to have replaced faith in technological and social progress, the sense of loss, of a lack of coherence, and a disquiet about the future, are features common to much cultural production. Modernism still has its followers, who appear unwilling to acknowledge the historicist basis of their continuing faith, but the popular signage of postmodernism with its dissonances and inconsistencies has descended into completely unironical pastiche. Rossi was as likely as any other to be the victim of pastiche, yet the very banality of his forms helps to crystallise the loss of validity and meaning, as they become representations of those absences. As Mark C.Taylor has noted:

Most important, both abstract and figurative artists and architects have regarded representation as problematic. The emergence of the problem of representation parallels the development of the question of language in twentieth century philosophy, and indeed these two issues are really different twists of a common problematic. Whereas language traditionally has been understood to be represent-ational, representation has gradually come to be interpreted in terms of language. Paradoxically, the more self-conscious philosophers, artists, and architects become about the media they use, the more opaque language and representation themselves become. Instead of a window on, or mirror of, reality, language and representation increasingly seem to form a screen or veil that obscures more than it reveals. As vision becomes questionable, representation changes from an ideal to be realised to a difficulty to be overcome.[15]

The immutability of Rossi's representations bring the observer up against the disillusionments of contemporary existence, regardless of the functions his buildings were intended to house. That the function of the example chosen here should be a city of the dead, the ultimate collective experience, only makes the issues of representation and language more resonant.

15. The abstract cube of the central sanctuary.
16. (opposite) Rossi's drawing of the various elements.

Drawing and building

The work of Rossi presents many paradoxes. There is the curious power of an essentially personal vision as a repository of public expression, the mismatch between his influential writing and his widely published design work, and finally the difference between what remains on paper and what is actually constructed. The relationship between design drawing and constructed building has been a subject of much debate. As Eisenman commented:

Within the realm of orthodox architectural drawing perhaps only Aldo Rossi has achieved such a critique of drawing in architecture today – an inversion of the mode of representation wherein a realised building becomes a representation of a drawing.[16]

The graphic language of Rossi's images is powerful enough to suggest a world independent of the experience of the building. This could be partially accounted for in the pragmatic uncertainties between design and construction which many of Rossi's projects experienced. He was aware that the drawings might be the only realisation, and therefore had to contain in them the full quality of the ideas which the project embodied, restricted to the sensual appropriation available through vision. Within the limited world of the page, the drawings contain many enigmatic elements which stretch far beyond the similarities to *Pittura Metafisica*. The conventions of orthographic projection are often manipulated to project an initially objective form into a subjective vision. Plans composed with geometric logic are much more than the distribution of building parts, for there is an implicit suggestion that they are representational of a body or a city, in an extension of the *Architecture Parlante* of Boullée and Ledoux. The very absence of figures in Rossi's elevations seems paradoxically to evoke a sense of passage along colonnades or the hidden presence of a pensive figure at a window. Sections, especially when heavily shadowed, reveal the 'intimate immensity' of an interior. And often in

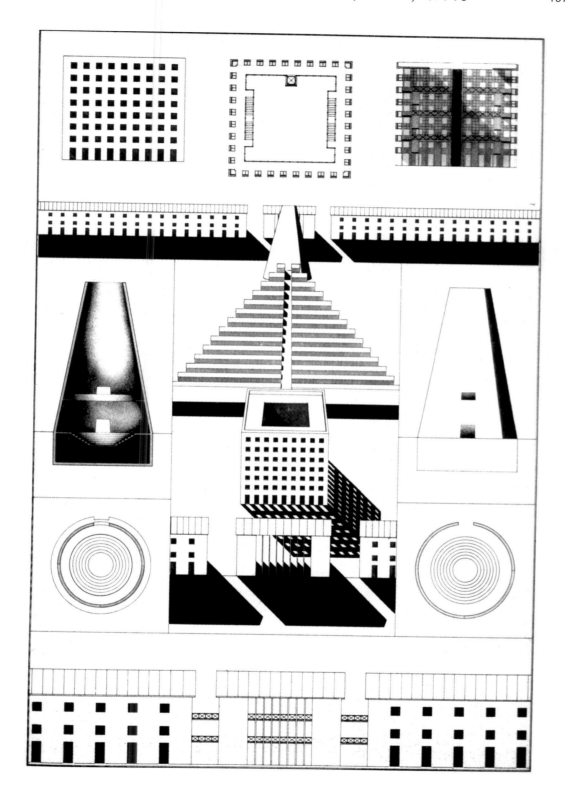

17. The new ossuary.

the drawings these architectural conventions are used to frame fragments of detail and to enhance atmosphere. The rigidity of the plan as frame might therefore be read as a metaphor for the framing of the daily life which the buildings were intended to accommodate. The drawings, especially when gathered in carefully composed panels, act as windows into the world of the project. Adding to the enigma, the critical discourse on the meaning of the drawings almost exceeded in volume the commentary on the built work, as demonstrated by Adjmi and Bertolotto's book published in 1993.[17]

The relationship with construction has also caused some difficulties of interpretation. Although in later projects fame brought Rossi the opportunity to use a rich palette of materials, he tended to envision his works at first in ordinary materials such as steel, concrete, brick and stucco. In realisation they often seem crude, for two reasons. On the one hand a disengagement between design and execution meant that supervision could be patchy. The cubic sanctuary at Modena, for example, was intended to be constructed of exposed brickwork. But according to Fabio Reinhart, Rossi's partner,

Gianni Braghieri, visited the site to discover that blockwork had been used instead, which required covering in stucco.[18] The change was accepted with equanimity, as a compromise which proved the authenticity of the project by showing its ability to withstand the unwitting intervention of the artisan. On the other hand, the buildings' constructional simplicity echoed a modernist attitude to materiality as typified by the abstraction of Le Corbusier's Villa Savoye (Blundell Jones 2002 Ch. 7), but it can also be connected to the specifically Italian attitudes of Arte Povera and Neo-Realism.[19] Arte Povera sought aesthetic value in material simplicity as an evocation of conceptual depth. Neo-Realism privileged ordinariness and actuality in direct contrast to the falsehoods and delusions that had supported Fascism: for example the contradictory pairing of Roman tradition with technological progress. Although the crudeness of Rossi's constructions has sometimes provoked comparison with Fascist architecture, his deliberate use of barely resolved junctions between concrete, stucco and steel can also be seen as an echo of the industrial landscape which was redefining Italian urban form during these years. Its rhetoric reflected a typically heroic left-wing view of working life and environment, a utopia of the ordinary, ostensibly devoid of fashion and materialism: this Rossi had witnessed in the Soviet Union.[20] The collective environment of the factory and the housing block provided the material expression for the image of the cemetery. Philosophically, this is not to suggest a policy of 'anything goes', but rather that a tolerant attitude to variety might best be accommodated in a self-effacing and robust frame with an enigmatic presence.

Later work

Rossi's subsequent career was conditioned by the dissemination of his drawings and then of his writings, as the English translation of *The Architecture of the City* did not appear until a decade and a half after its first publication. Thanks to the inefficiency of the Italian construction industry, the buildings took even longer to appear, though international commissions played an increasing role. Rossi's drawings, with their intense shadows, violent juxtapositions of scale and bright colours, presented a much more immediate and evocative experience (generally urban) of familiar elements in unfamiliar combinations. Intriguing and easy on the eye, and quickly associated with

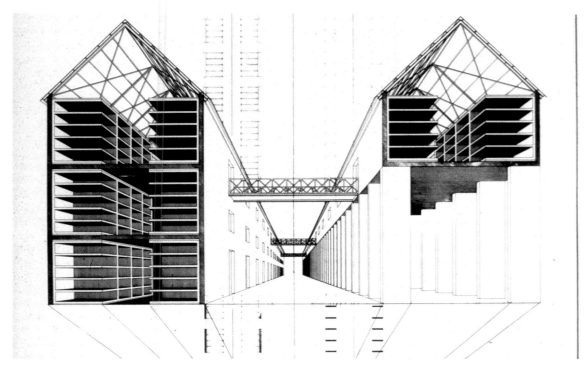

18. The archetypal power of a factory-like building.

postmodernism, they were soon appropriated by Milanese design culture, but in a superficial way and without reference to the underlying theory.

However, Rossi's urban theory, for which the cemetery plan provides a metaphor, found an opportunity for expression in La Nuova Piazza at Fontivegge on the outskirts of Perugia. Partially built from 1982 onwards, this new square took as its source the central space of historic Perugia, Piazza IV Novembre, where monuments of church and state oppose each other uncomfortably across a rising space. In his new square, Rossi combined a familiar vocabulary of colonnade, steps, corner column and monumental clock to create a disquieting space. But the preferred forms interfered with the transmission of his ideas, reducing the impact of the space, leaving it a sterile replication of the historical spaces from which it was derived.[21]

Where it took the form of theory rather than image, Rossi's legacy has proved more successful. Various individuals and groups have been inspired by him, but two in particular stand out, both distant in space and climate from Italy. Through his teaching in the United States, Rossi's ideas influenced the 'School of Miami' providing inspiration for the

development of the new urbanism, particularly the typological distinction between public and private spaces within a tightly organised pattern, and the evocative potential of traditional and familiar forms.[22] Secondly, in Dublin a generation of young architects became interested in Rossi's ideas through exhibitions of his drawings. This resulted not only in theoretical pursuits like the analytical classification of vernacular forms as an expression of primitive classicism, but also in built work, particularly the regeneration of the Temple Bar quarter.[23]

Rossi's research on typology took place in a context as much physical as cultural, and it was here that his deftness of touch came to the fore. The architectural milieu of modernism which he met at the opening of his career placed value on precision of detail, and the issue of place was seen as a distraction. He saw that the stained concrete and cracked plaster, the metal stairs and grilles, the scale redundant or perhaps significantly oversized, were elements of the typical environment from which an architectural and urban typology might be defined. Its very banality was a sign both of its ubiquity and its comprehensibility.

200

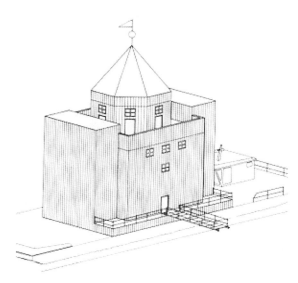

19. Teatro del Mondo, a theatre on a barge, Venice, 1980.

Rossi's intellectual position was more discrete than those of American contemporaries like Eisenman and Venturi (Chapters 17 and 19) who were more overt in their employment of literary and popular forms. Rossi saw in his forms a degree of inevitability which simply presumed acceptance. The very muteness, the total lack of rhetorical flourish, is his work's most tender and enduring quality.

Rossi died as the result of another motor accident in September 1997. His work had ceased to be fashionable, probably as a result of overexposure in the 1980s. Apart from the Teatro del Mondo for Venice in 1980, few of his larger late projects had the pregnant power of the Modena cemetery. But his drawings live on. Following a major exhibition in Rome, 2004, of a collection acquired by the Italian State, a reassessment of the four decades of his *oeuvre* as a historical phenomenon became possible, and like one of the urban artefacts praised in *The Architecture of the City*, it exerted its own unique influence on the environment in which it was formed.

EC

Notes

1. See in particular the social housing complex at Tuscolano, Rome of 1950-54 in Garofalo and Veresani 1992, pp.149-155. For Moretti see Bucci and Mulazzani 2002.
2. For the monument to the deportees see Strathaus and Reichlin 1995. For the Torre Velasca see Brunetti 1996.
3. See Bottoni 1954, pp. 196-241.
4. Foot 2001.
5. Adjmi and Bertolotto 1993.
6. Rossi 1982 a.
7. Ibid, pp. 29-32.
8. Durand 1802-05.
9. Rossi 1982 b, p. 11.
10. Rossi was influenced by writings of Emil Kaufmann such as *Three Revolutionary Architects: Boullee, Ledoux and Lequeu* The American Philosophical Society, Philadelphia, 1952. He commented on them in 'Emil Kaufmann e l'architettura del' Illuminismo' in *Casabella - continuità* No. 222, November 1958, pp. 42-47.
11. Aldo Rossi, '*The Blue of the Sky*' (1971) in O' Regan 1983, p. 42.
12. Peter Eisenman, '*The House of the Dead as the City of Survival*' in Frampton 1979 pp. 4-15.
13. Rossi (1971), as cited in n. 11, p. 47.
14. Eisenman 1979 op. cit.
15. Taylor 1992, p. 8.
16. Eisenman 1979 op. cit.
17. Adjmi and Bertolotto 1993. Following his death in 1997 some of Rossi's sketchbooks were published by their new owners in a facsimile edition, *I Quaderni di Aldo Rossi 1990-97* Getty Trust Publications, Los Angeles, 2000.
18. Annalisa Trentin interview with Fabio Reinhart in 'Dopo Aldo Rossi' *d'Architettura* no. 23, May 2004, p. 181.
19. See Jacobson 2001.
20. Rossi 1982b.
21. See Canniffe 2006, pp. 153-4.
22. Dutton 2000.
23. Quinn 1996.

Chapter 16. Peter Eisenman: Wexner Center for the Visual Arts, Columbus, Ohio, 1983-89

Following the establishment of the Modern Movement in the 1920s, much twentieth century architecture treated the building as a free-standing object set in an open field or lightly juxtaposed with others (Blundell Jones 2002, Ch. 3 and 7), and this became the dominant mode in modern planning. When that modernist inheritance came into question in the 1970s some architects, including Peter Eisenman, attempted conscientiously to disintegrate the material presence of their buildings as objects, instead playing on the ambiguity of whether they are seen as self-sufficient entities or as components of some larger structure which constitutes the urban context. That this issue should have gained such a crucial role in contemporary architectural thought is a result of the cultural condition known as 'postmodern'. This term, which merely denotes a period following the modern and connected to it through reaction, has been overused in the last three decades, applied *ad nauseam* to every kind of cultural manifestation from elite fine arts to popular modes.[1] In architecture it does not lend itself to easy definition through the use of specific forms, but shows itself rather in a knowing use of them which signals a self-reflexive interest in the concept of play.[2] Some critics have felt that the postmodern is not the advertised self-consciously ambivalent game of manipulation, but rather, as Hal Foster has claimed:

a basic opposition which exists between a post-modernism which seeks to deconstruct modernism and resist the status quo, and a postmodernism which repudiates the former to celebrate the latter: a postmodernism of resistance and a post-modernism of reaction. [3]

His language carries an obvious code, for that description belongs to the early 1980s when, in the era of Reagan and Thatcher, to any politically correct academic the designations 'reaction' and 'resistance' had political equivalents in right and left. But a quarter of a century later the Cold-War scenario has been usurped by the collapse of the Warsaw Pact, economic globalisation, and the 'war

on terror'. This new situation has made definitions of left and right much less clear, as well as eroding the difference between resistance and reaction. Political extremism and factionalism now present a far more threatening instability than any concept of a 'postmodernism of reaction'. As so often happens, reality has displaced the neat intellectual models of the academy.

All the same, we should not dismiss those figures who sought to create an architecture expressive of that uneasy *Zeitgeist*. Drawing on the difficult and conflicting disciplines of philosophy and semantics, they moved from the isolated world of professional debate to a position more deliberately engaged with the cultural context. Amongst them, Peter Eisenman has been a vocal leader, the protagonist of an autonomous architecture which existed in drawings and academic discourse long before his success in the 1983 competition for a Visual Arts Center at the Ohio State University in Columbus, Ohio, precipitated a move into substantial architectural practice.

1. Wexner Center. Detail of the reconstructed Armory which serves as entry pavilion to the new building.

Born in 1932 in New Jersey, Eisenman was educated at Cornell and Columbia Universities before undertaking a doctorate at Cambridge University.[4] Returning to the United States in 1967, he founded the Institute for Architecture and Urban Studies in New York which, with its journal *Oppositions*, became an international platform for architectural debates in the 1970s, attracting figures like Kenneth Frampton, Aldo Rossi and Rem Koolhaas. As an architect of domestic buildings, he was also associated with a group called 'The New York Five' – the others being Michael Graves, Charles Gwathmey, John Hejduk and Richard Meier – mainly because of aesthetic similarity between their works as reinterpretations of pioneering modernism. 'The Whites' as they were also known, gathered under the aegis of the influential architectural fixer Philip Johnson, who with Henry-Russell Hitchcock had curated the International Style exhibition at the Museum of Modern Architecture in New York in 1932. In the early 1970s, a time of social and political turmoil in the United States, this new architectural elite established their careers in opposition to their immediate predecessors as protagonists of an autonomous architecture. Arthur Drexler, Director of the Department of Architecture and Design at the Museum of Modern Art, wrote of the aspirations of this new generation in the following terms:

Brutalism, architecture in blue jeans, and other effete mannerisms of proletarian snobbery, impress these architects no more than Mies's elegant but arbitrarily pure structure. Instead they have picked up where the thirties left off, pursuing what was implied before an architecture of rational poetry was interrupted by World War II and its subsequent mood of disenchantment, restlessness and resentment. The resentment, we all know, has good reason. We are all concerned, one way or another, with social reform. But the concern for reform has flavoured all discussion and criticism of anything that claims to be architecture first and social reform second. That architecture is the least likely instrument with which to accomplish that revolution has not yet been noticed by the younger Europeans, and in America is a fact like a convenient stone wall against which architectural journalism can bang heads.[5]

Whatever the accuracy of this local assessment of the architectural profession, the five architects all went on to establish positions in architecture and education that offered a coherent alternative to the corporate mainstream.

Architecture as language

During the 1970s, Eisenman worked on a series of house projects, some built, others remaining on paper, which explored in physical form the linguistic analogy he had developed in his Ph.D. thesis. He had analysed the work of Giuseppe Terragni (Blundell Jones 2002, Ch. 10) to which he had been introduced by Colin St John Wilson before visiting the buildings in Como with Colin Rowe: both mentors were teaching at Cambridge. From the geometric compositions of this key rationalist architect he derived a vocabulary and syntax of architectural elements, isolating them as self-referential motifs.[6] Reapplied in his own work, this formal system gave an impression of sober modernist orthodoxy, but close inspection reveals no machinist symbolism like that found in the work of Le Corbusier or Mies van der Rohe, nor any of their elegance in spatial composition. Eisenman's beams, columns, walls, and floors are spare and inexpressive. Their positioning gives no indication whatever of the function to be accommodated: indeed, he considered the negation of functionalism essential in his bid to distil the essence of architecture.[7]

Eisenman developed his analogy between architecture and language under the influence of contemporary linguistic theories of structuralism and deconstruction. These theories were important for concentrating interest not on the content of a given text but on its form, and particularly on the syntactical relationship between words, implying that meanings could be transferred at many levels obscured below the surface.[8] Terragni's architectural vocabulary seemed to provide an ideal parallel, for the reduced and emblematic nature of his frames and surfaces suggested a similarly hidden set of architectural values. Among the projects which Eisenman built was House II in Hardwick, Vermont (1969-70), where the architectural idea centred on the mutual redundancy of two sets of structures, a grid of columns and a set of planar walls, creating a complex matrix of space. In House VI in Cornwall, Connecticut (1972-76), this redundancy was made explicit by a suspended red stair hanging over the actual green stair of the house, more explicitly questioning the architectural conventions derived from gravity. Eisenman's abstraction was indebted also to New York minimalist art of the period, such

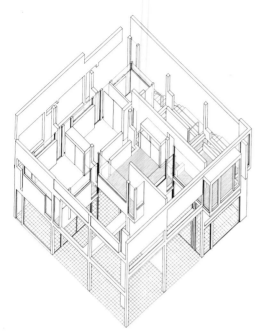

2. (left) Axonometric projection of House II, Hardwick, Vermont, 1969-70.

3. (above) Social housing at Checkpoint Charlie, Berlin, 1980-88, constructed as part of the Internationale Bauausstellung.

as the sculpture of Carl André and Sol Le Witt. As Drexler claimed, such intensely aesthetic concern removed the last vestiges of social engagement from the field of architectural debate. But since it drew so heavily on modernist precedent, the formal vocabulary of Eisenman (and of the other four members of the New York Five) made it just as much self-conscious historicism as the more eclectic postmodern work of Charles Moore and Robert Venturi. A change in Eisenman's work came with the invitation to participate in the Venice Architecture Biennale with an unbuilt project for Cannaregio town square in 1978, and with social housing at Checkpoint Charlie, Berlin, of 1980-88. In both cases the history of the site provided a foundational datum out of which the familiar abstract cubic forms arise. Eisenman had discovered context, and his subsequent work was increasingly to depend on ideas of memory derived from geometrical analyses of the site.[9]

The Wexner Center
The invited competition to design a new university visual arts centre in Columbus, Ohio was held in June 1983 and the building was opened in 1989. The competition, judged by Harry Cobb (partner of I.M. Pei and Chairman of the Architecture Department at Harvard) received entries from an illustrious group including Cesar Pelli,

Michael Graves, Kallman McKinnell and Wood, and Arthur Erikson, but Eisenman's 'non-building' was chosen as best representing the desire to integrate teaching, research and exhibition.[10] The site at the edge of the University's oval campus was already occupied by two large auditoria set perpendicular to one another but aligned with the general grid of the campus. This was also the point where the University's grid met that of the town, displaying a 12.25° difference of alignment. This angle shift furnished Eisenman with a starting point for a recurrent theme in his work: the exploitation of conflicts and disjunctions between two systems, each of which undermines the validity of the other's presence.[11] The idea had been explored in the aforementioned projects for Cannaregio and Checkpoint Charlie, but in those cases the treatment of the ground plane, involving an artificial 'archaeological excavation', was made to serve as an explicit metaphor of the site's history.

In the case of the Wexner Center, the contextual material was more resonant, for the whole territory of the State of Ohio was defined and described by the imposed Jeffersonian grid.[12] By overlaying the conflicting grids, Eisenman subverted their power, with the novelty that the grids were no longer mere intellectual games, but physical manifestations of forces that had shaped the site. As Rafael Moneo explained:

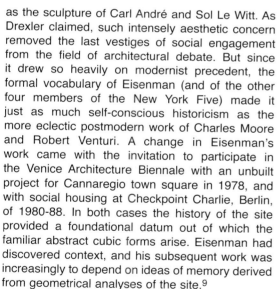

4. Entrance to the Wexner Center from the lawn of the Ohio State University campus showing from the right: the existing auditorium, the scaffolding grid, and the reconstructed Armory.

5. Public route between the existing auditoria. Note that the ground level is a horizontal path while the scaffolding frame is trapezoidal in section.

Eisenman's former reluctance to admit that such circumstances (that is, site and programme) affect architecture has, at least implicitly, changed. His work now starts to take shape either from considerations that have contextual issues at their base or from interpretations of the program that allow him to incorporate current literary ideas into architecture. One wonders if this change in attitude was simply his answer to the post-modernist pressure of the late seventies and to the recent interest in incorporating literary criticism into architecture. But one might also understand this new interest in site and program to be the consequence of approaching broader and more complex projects. As a result Peter Eisenman seems to have discovered that architecture needs to include outside parameters in order to be produced, and that only in the frame of its external circumstance does it acquire meaning.[13]

Without changing his preferred architectural forms, Eisenman had moved from an internalised intellectual framework to an externalised one. He used the grid of the city as a device to weave a route between the two existing auditoria. This route is both open to the public and enclosed from the weather, making the public the link which unites the exhibition spaces below ground. It is marked by an open gridded framework, the spatial echo

6. The scaffolding grid emerging to the rear of the building where its raked form is clearly visible.

of the grid shift in plan, which is distorted as a shearing, rising form. The principal entrance to this link is perhaps the most controversial element in the complex, for where the long gallery crosses routes perpendicular to it lies an entrance pavilion presented as a fragmented recreation of the Armory, a nineteenth century Gothic Baronial structure demolished in the 1960s to make way for the lesser auditorium. In the competition proposal the Armory was recreated whole, albeit shifted and with the trace of its original position excavated; but by the time of construction, a further stage in the decomposition of the authentic architectural text had taken place, by allowing the new Armory to be affected by the grid which incises itself on to the brick surface, rupturing the consistency of its historical form. The pavilion is further penetrated by another errant grid, which frames the main stair and is itself subverted by a hanging column, the kind of redundant device Eisenman had used in previous projects to declare 'Architecture' (i.e. precisely that which **is** architecture but **is not** building). In Eisenman's usage the grid is an element of language which retains its validity even as a fragment; indeed its fragmentary quality implies its potential completion at any scale from building component to city, or even to continent.

According to Moneo, the building:

'...tests the ability of the theoretical methods to deal with large scale construction. This analytical attitude allows problems to be approached with a high degree of generality. The insistence on the grid and the architectural strategies which evolve from it have given them the means to create a continuum which can also embody pieces of a disjointed reality. The idea of a single building has vanished, and instead there appears a complex reality closer to the perception of the idea that we have of our cities today, rather than towards traditional buildings. The instability of today's cities seems to be reflected in the [Wexner] Center and that leads me to say that Eisenman's work, without explicitly pretending to do so, replicates the reality of today's cities. Perhaps paradoxically, some of those procedures that Peter Eisenman might like to call deconstructivist are in fact not so far from the formal mechanisms used by cities in a rather unconscious but rational way as they themselves evolve. In other words, it could be said that some devices that Peter Eisenman has explored through the last years were implicit in the strategies assumed by cities in their unconscious development through time. Unexpectedly, Eisenman's research seems to coincide with a description of the actual city.[14]

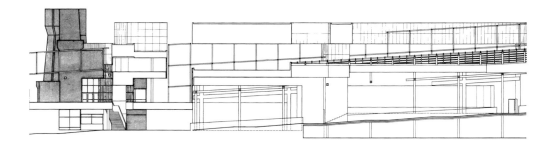

This unconscious, automatic exploitation of process is a phenomenon which Eisenman has explored throughout his career, but the Wexner Center was his first large work successfully to apply this theoretical method to an urban environment, thus going beyond imitation to appeal to a larger order which Jean-Louis Cohen described as 'hypercontextuality'.[15] Ignoring the differences between figuration and abstraction, the Wexner stands outside conventional categorisations of architectural language, occupying an ambiguous middle ground. It is neither traditional, i.e. governed by the form of the room; nor modernist, i.e. relying on a fluid spatial continuum; nor functionalist i.e. determined by use. Instead the Wexner Center displays a general ordering principle which overlays the site and works downward in scale. In Eisenman's use of what might be described as artificial history, for example the Gothic Baronial of the entrance pavilion, we are introduced to elements revived

and reinterpreted; intimate site-specific elements. That these should be intentionally scenographic and even picturesque is underscored by their uncomfortable attachment to adjacent black glass elevations, which by their very muteness declare by contrast that the adjacent features are to be read as bearers of meaning.

There is also significance lodged in the illusion-istic distortion of space of the Wexner's open gridded framework (or 'scaffolding' element). In his House X project (1975) Eisenman ended up with an axonometric model distorted out of its orthogonal relationships to simulate a two dimensional architectural projection when seen from one specific viewpoint.[16] Axonometric projection rather than perspective is his preferred convention for two-dimensional representations of three-dimensional form because sizes remain constant. At the Wexner Center the non-orthogonal distortion of the scaffolding is played against the

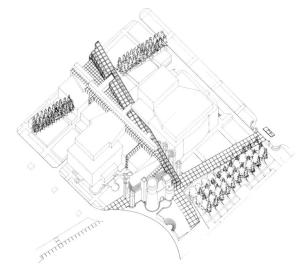

7. (above) Partial section showing the reconstructed Armory and the main interior levels of gallery and basement.

8. (left) Axonometric projection of the Wexner Center showing existing auditoria, conflicting grids, and reconstructed Armory.

9. (above opposite) Site plan of the Ohio State University campus showing the dislocation of grids between the city and the campus. The red line marks the axis of the Jeffersonian grid, linking a sports arena to north with the street network to south.

10. (below opposite) Plan of the entrance level showing the existing auditoria and the public route between them.

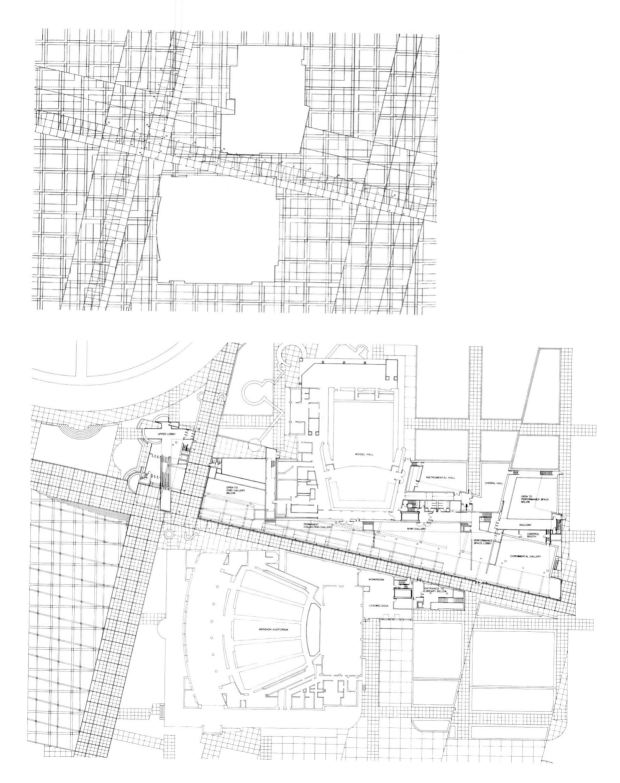

11. Interior by the entrance with the hanging column.
12. (opposite) Interior of the main gallery.

orthogonal grids of the glazing and of the spaces to create a series of distorted vistas. The architect plays with the assumed coherence and consistency of architecture by making buildings in which an application of one device immediately provokes a disjunction with another. This type of exaggerated and warped space became a feature of designs following in the building's wake, such as the first project for Daniel Libeskind's Jewish Museum in Berlin of 1989, the year in which the Wexner Center opened.[17]

The question of drawing conventions brings us to the issue of representation in Eisenman's work, and its continuing presence as the filter through which the work is made and interpreted. The super-imposition of layers through the analytical method became the principal representational motif. This occurs frequently in graphic form, particularly in the non-gravitational axonometric projections, the 'symbolic form' of modernist architecture in which layers of context are exposed. (But Eisenman's usage contrasts with that of pioneering modernists like El Lissitsky who employed it to remove context). Traces of the overlay technique occur again in the forms and spaces actually realised, apparent through their repetition at different scales, in the scoring of surfaces to represent the presence of an absent element, and in the ubiquitous employment of the grid-shift to communicate contextual references (Fig. 11).

Mannerist reinterpretations of modernism?
The strategies which animate Eisenman's later work suggest a dissolution and reconfiguration of norms typical of mannerism.[18] That a pioneering phase in architectural history should be followed by a decadent phase, rearranging or subverting the former's expectations, presents a tempting parallel with sixteenth-century Italy. At that time the search for harmonic completion and stasis, as defined by the theory of Alberti, gave way to strange progeny in the work of Giulio Romano, with its exaggerated delicacies and contrasting roughness as seen in the courtyard of the Palazzo Te. Representing the opposition between culture and nature, such contrasts presented the aspirations of civilisation as if under threat by forces of chaos and disorder.[19]

Another historical parallel is the creation of an attenuated space to bestow new value on an existing situation, as witnessed by mannerist urban interventions like Vasari's Uffizi in Florence.[20] Unlike that of his contemporary Michael Graves, Eisenman's mannerism was not expressed by imitating mannerist forms, adopting syncopated columnar rhythms, forming surfaces by laminating veneers of architectural members, or creating an implication of perspective in depth. Eisenman remained indebted to the formal abstraction of the modernism he had first analysed.

The literary metaphor employed throughout Eisenman's projects is the palimpsest, which originated in the medieval practice of reusing precious parchment by erasing one text to impose another. This act of suppression, leaving fragments of hidden meaning not necessarily connected to the overt message, is part of the psychological foundation of critical theory, where ostensibly random circumstance can be woven into a rich narrative of indirect meaning and communication. As a literary device, this became a commonplace in novels like Umberto Eco's The Name of the Rose, while in urban terms it renewed interest in the sedimented layers of historical form. The palimpsest presented a perfect model, its lack

13. Exterior showing the juxtaposition of the fragments of the reconstructed Armory and the new building elements.

14. Detail of the end of the scaffolding grid which marks the public route across the site.

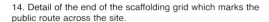

of a single authorial voice allowing for a meaning to emerge that was authentically obscure, perhaps only half known, suggesting hidden depths. It added dimensions that could be unconsciously sensed, and that did not trouble the author, observer or designer with the need to create. All that was apparent, in its inconsistencies and discontinuities, had simply been revealed and awaited its interpreter. This allowed a passivity in the face of circumstances, a passivity in marked contrast with the calls for action associated with modernism. Despite all such disorder, however, Eisenman was able to summon an architectural language that was identifiably his own. (Fig. 14)

The principal architectural palimpsest interpreted by Eisenman was the work of Terragni, and his primary object was the Casa del Fascio in Como (Blundell Jones 2002, Ch.10). In Eisenman's reading the political content of the work was totally ignored in favour of its formal qualities. For an architect apparently so concerned with the eschatological significance of the Second World War – in relation to the Holocaust and Hiroshima at least – this might seem strange: but such is the power of cultural context as defined by post-structuralism that any ethical charge can be dispersed in the focus on form.[21] The particular character of Italian modernism was its self-conscious attachment to history, required by the Fascist regime, which was distinct from the distancing attitudes adopted by French and German modernism. The abstract forms, far from the formalist/ functionalist rhetoric of Le Corbusier or Mies van der Rohe, explicitly referred to the history of architectural culture. In Eisenman's early work, the white cubic forms have to be considered as emanations of the Terragni inheritance which are implicitly present, if only explicitly understood by the initiated. The later work, less constrained in its forms, merely makes the relationship to Terragni more explicit. The syntactical analysis developed in the study of the Casa del Fascio, for example, provided the layered methodology through which, two decades later, the palimpsest of a site could be excavated.

As the Wexner Center approached completion, Eisenman's work featured in the *Deconstructivist Architecture* exhibition at the Museum of Modern Art in New York in 1988, a self-conscious attempt to recreate, with a newly defined architectural school, the effect of the International Style exhibition held there in 1932. As with that precedent and the 1970s promotion of the New York Five, Philip Johnson gave the new style his considerable support. Displayed alongside work by Frank Gehry, Daniel Libeskind, Zaha Hadid, Coop Himmelblau, Bernard Tschumi and Rem Koolhaas, Eisenman's contribution was less dependent on confidence with form as displayed by Gehry and Hadid, or on an ironic attitude to the commercialisation of modern architecture as demonstrated by Koolhaas. Instead, the intellectual basis of his work, its provocative juxtaposition of forms, the scaffolding of its design-as-process, suggested an architecture struggling with contradictions, less self-sufficient than its modernist predecessor and, despite the disquieting characteristics of distortion, engaged with its context.

Later work

The Wexner Center's blurring of the boundary between inside and outside, between object and context, recurred in subsequent projects such as the University Art Museum at the California State University at Long Beach of 1986 (unbuilt) and the Aronoff Center for Design and Art in Cincinnati, Ohio, of 1988-96. There was also an unbuilt collaboration with the philosopher Jacques Derrida entitled Chora L Works, 1985-86, as a contribution to the Parc de La Villette in Paris by Bernard Tschumi, which led to an acrimonious dispute

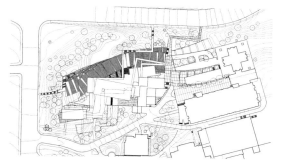

15. Aronoff Center, 1988-96.
16. (below) Model of Chora L Works project (1985-86), a collaboration with Jacques Derrida (unbuilt).
17. (bottom) 'Garden of lost footsteps' in the courtyard of the Castelvecchio Museum, Verona, 2004-05 as part of the Venice Architecture Biennale 2004.

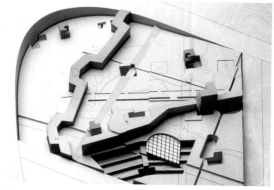

212

18. Memorial to the Murdered Jews of Europe, Berlin 2005

between the two architects about the origins of the park's design.[22] The elaboration of these 'non-building' projects – where conventions about the upright nature of the architecture were challenged by ambiguity of ground planes, overlapping of forms and the compositional technique of 'artificial excavation' – all developed from the strategies employed at the Wexner Center.[23] Its repetitive, serial overlapping ambiguity was derived from cubist composition, but the advent of complex computer modelling techniques allowed ever more complex forms in the following decades. The computer's tendency to repress human scale and signs of occupation was prefigured in Eisenman's hand-drawn work, and this later became a feature of public works like Gehry's Guggenheim in Bilbao (if without the intellectual argument which Eisenman requires). Eisenman himself continues to experiment with architectural, urban and landscape form, as the 'Garden of Lost Footsteps' installation in the courtyard of the Castelvecchio in Verona demonstrated in 2004-05.[24] Most provocative of all is his Memorial to the Murdered Jews of Europe, inaugurated in Berlin after much delay in the spring of 2005. Here landscape and memory combine to evoke the kind of resonant idea which lies beneath all his work as an architect and theorist.

EC

Notes

1. In the fields of architecture, culture and urbanism: see for example Jencks 1977, Foster 1985 and Ellin 1995.
2. See Jencks 1977, pp. 87-90. With specific reference to Eisenman see Kenneth Frampton 'Eisenman Revisited: Running Interference' in *Peter Eisenman, Architecture and Urbanism,* Extra Edition, August 1988, pp. 57-69 which begins with a quotation from Johannes Huizinga's *Homo Ludens.*
3. See Foster 1985, pp. xi-xii.
4. Peter D. Eisenman, *The Formal Basis of Modern Architecture,* Ph.D. thesis, University of Cambridge, 1963, later published by Lars Muller Publishers, Baden, 2006.
5. Drexler 1975, p. 1.
6. The analysis on Terragni was published in a series of essays but eventually was comprehensively collated in Eisenman 2003.
7. See Eisenman 1987.
8. See Mario Gandelsonas '*From Structure to Subject: The Formation of an Architectural Language*' in Eisenman 1982, pp. 7-30.
9. Moneo 2004, p. 175.
10. The competition entries are published in Arnell and Bickford 1984.
11. Exploitation of this kind of angle shift existed in early modernism, for example in the diagonal disposition of a square volume in Le Corbusier's unbuilt mass-production artisans' dwellings of 1924, where it is justified by the claim to create the illusion of a larger space (Le Corbusier 1927, pp. 236-7). It can also be seen in Hans Scharoun's project for Mannheim Theatre of 1953 (Blundell Jones 2002, Ch 13) and be traced back to the same architect's Schminke House, Löbau, of 1932-3. Eisenman had employed a shifted geometry in House III in Lakeville, Connecticut (1969-71).
12. The Jeffersonian Grid refers to Thomas Jefferson's Land Ordinance Act of 1785 which established the graduated gridded nature of the American urban and rural landscape. See Pope 1996, p. 51.
13. Rafael Moneo '*Unexpected Coincidences*' in Moneo, Vidler et al. 1989, p. 40.
14. Ibid., p. 45.
15. Jean-Louis Cohen in Bedard 1994, p. 120.
16. See Eisenman 1982, pp. 158-66.
17. Libeskind 1991, pp. 85-107.
18. Pier Vittorio Aureli '*Mannerism, or the Manner at the time of Eisenman*' in Eisenman History Italy, Marco Casamonti (ed.) *Area,* No. 74, May-June 2004, pp. 78-85.
19. See Hauser 1965.
20. See Eamonn Canniffe, *Mannerist Interventions: Three Sixteenth Century Italian Squares,* Urban Design Studies: Annual of the University of Greenwich Urban Design Unit, Vol. 1, 1995, pp. 57-74.
21. Johnson and Wigley 1988.
22. See Kipnis and Leeser 1997, pp. 82-5.
23. See Bedard 1994.
24. Forster et al. 2004.

Chapter 17. Karljosef Schattner: Waisenhaus, Eichstätt, 1985-8

In an age when cities compete to decorate themselves with works by international architectural heroes and reputations are measured in air-miles, Karljosef Schattner has been the opposite: a local architect executing almost his entire *oeuvre* in a small town of only 13,000 inhabitants.[1] Eichstätt lies between Munich and Nuremberg in northern Bavaria, its historic importance due to the Roman Catholic Church. A monastery was set up there in the eighth century by St Willibad of Wessex, and the town later became the seat of the Prince-Bishops of Bavaria, one reaching the status of pope in the eleventh century. After medieval Eichstätt was sacked by the Swedes in 1633-34 during the Thirty Years War, it was rebuilt by Baroque masters from Italy under the patronage of the Church, and the bishops remained largely in charge until their territorial holdings were turned over to the *Land* in the early nineteenth century. Thereafter it stagnated as a small market town, avoiding the industrial and commercial development that swamped better connected places, and spared the curse of highway engineering. But as a religious centre it retained its traditions and memories, its piety and integrity. Wedged into the tight valley of the river Altmühl, it has a picturesque setting that can still be appreciated despite modern suburbs, and the old kernel is unusual in combining Baroque architecture with a medieval plan. The walls and gates survived into the nineteenth century.

When Karljosef Schattner took up the post of Diocesan Architect in 1957 at the age of 33, he was pleased to get a secure job in the place that he had made his home. He looked forward to a relatively quiet professional existence, maintaining the church's many historic buildings, making extensions and alterations, and adding the occasional new one. But only a year later in 1958, the bishops decided to found a Pädagogische Hochschule, which was later expanded with state support into the Catholic University of Eichstätt. This relatively small institution, with seven faculties and 4200 students of all faiths, brought Schattner his first substantial new-build job. Fortunately plans to start a completely new campus north of the town, initially supported by Schattner in line with current wisdom, were abandoned in favour of a closer site just east of the old centre.[2] The university was subsequently integrated into the town, able to grow up little by little across the 34 years that Schattner held the post. It brought funding for restorations and for conversions of several historic buildings as well as for a handful of new ones by Schattner and by others under his patronage.[3] The case study considered here was among his later conversions.

It was these conversions that made Schattner famous and put Eichstätt on the map for architects in the 1980s. Most striking were the fine quality of detail and the intentionally stark contrast between old and new, but these were just the most visible

1. City of Eichstätt as seen in an eighteenth-century engraving.

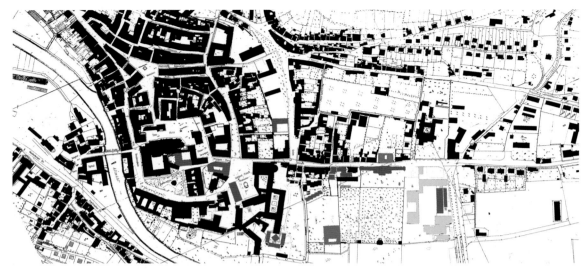

fruits of a significant continuity of approach which stretched from the silent maintenance and repair of old buildings through to the construction of completely new ones. The work takes place within such a small area that in effect every addition belongs to the same compositional whole and each gesture is part of a cumulative repertoire. Schattner's work grew in scope and confidence as he came to know the fabric and history of Eichstätt with increasingly intimacy, trying one architectural experiment after another. Ruled by a mere four bishops during his period of office, he was fortunate in a client used to patient discussion and rational argument, geared to long-term aims, and with an uncommercial concern for quality. He had time to plan developments carefully and to maintain an office with a consistent workload. He was able to engage in a long and fruitful dialogue with the same local contractors, and with metalworking firms who rose to his exacting standards, finding ways to achieve them without excessive costs. Also at his disposal was his own *Dombauhütte*, a team of around twelve specialist craftsmen including masons, a joiner and painters, initially convened for restoration, but who could also be deputed for special duties on new work. These working conditions were by today's standards old-fashioned and almost romantically small scale, yet many architects would envy them as close to ideal, and the quality in the result tells.

Schattner's background
Born in 1924 in East Germany, Schattner was a schoolboy at the outbreak of the Second World War, and was called up as a solider in 1942 at the age of 18. He was wounded and brought to convalesce in Ingolstadt, and he married his nurse from nearby Eichstätt, settling in her home town. The war delayed his architectural studies, which began at the Technical Univeristy of Munich in 1949. A leading figure there was Hans Döllgast, the architect for the restoration of Munich's art museum, the Alte Pinakothek, which was being carried out right through Schattner's time as student. This was a key work in the layering of new and old, for Döllgast chose to fill in Klenze's bombed stone facade in brick, fulfilling the form but preserving the wound. Also present as professor was Martin Elsaesser, who had been a key figure in the New Frankfurt and had studied under the great exponent of *genius loci*, Theodor Fischer.[4] As a student, Schattner helped mount an exhibition on the work of Frank Lloyd Wright and to organise trips to Switzerland and Scandinavia, the fashionable destinations for German architectural students at that time. In Denmark he imbibed the work of Arne Jacobsen, and in Sweden Gunnar Asplund's Gothenburg Law Courts of 1937, the key early modernist work setting new and old in clear contrast (Blundell Jones 2002, Ch. 11).

Later, in the 1960s, Schattner made his own architectural pilgrimages to Italy, where he admired particularly the emerging work of Giancarlo De Carlo at Urbino (Chapter 13) and of Carlo Scarpa in Verona (Chapter 9). Scarpa's way of separating the preserved historic substance from new work 'with a scalpel', as Schattner described it,[5] was

2. (opposite) Plan of Eichstätt with centre and river to left, north-east road to first suburbs on right. Waisenhaus is picked out in red.

3. (right) The new university complex of 1960-65, shown yellow on plan opposite.

4, 5. (below) The seminary library of 1963-5, shown green on the plan opposite. Other buildings by Schattner are picked out in blue.

a crucial inspiration, and he also learned from Scarpa's details and uses of materials, particularly the waxed render *stucco lustro*.[6] Schattner's reforging of an Italian connection to Eichstätt was happily appropriate, for the three leading Baroque architects who worked in the town in turn between 1670 and 1799 – Jakob Engel, Gabriel de Gabrieli and Maurizio Pedetti – were all Italians. Such cultural exchange across the Alps has long been fruitful. Schattner's first group of buildings for the new Catholic University in 1960-65 were newly built on the eastern side of town next to the bishop's former summer residence. A series of well-placed slab blocks of various sizes stood around a big grass court as an extension of the former bishop's garden. The strict, sober and fastidiously detailed architecture followed the brutalism of the time in its exposed concrete frame and local Jura-stone infill.

The state and seminary library followed in 1963-5 on the opposite side of the bishop's garden. Here a rigid cube was set within its own walled garden, contrasting the solidity of the bookstack with the contemplative void of a cloister-like court. Though sensitively integrated into the context, neither building made any stylistic reference whatever to the Baroque surroundings: indeed for a visiting architect at the time the likely references would have been Mies (steel detailing), Kahn (plan geometry) and Aalto (rooflights).

In the mid-1960s Schattner started with conversions. Among the first was the former Cathedral Deanery, a barn-like structure of medieval origin that had been reworked in the Baroque with painted stucco facades, corner bays and a curly gable. Since the fabric was in a poor state and there was pressure to extend the accommodation

6. The converted Ulmer Hof, former external court made into a library.

7. The new entrance to the converted Deanery.

into the roofspace, the interior had to be gutted, and efficient use as ecclesiastical offices (including Schattner's own) necessitated a new side entrance. Schattner added a new frame in hand-carved stone which follows the Baroque facade rhythm while indicating the upward connection. It leads within to a triple-height hall with exposed concrete frame, bridge-like landings, and steel stairs, a daylit space that reveals the building's organisation and allows dignified progress to offices via short passages. To the casual visitor Schattner's alterations are not prominent, yet his moves were deft and choices about what to preserve crucial for the building's character. Although the vocabulary changes between outside and in, there is no sense of a loss of quality nor of compromise in the insertion of new functions. Other equally subtle conversions followed, but also some bolder ones. Schattner hit the international architectural press with the conversion of the Ulmer Hof in 1980. This three-storey building with fine Baroque facades lay in the centre overlooking Leonrodplatz, and was to become the Theology Faculty. Its three gently preserved wings surrounded a rear court which Schattner roofed over and turned into the library, closing the fourth side with a wing of bookstacks. He played up the liminal nature of the space by preserving the old outer facades with their windows and painted decoration, even preserving the corner outdoor clock face. At the same time he showed off the freshly detailed new work in naked steel, concrete, and glass: new bookstacks, spiral

staircase, roof trusses and structural supporting frame for the old arcade. Investigation of facade paint revealed many layers which at one point were left nakedly on display like a sample-board, and various versions of the painted window surrounds were reproduced on the facade, along with some section drawings. The building's faces to the town quietly retain their Baroque form, but there is no calm unity in the former court: instead the layers of history reveal themselves, peeled back one by one, and the new layers are visibly added.

The Waisenhaus (Orphanage)

The building chosen for close study here is a conversion of a conversion, a unique architectural anomaly. It lies in the former eastern suburb of the town across the road from the bishop's summer residence, which it pre-dates. As in many old towns, growth beyond the walls had taken the form of ribbon development along main outgoing roads, this one heading south-east along the valley of the river Altmühl. A large Renaissance house had been built on the site in 1581 and survived the conflagration of 1633: another was added in 1695. They were similar in size with gables to the street but set at slightly different angles, and an alleyway ran in between. They were bought up by the town and combined into an orphanage in 1758 by Maurizio Pedetti, one of the Italian Baroque architects who rebuilt Eichstätt. He linked the two gables with a new classical facade, adding a

8. The restored Baroque facade of the Waisenhaus.

central entrance, but he kept the original structure and the two independent staircases. The symmetry served the division of the sexes, with girls in the right hand house and boys in the left, while the new entry axis between the former houses ran through a light-well, terminating in a chapel at the back of the plan. Children could participate in religious services without leaving their respective houses by gathering on first floor galleries. One house was deeper than the other, which would have played havoc with Pedetti's roof geometry, so he built a new back wall to square it up, the space between serving variously as an enlargement of the rear rooms, as a loggia, or for a poché of storerooms and lavatories. The whole arrangement survived as an orphanage well into the twentieth century,

9 Interior of the restored building.

with some renovations carried out in 1910. It became redundant after the Second World War and was used temporarily as a kindergarten. Later it became a hostel for the homeless before being left vacant for more than a decade. It had fallen into a sorry state when taken over for reconstruction, though the walls and original roof structures of the two houses remained sound. Being architecturally so 'impure', it was not recognised as a monument and would probably have been pulled down without further consideration had not Schattner taken an interest. In the mid-1980s he was developing the site almost opposite for the Faculties of Psychology and Journalism, supplementing the two Baroque orangery buildings of the summer residence with new blocks of his own, but the programme was too large for the site, prompting the need to dig deep basements for the large studios. He saw the possibility instead of decanting the offices and seminar rooms of the two faculties into the Waisenhaus, and he persuaded the bishop to buy it.

Three historical phases

If it was the Baroque phase that gave the Waisenhaus its peculiar character and scale, turning it into a major landmark on the approach to the town centre, the presence of the Renaissance houses could still be felt in the strange roof, kinked facade, and internal arrangements. When the Baroque render was stripped off, areas of wall-painting were found to prove that the houses too had been grand in their day, and this prompted a familiar question faced by restorers of historic buildings: which period? It would go against the institutional nature and scale of the university's programme to remove Pedetti's link and return to the two houses, but it would also be a pity to cover up the evidence of the earlier phase. Nor would an accurate restoration to the Baroque form be well suited to modern needs, there being nothing required of such hierarchical significance as Pedetti's chapel.

Clearly both strata of history were of interest, and with conversion to a new programme, Schattner was obliged to add a third. He restored the extraordinary Baroque facade with all its windows, paint and mouldings, replacing lost elements on the basis of Pedetti's drawings and on the evidence of other works. He also restored many old interiors, including repairing murals and reconstructing plaster ceilings where only parts remained, patching up brick vaults on the ground floor. But he was also obliged to reinterpret. He made sense of the symmetrical divide with the two university departments: Psychology on the left, Journalism on the right. He cleared out the chapel to regain the memory of the former alley, glazing the end and top, and adding a new main staircase as the principal architectural gesture, shared between the two sides. The voids left by the old staircases could then be occupied by stacks of modern lavatories, conveniently central but necessarily artificially lit and ventilated.

He decided to remove Pedetti's added rear wall and clutter of rooms, rediscovering the original backs of the Renaissance houses with their painted corners, and re-exposing the change of angle between them. To reunify the rear of the building he then added a rendered masonry screen wall, with regular window like holes lined in steel frames. This free-standing facade recalls the abstraction of contemporary neo-rationalists such as Aldo Rossi (see Chapter 15), but it also defines a spatial layer, a roofed space between the outside world and the true interior. Steel fire-stairs are placed at either end,

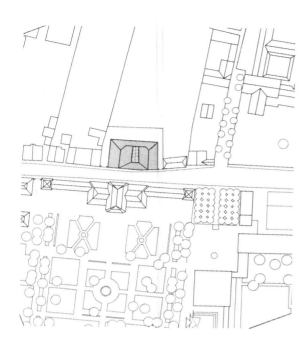

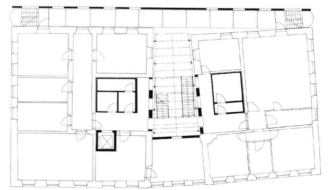

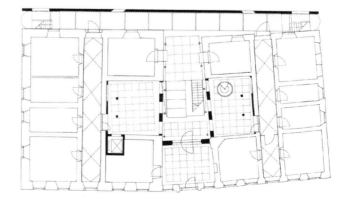

10. (top) Site plan, with bishop's former summer palace across the road. Town centre is to left.

11. (top right) Axonometric projection of the Waisenhaus from the rear, showing screen wall and central hall.

12. (above) The eighteenth century ground plan.

13. (middle right) Plan of upper floor as converted.

14. (right) Plan of lower floor as converted. Street entrance is centre bottom.

15, 16, 17 (overleaf) Contrasting views of the porch and entrance hall, showing the effect of the inner threshold.

nicely integrated into the building but also revealed in the portal-like gap and upper pattern of small square apertures that accentuates each end. Two normal-sized doorways with steel jambs slanted in the direction of travel lead through to the ground floor corridor exits of the respective departments. The screen wall is tied at the top to the rest of the building by a seemingly continuous tiled roof which rises into a hip on each side, though the middle part is merely an empty monopitch.

A dramatic spatial progression

The experience for the user is rich: approaching the building from the street, one is confronted with the perfectly restored Baroque facade complete with gilded coats of arms and inscriptions from the orphanage phase. The pilasters and canopy of the doorcase frame an inner stone arch, and only at this point does modernity intrude, with a steel door hung asymmetrically in a wooden frame soberly headed KATHOLISCHE UNIVERSITÄT. The door is in fact glazed, and from close to it allows a glimpse into the vestibule, but its external plane is stated by a close-knit black steel grid with dominant verticals. It is obviously modern yet sufficiently archetypal to blend with the Baroque context. As it opens, one discovers that it swings across a

mat-well whose square of floorspace is reiterated, implying a kind of aedicule, by a hanging gridded canopy above, this time in hardwood. But this is noticed more on the way out. One's attention on entering is grabbed by the view ahead on axis, through the intermediate glazed door and on into the light-filled central hall. The inner door, of frameless glass, is set in a black steel half-round arch, which on the inner side continues the circle to meet the rectangular door at knee level. Here again is archetypal geometry, and perhaps the memory of a Chinese moongate, but nobody can avoid the sense of a very special threshold – the most important in the building. In contrast with the street door, it offers quite another interplay of solid and void, the door proper persuaded almost to disappear in favour of the circle incised in black. There is also play with depth, found not only in the treatment of the wall thickness and contrast between back and front, but also in a change of texture of flooring from shiny to matt, leaving a border on each side.

The view through the opening is of the hall, its glass wall, and the rear screen wall beyond with its window holes. The main staircase runs mainly from the rear of the building forwards, and its rising edge is visible, but it is announced by four initial stone steps which end in a platform – the first landing.

18. Rear of the converted Waisenhaus, showing the abstract screen wall which unifies the two original houses.

The thickness of the steps is shown and shadow gaps accentuate the progression, but more dramatic still, the floor seen at the sides – standing in for the ground beneath – slopes markedly. It is as though a natural slope were present and stepping stones had been offered to speed one's way. At the back of the platform, glass wall and roof allow views through to the rear screen-wall and the monopitch roof above: building within a building. As one turns to take in the view back towards the street and on up to the floor above, one discovers that the stone treads continue, now trapped within the steel cage of the staircase, guiding one on up to higher levels.

The sides of the hall space are the original external walls of the two Renaissance houses with the original window holes, some of which became viewing galleries for children partaking in services held in the orphanage chapel. Schattner restored the old windows and the painted walls, adding metal grilles in voids where safety demanded. The glazed roof and staircase he treated as a new and separate structure on five pairs of steel columns, placed within the edges of the space with ties across into the wall for stability. The slenderness of the steel made it possible to retain a high degree of visibility, allowing the impression of one building inside another. It also lent itself to a vocabulary of detail with rules quite independent of the old building. The use of bunches of steel angles placed back-to-back for vertical columns, for example, allowed for many different kinds of junctions to accept changes in angle and variations to accommodate the stairs, as well as making modern versions of capitals and bases. In contrast with the black steelwork structure, the tubular handrails were made in round stainless steel tube, precious silver inviting contact.

The stair-hall, bathed in light and criss-crossed with shadows when the sun is out, opens dramatically and draws one through. Since the building consists largely of traditional rooms behind closed doors, it provides a much needed sense of centre and focus for orientation. Penetrating into the offices and seminar rooms, one finds some noble chambers with fine ceilings, but even the plain ones are pleasant and well-proportioned. Timber windows made on a traditional pattern were unobtrusively triple-glazed, providing good sound-proofing on the street side,[7] while lighting and services were provided discreetly through the floors, avoiding too much hacking away of old wall surfaces. Detailing was of high standard, with every junction studied and nothing left to chance.

19. Rediscovered wall painting in an upper room.

20. Original house walls with painted decoration and the new rear screen wall.

Restoration or reinterpretation?

Although fêted among architects for his sensitivity in dealing with old buildings, Schattner has met a surprising degree of opposition from conservationists.[8] They are understandably concerned about what is lost in the course of conversion, for much historical and archaeological evidence is bound to be destroyed even in 'sanitising', as the Germans call it.[9] But they are also worried about the arrogance of reinterpretation, about the sharp juxtaposition of old and new. For some it would seem to be more polite to stick to the principal style of a building, adding new parts in a 'Gothic' or 'Baroque' way so that they blend in. The problem with this apparently obvious approach is not just that we can never really know what our ancestors would have done, or properly emulate their craftsmanship: it is that we muddy the waters, leaving the real old almost indistinguishable from the fake old.[10]

Many monuments were irrevocably damaged in the nineteenth century by such enthusiastic 'restoration', and precisely in reaction against this William Morris and Philip Webb set up the Society for the Protection of Ancient Buildings, nicknamed 'anti-scrape'.[11] Their policy of bare minimal preservation as opposed to historicising restoration is now almost universally accepted, and is surely appropriate for major monuments kept at the state's expense for their intrinsic cultural value. But relatively few buildings can be afforded this privilege, and there are very many more worth preserving if ways can be found to let them earn a living, as in the case of the Waisenhaus. Arguably all buildings carry memories and contribute to places,[12] and often their lives can be usefully prolonged with a saving of energy, but many conversions are done in pragmatic and careless ways, ignoring history and shoe-horning in the new programme, letting the pain show. Schattner's type of conversion is much more difficult and reinterpretation is essential, both to find a fit between contents and vessel that is unstrained, and in celebrating the public areas – the parts of the building you must pass through to get to your room and to communicate with others. When he adds a strong new layer to the building's history, the old layers are not so much cancelled or contradicted as set in chronological perspective, while the newness allows the inhabitants to enjoy their fresh habitat without feeling shortchanged. A relatively dull programme of offices and meeting rooms, which by itself would not perhaps have inspired much architectural expression, easily becomes enlivened by a dialogue with the old context, and a strong sense of place is preserved.

224

21. Stair and openings in the main hall: detail.

Eichstätt is a small provincial place, yet Schattner's architecture depends on world sources and is now known worldwide.[13] Both the current star-system and art-history's traditional emphasis on individual creativity would attribute much to his talent, yet the special conditions of being Diocesan Architect, of studying every stone over decades, of having a sympathetic clients with an adequate purse and a team of craftsman at one's disposal, should not be underestimated. If a sense of *genius loci* is urgently needed in a world increasingly made of 'non-places',[14] this is clearly one way to preserve it, and it is evidently the opposite of calling in an international superstar who is bound to be ignorant of the place, expecting him or her to work some magic within days. Also in such cases, execution is difficult because of distance and lack of prior relationship with builders. It would be better if every town had its own Schattner and was given a similar chance to develop its architecture in response to local conditions.

Notes

1. Relatively unaffected by modern commerce and industry, its population only just doubled between 1807 and 1966, rising in the latter year to a mere 10,500. This information and much that follows, from *'Ort und Stunde: Eichstätt heute'*, by Günther Kühne, in Conrads 1983. The other main source is Pehnt 1999.
2. A happy accident, entirely due to the town wanting to capitalise on its property holdings there, see Pehnt 1999, p. 21.
3. Notably the university library by Günter Behnisch and Partners, 1987, winner of an open competition: see my article in *The Architectural Review,* March 1988, pp. 28-36. It is a tribute to Schattner's tolerance and broad-mindedness that he supported this alternative direction which Pehnt (1999, p. 29) has condemned as a 'jam-session' in the middle of his 'chamber-music'.
4. Significant because Fischer was the great exponent of *genius loci* and the teacher of many important modernists on the organic side, including Hugo Häring, Bruno Taut, Erich Mendelsohn and Dominikus Böhm. See Nerdinger 1988.
5. Pehnt 1999, p. 20.
6. The technique of *stucco lustro* is as follows: first the wall is rendered with sand and cement to a smooth finish, then it is sandpapered and treated with a filler, sanded down again and filled again. The filler contains mineral pigments as traditionally used, and the multicoloured effect is achieved by the sanding off which partly reveals deeper layers. The surface is finally treated with wax.
7. Double windows are of course traditional in Germany, but triple glazing is achieved by using a sealed unit for the inner light. This neatly sidesteps the problem of how to achieve traditional subdivisions, for the outer light which carries them can remain single glazed.
8. I was told this by Jörg Homeier, Schattner's assistant and later successor, on a visit to Eichstätt in 1988. It is also discussed in Pehnt 1999, pp. 21-3.
9. 'Sanierung' is the general word for rehabilitation of old buildings.
10. See my article on Quinlan Terry's Richmond Riverside, *The Architectural Review,* November 1988, pp. 86-90.
11. For a good summary of the origins of the SPAB see Kirk 2005, pp. 166-77.
12. The listing process for historic buildings is a curious progression: under 30 years reputations are not yet regarded as firm, but thereafter the main criterion is 'quality' as measured by publication and peer opinion. Beyond about 300 years everything seems to become valuable, simply because it is old and has survived, and for archaeologists rubbish dumps are treasure. In between there is a gradual exchange from the exceptional to the typical, as examples of the typical become increasingly scarce. While ceremonial buildings such as churches are obvious candidates for preservation, industrial buildings, which may have shaped places just as much, tend to be lost.
13. Schattner managed to be a local architect without being in the least parochial: he took part in symposia, followed the international scene in the press and through conversations, and visited the work of other architects. For example, in a work under construction in 1988 there was a window obviously inspired by Lewerentz.
14. See the book of that title by Marc Augé, 1995.

Chapter 18. Robert Venturi and Denise Scott Brown: Sainsbury Wing, National Gallery, London, 1986-91

Robert Venturi made his reputation with the ground-breaking book *Complexity and Contradiction in Architecture* published by the Museum of Modern Art in New York in 1966. It was described by Vincent Scully as: *'probably the most important writing on the making of architecture since Le Corbusier's* Vers une Architecture *of 1923',*[1] but in contrast with Le Corbusier's, Venturi's book was no universal theory pronounced in messianic terms: it was a 'gentle manifesto' claiming that the pleasure in architecture lay in the incidental, the accidental, juxtapositions and inconsistencies. His proposal stood against the intervening four decades of architectural theory, which had favoured rationalism and decried the intuitive. 'Less is more' had been Mies van der Rohe's dictum, to which Venturi's only partly facetious response was 'Less is a bore'.[2] Team Ten had sought to reanimate post-war architecture with appeals to existing social patterns, aggressive expression of form, and the exploitation of characterful materials. In contrast Venturi's prescription was for ambiguity, double functioning elements, conscious historical illusion and 'the difficult whole'. As Scully put it: *'that whole is new – hard to see, hard to write about, graceless and inarticulate as only the new can be.'* [3]

Robert Venturi was born in Philadelphia in 1925 and was educated at Princeton University, where his teachers included the Beaux Arts master Jean Labatut. This basic professional training was enhanced by a period at the American Academy in Rome, sandwiched between work for Eero Saarinen and for Louis Kahn.[4] This mixture of classical and modernist influence, including its inherent conflicts, was the ground for Venturi's reinterpretation of architectural theory as presented in his famous book. His wife and professional partner Denise Scott Brown was born in South Africa in 1931 and grew up in an atmosphere imbued with the influence of European modernism. Her mother had been a fellow architecture student with Rex Martienssen who corresponded with Le Corbusier. Completing her architectural education at the Architectural Association in London, she and her first husband Robert Scott Brown (d. 1959) were recommended by Peter Smithson for graduate study at the University of Pennsylvania under Louis Kahn.[5] But she chose to sidestep architecture in favour of city planning, particularly its social aspects. At Philadelphia she met Robert Venturi, identifying with his dissatisfaction about

1. The Sainsbury Wing in the corner of Trafalgar Square, London, as backdrop to a peace rally. The old gallery is on the right.

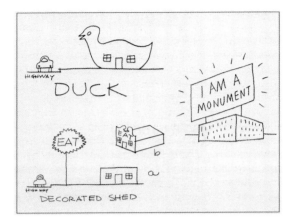

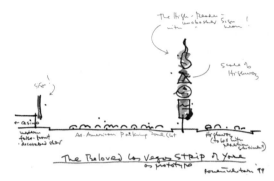

2. (left) Duck versus Decorated Shed.
3. (above) The beloved Las Vegas Strip of yore.
4. (opposite) Vanna Venturi house, 1961-64, plan and elevation.

contemporary architecture and urbanism, and together they developed a critique which fuelled their subsequent career together. They condemned as sterile the architecture and urban planning then discussed in academic and professional circles, for the creed of functionalism masked a rigid formalism and failed to provide an environment supportive of the variety of human activity.[6] The utopia promised by the modernists was simply not visible in the urban environment then being created, certainly not in the developing American city. Their joint interest in the expressive effects of Italian mannerism presented them with a historic model of how a discrete system of architecture could evolve into a less remote language, adaptable to changing circumstances. The need for a communicative architecture seemed to them more pressing than the spatial experimentation conducted by their contemporaries, and they regarded generic spatial solutions as preferable because, as the result of historical evolution, they were implicitly functional and inherently economical.

As discussed in Chapter 1, the rise of modern architecture in American schools was particularly associated with a wave of émigrés escaping Nazism and Fascism: Walter Gropius, Marcel Breuer, Ludwig Mies van der Rohe and Josep Lluis Sert. In contrast Venturi's educational experience was somewhat old-fashioned. Its predominantly Beaux Arts inspiration provided him and his fellow students with a solid if conservative education in the composition of buildings in plan and elevation.[7] In Louis Kahn, a fresh architectural talent if rather a late developer, Venturi found a mentor with the same Beaux Arts background, who was struggling to develop an architecture that went beyond the prevailing functionalism to seek a poetic content. Kahn's own brief period at the American Academy in Rome had encouraged him to focus on the development of an elemental architecture inspired by ruins. Venturi's later experience of the same city alerted him to the juxtaposition of ancient and modern, and the consequent inconsistencies of scale and use. Complementing these architectural influences was the literary analogy of William Empson's *Seven Types of Ambiguity*, source of some critical tools employed by Venturi in his analyses in *Complexity and Contradiction*.[8]

Another important influence came from contemporary American figurative art, especially Pop Art, which drew on advertising and graphic imagery to produce a more engaging alternative to the cool, impenetrable muteness of Abstract Expressionism. The celebration of popular imagery was particularly apparent in the later book *Learning from Las Vegas*, written with Denise Scott Brown after they had married. Quite apart from its intended shock effect of taking seriously a banal kind of architecture normally dismissed by architects, this book was also a hymn of praise to the sign. Venturi, Scott Brown and their co-author Steven Izenour had made a famous distinction between the 'duck' and the 'decorated shed', the 'duck' being a building that expressed its function through its form, the decorated shed a standard mute box to which identity was given by an added sign.[9] The gap between the generic building – the loft or shed – and the expressive signage of the exterior, became a significant motif in their work. It helped give priority to the hierarchical distinction between public and private realms, both in the urban context and within the building, and it

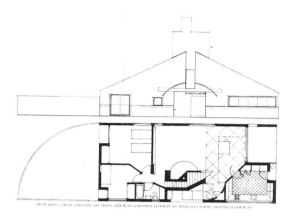

FROM ABOVE: CROSS AND LONG SECTIONS; SITE PLAN AND FIRST-FLOOR PLAN; MAIN ELEVATION; GROUND-FLOOR PLAN.

reflected a conscious separation of content from appearance. From our historical perspective it is perhaps difficult to appreciate the countercultural aspect of Venturi and Scott Brown's critique, since their teaching has since become so widely absorbed into architectural discourse. By the time *Complexity and Contradiction* was written in the mid 1960s, the contemporary forms of Modernism in architecture and Abstract Expressionism in art had been appropriated by corporate and governmental America to represent the individualism encouraged by the capitalist system, a tendency identifiable two decades earlier in the work of Eames (Chapter 1). The Venturis' sources were quite as eclectic as the Eameses', but they were not neutralised as elements in a formal system. Instead they were juxtaposed and integrated with each other, like the hybrid paintings and sculptures produced during the same period by Jasper Johns and Robert Rauschenberg. Embedded in American culture, such work was less knowingly banal than that of Andy Warhol which followed and overshadowed it. The exploitation of popular imagery by these artists was never a simple endorsement of conventional values, for in the gallery context it retained an iconoclastic and shocking edge. The same could be said of similar usage by Venturi and Scott Brown, though the architects supplemented popular imagery with ingrained academic habits left by their education and professional experience.

In the final section of *Complexity and Contradiction*, Venturi demonstrated his theories in his own design work, including the house he had built for his mother in Chestnut Hill, Pennsylvania between 1961 and 1964. The Vanna Venturi House breaks decisively with Modern Movement

attitudes by concentrating its efforts on producing an image which is recognizably that of 'house' rather than 'machine'. As Venturi wrote: '*The front, in its conventional combinations of door, windows, chimney and gable, creates an almost symbolic image of a house.*'[10] Underneath this simple form were a multitude of eclectic references. The facade derived from the grotto at Palladio's Villa Barbaro at Maser (1550s), the silhouette of its surface detail from Michelangelo's Porta Pia in Rome (1561-64). It was symmetrical but not perfectly so, and its asymmetrical fenestration recalled McKim, Mead and White's Low House in Rhode Island (1887), mentioned in *Complexity and Contradiction*. The gable was broken, referring to the Mannerist device of the split pediment, allowing it to be read as a unity or a duality, which recalls Luigi Moretti's Casa del Girasole, Rome, 1947-50, also cited in the book.[11] These layers of reference are largely resolved on the outside, but they seem to be left deliberately awkward inside, for inflections and distortions elaborate the spatial complexity of what appears at first glance a simple house. This work places Venturi in a decidedly ambivalent position. The modernist principle of spatial continuity between interior and exterior is rejected, but it is replaced not by a spatial method that is recognisably historicist, but by one that plays disjointed games with the tradition of major and minor spaces. It is unthinkable without the experience of modernism because it consciously contradicts modernist principles, in the same way that Le Corbusier's Five Points deliberately contradicted earlier tradition. The Vanna Venturi house, and larger buildings that followed, celebrated the distinction between interior and exterior, but also reflected a reading of the city as form in continuity:

Venturi's primary inspiration would seem to have come from ... the urban facades of Italy, with their endless adjustments to the counter requirements of inside and outside and their inflection with all the business of everyday life: not primarily sculptural actors in vast landscapes but complex spatial containers and definers of streets and squares.[12]

Vincent Scully's description of Venturi's general design principles seems as applicable to his work when first published in 1966 as it did a quarter of a century later with the opening of the Sainsbury Wing of the National Gallery in London.

The Sainsbury Wing

The new wing to London's National Gallery had a complex history long before Venturi and Scott Brown arrived on the scene. The Gallery occupies the north side of Trafalgar Square, one of the best known public spaces in London. The original building by William Wilkins of 1832-38 had already been extended somewhat anonymously to the rear, but with more gallery space needed the obvious place to expand was to the west, onto the so-called Hampton site, named after a furniture store destroyed during the Second World War, and since used as a car park. Besides marking the north-west corner of the square, this site also occupied the point where the urban grid changes its orientation to meet the famous street of Pall Mall. Added to the problems of this complex and difficult site was the self-sufficiency of the existing building in a symmetrical neo-classical style. The site was purchased for a future National Gallery extension in 1958. The next year a competition for a new building was organised by the *Sunday Times*, but failed to attract Government support. Two decades later, in 1981-82, a more serious competition was won by British architects Ahrends, Burton and Koralek, who were asked to develop a final design.[13] There was an element of compromise since, with Margaret Thatcher's recent ascendancy to power, it was set up as an architect/developer competition and was supposed to pay for itself by incorporating lettable office accommodation. ABK produced a revised design in 1983, but the Prince of Wales was launching his foray into architectural criticism and selected it the following year as a subject for special scorn in his Hampton Court speech, dubbing it *'a carbuncle on the face of a well-loved friend'*. [14] The design was hastily dropped and, in recognition of the contradiction at the heart of the brief, a patron was sought to fund the building. The politically influential grocery magnates of the Sainsbury family agreed to take on this role, and a new shortlist of architects was drawn up for a second competition. They were Harry Cobb of I.M. Pei, Colquhoun and Miller, Jeremy Dixon with BDP, Campbell, Zogolovitch, Wilkinson and Gough, James Stirling and Michael Wilford, and the eventual winners Venturi, Rauch and Scott Brown.[15]

The Venturi design was constrained by negative opinions gathered during years of controversy. During the stalled design process a decision was made to rebuild the site diagonally across the square called Grand Buildings, and the chosen project was externally a facsimile of its Victorian predecessor. The scale and form of the gallery's extension was required to defer to the height of William Wilkins's National Gallery (1832-38) and also to complete the corner of Trafalgar Square in a way that complemented James Gibbs's St Martin-in-the-Fields (1720-26) at the opposite side. The galleries inside were meant to provide an appropriate backdrop to the early Renaissance collection. To resolve the differing contextual requirements of square and gallery, Venturi replicated elements of Wilkins's elevation and stretched them along the elevation to the square, allowing the complexity and detail to disappear as it retreated from the main building.

Venturi's strategy is cleverer than it looks, because behind the games with columns lies a crucial shift of a troublesome corner. He moves it to a position where it can echo the south-west corner of the old building, giving it a convincing *raison d'être* framing the now symmetrical entrance to Jubilee Walk, enhancing the identity of this pedestrian street which runs through to Leicester Square. This symmetrical figure centred on a void, the street, is in direct conflict with the symmetry of the elevation of the National Gallery as a whole, a solid; but Venturi is bargaining on the fact that the elevation is so long that it is not normally looked at as a whole. Jubilee Walk has a pair of gates, and the strong sense of threshold produced at this point gets Venturi around the corner allowing him to switch to a modern glass facade, since it belongs to a different space.

Internally, the gallery floor space was divided into a series of rooms with lantern-like ceilings derived from the architecture of Sir John Soane: specifically the Dulwich Picture Gallery of 1811-14. For the main rooms of a national institution these galleries are deceptively modest, though the details of their openings and skirtings are made from Tuscan pietra serena (as used by Brunelleschi at San Lorenzo and Santo Spirito in Florence) so that the interiors offer, through their lighting and form, the illusion of a Renaissance church interior as a vaguely appropriate setting for the collection. The connection between the facade and the elevated galleries is provided by a grand staircase which ascends along the glazed wall adjacent to the National Gallery side elevation, placed parallel with the public route connecting Leicester Square and Trafalgar Square, a route straddled by the upper level rotunda bridge link between the two buildings.

5. Ahrends, Burton and Koralek's National Gallery extension project (first stage), 1982.

6. (right) Site plan of London's Trafalgar Square showing the principal gallery level of the original building on its north side, the church of St Martin-in-the-Fields to right, and the Sainsbury Wing to the left. The south end of Leicester Square is at top left.

7. Facade of the Sainsbury Wing showing the relationship of its articulation to the Wilkins facade.

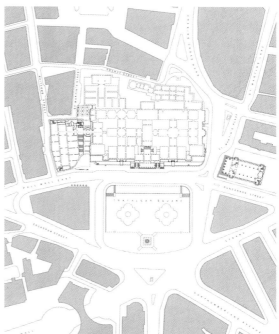

8. Section through the Sainsbury Wing showing principal gallery level and its service zone above. The grand staircases on the right connect past the mezzanine café to the entrance floor and temporary exhibition galleries in the basement.
9. (below) View of sequence of galleries.
10, 11, 12, 13. (opposite) Plans at every level, clockwise from top left, principal gallery level, mezzanine cafe level, basement plan with auditorium and temporary exhibition galleries, and entrance level.

Irony and contradiction

Three elements which seem in cold description simple and self-effacing, the facade, route and galleries, are treated by Venturi in an ironic manner. Though composed of elements taken from Wilkins's vocabulary, the facade is designed to subvert classical decorum. The smooth membrane of the wall plane is hollowed out at ground level, reducing the area of plinth on which (in classical terms) it might be deemed to sit. The openings are cleanly cut into the plane with no expression of load-bearing structure; no lintels or voussoirs. On this folded, cranked plane, concertina-like, a selection of coupled and layered pilasters and a single engaged half-column provide the vertical continuity. Wilkins's main string course is repeated by Venturi, although it and other subsidiary elements peter out before they reach the half-column. The string course supports a series of increasingly shallow blind windows. In a further twist, the large window acknowledging Canada House across Pall Mall fails to penetrate the gallery space, although this contradictory element was introduced at the behest of the curators so that attention was not distracted from the paintings. The facade also betrays other influences; for example the treatment of the ground floor loggia is similar to the curved loggia of Baldassare Peruzzi's Palazzo Massimo alle Colonne (1532-38) and Armando Brasini's colonnade at his church 'Cuore Immacolato di Maria' at Piazza Euclide (1923), both in Rome and

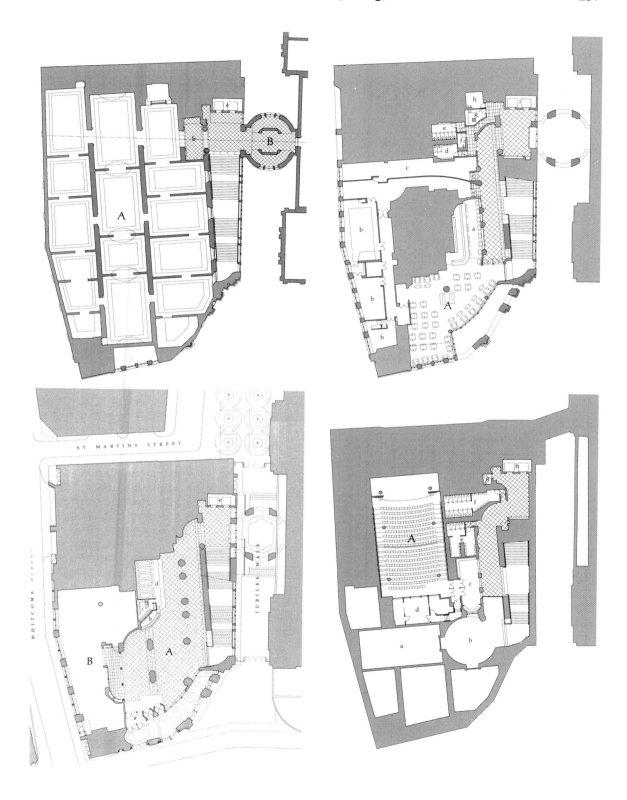

14. View towards the bridge link rotunda showing the pairing of new and old facades.

15. Glazed facade to the main stair (with a reflection of Nelson's Column), and the portico of Canada House beyond.

both cited in *Complexity and Contradiction*.[16] The galleries are far from the conventional rooms they pretend to be, often deflected by the alignment of the rooms within the site outline. Their staggered network is penetrated by a non-orthogonal vista connecting new and old galleries. This route takes the form of a *trompe l'oeil* diminishing perspective which terminates punningly on Giovanni Battista Cima da Conegliano's painting *The Incredulity of St Thomas* (1502-04). The quasi-Tuscan columns framing the view are sliced and tucked uncomfortably into the thickness of the wall, while the arches above, diminishing in height, cut at different depths into the inclined plane of the ceiling. Venturi's diminishing vista in perspective relates to a long tradition in Renaissance and Baroque architecture, but his demonstration with arched openings shows ambivalence to the theatrical convention of a willing suspension of disbelief. If the postmodern condition – mentioned in opening the previous chapter – no longer permits belief, how can there be disbelief, which is the subject of Cima's painting? Venturi underscores the paradox.

The staircase, like that in the Vanna Venturi house, widens as it ascends. It sits between an external wall which is fully if rather heavily glazed,

and an internal wall faced in the stone of the exterior and relieved with a series of windows which echo those on Wilkins's building opposite. Above, ungainly steel arches are suspended from the ceiling. These stand in many ways for the treatment of the whole building. Each element is virtually detached both in function and meaning from its context, as if to heighten its quality as decoration. This language of disengagement dominates only what could be described as the public route – the facade, stair and gallery vista – since within the galleries this architectural attention-seeking largely ceases. It is as if the new conventions of the postmodern idiom wither in comparison with the great Platonic certainties of the Renaissance. This seems to contradict Vincent Scully's assertion that Venturi's fascination with surface relates inside to outside. Rather, the surface is reduced to an independent plane indicating its own concerns, not engaging larger issues of interior and exterior context.

Venturi and Scott Brown's transposition of architectural language between private domestic sphere and public urban realm may simply reflect changing opportunities in a developing architectural career. But the similarities between the small

16. Interior of grand stair with glazed facade and a view of the Wilkins elevation.

17. View from gallery level showing suspended steel arches and internal / external windows which open from the galleries.

Vanna Venturi House and the National Gallery extension considered as a set of motifs and spatial experiences that are self-consciously unresolved are striking. While to a certain extent this suggests the creation of an artificial history, similar to the reworkings of a building often found in historic Italian environments, there is no attempt at falsification in the detailed expression. The provisional nature of the work of architecture, dependent on its context, serving conflicting formal and functional needs, not so subtly subverts the authorial claims to architectural genius.

Many properties of the Sainsbury Wing can be traced back to specific concerns seen in Venturi and Scott Brown's earlier researches. The gallery spaces, treated in a traditional way, are in the architects' terms 'generic' spaces, window-less and top-lit. Despite the support of much concealed technology to control the light level, they are essentially the type of picture-viewing space which developed in the nineteenth century from the tradition of the palazzo, in contrast to the radical alternatives attempted under the patronage of the same family by Norman Foster at the Sainsbury Centre in Norwich. The public route, connecting the street entrance to the existing promenade of

galleries at the upper level, consists of a set of distinct episodes, juxtaposed rather than seamlessly connected. These are the drum/bridge link, the false perspective view, the grand stair with its discreetly attendant lifts, the inscribed internal/external wall backing on to the rusticated wall of the ground floor lobby, and the entrance loggia which opens to the square. All occupy perimeter zones of the new structure, wrapped around a core of gallery space. The actual perimeter – the framed glass wall reflecting the original building, the brick walls to north and west (homage to the plain exterior of Soane's Dulwich Gallery) and the stone entrance facade – all contribute to the accumulation of incidents from which the story of the gallery can be deduced. The circuitous and contradictory nature of this story suggests a type of artificial history associated with the most recent of Venturi's English architectural heroes, Edwin Lutyens.[17] The same kind of fiction can be found in the relation to the parent building. The Sainsbury Wing's facade's continuation of Wilkins's motifs, synthesised from Peruzzi and Michelangelo, suggest an abandoned project for aggrandisement. The grand stair, running up the internal/external stone wall recalls the fully external

18. Detail of the articulation of the facade. Note discontinuation of the dentil course, right to left, as it retreats from the original building.
19. (opposite) Cross axial vista in diminishing perspective towards Cima da Conegliano's *The Incredulity of St Thomas*.

staircases of central Italian palazzi, such as the Palazzo Comunale in Todi, as if the staircase had later been roofed-in by the suspended steel arches and enclosed by the Miesian glass wall. The arches recall the suspended hollowed arches of Soane's own house. The discontinuities in Venturi's work, however, distinguish his adoption of classical elements from the full-blooded classicism of Quinlan Terry's Howard Building at Downing College Cambridge (1985-89) which treated a neo-classical campus dominated by original buildings (also by Wilkins) to an essay in modest English Baroque.[18]

The Sainsbury Wing in London bears a strong similarity to the Seattle Art Museum (1984-91) designed by Venturi's practice during the same period. A similar configuration of site and section is complemented at Trafalgar Square by elements which connect the building directly to its parent structure and thereby undermine its independence as a unique monument. The facade treatment, the axial connection to the main galleries, and to a certain extent the more subdued treatment of subsidiary elevations, all support the camouflaging of the new building. In contrast, the detail of cookie-cutter openings, flat pressed ironwork and Egyptian lotus capital details counteract the building's dissolution into the urban fabric, instead signalling its novel status. If this ambiguity is a conscious strategy, and no evidence suggests otherwise, the oscillation between embeddedness and isolation can be traced back to works identified in *Complexity and Contradiction*. This characteristic is evident not only in historic architecture but also in twentieth century examples cited such as the Casa del Girasole and Brasini's church at Piazza Euclide. To a modernist eye, which ignored the significance of classical elements, such buildings simply presented inconsistency rather than complexity, and Venturi's advocacy of architectural eclecticism could be mistaken for a policy of 'anything goes'.

Venturi's impact

Though it followed the publication of *Complexity and Contradiction* by no less than twenty-five years, the Sainsbury Wing presented a form of 'retroactive' manifesto for Venturi's ideas on a very public stage. Its critical reception was disdainful, especially by a British architectural audience still smarting from princely and public disapproval.[19] Venturi's architectural language, seen as both unfashionably conservative and clumsily primitive, won few followers in Britain. Within a few years, though, its strategies spread into other locations as money from the National Lottery instituted in 1993 redefined the cultural infrastructure of Britain. Ashlar stonework, monumental inscription, pseudo external grand staircase, glass skin and new use of the classical orders even featured in Norman Foster's project for the Great Court of the British Museum opened in 2000. Further north, Benson and Forsyth's design for the Museum of Scotland in Edinburgh, completed 1998, showed similarities to Venturi's work, notably in the disjunction between a modernist core and an eclectic exterior conditioned by the historical context. Venturi's building played a significant role in the redefinition of British public architecture, so that by the time new opportunities began to appear in the mid-1990s, architects had become more aware of the need for public approval. Other museum authorities in London were keen to create new images for their institutions, but turned to a younger generation of architects, to Daniel Libeskind for the yet unbuilt extension to the Victoria and Albert Museum (1996) and to Herzog and de Meuron for Tate Modern (2000). The divergence of approach and toleration of difference owe much to Venturi's undermining of a modernist orthodoxy that had lost all purpose beyond its own self-perpetuation. His admission of interest in pre twentieth-century history encouraged architects not only to enrich their work with cultural references but also to express irony, almost as a duty. He had declared in 1966 that:

The architect who would accept his role as combiner of significant old clichés – valid banalities – in new contexts as his condition within a society that directs its best efforts, its big money, and its elegant technologies elsewhere, can ironically express in this indirect way a true concern for society's inverted scale of values. [20]

EC

Notes

1. Vincent Scully in the Introduction to Venturi 1966, p. 11.
2. Venturi 1966, p. 25.
3. Scully op.cit., p. 11.
4. See Brownlee and De Long 1997, p. 72. On his return from Rome in 1956 Venturi joined Kahn's office until the establishment of his own practice the following year.
5. See Venturi and Scott Brown 2004, pp. 105-7 and 109-14.
6. See Moneo 2004, pp. 52-5.
7. For a brief discussion on the Beaux Arts method as applied in America and its influence on Kahn see Brownlee and De Long 1977, pp. 13-15. Venturi has acknowledged its influence in Venturi and Scott Brown 2004, p. 7.
8. Empson 1930. For its use by Venturi, see Venturi 1966, pp. 27-30.
9. Venturi, Scott Brown and Izenour 1972. Venturi summarised the distinction between duck and decorated shed in Venturi and Scott-Brown 2004, p. 35:
On of the most vivid ideas to evolve from our Yale/Las Vegas Studio study of the quintessential strip was our distinction between the Duck and the Decorated Shed as architectural prototypes for our time: that is, the building is itself a symbol, exemplified by the Long Island Duck, a roadside stand we made famous (Peter Blake had first made it infamous) and that is now on the National Historical Register, and the building as generic loft whose aesthetic derives from its decorative or iconographic surfaces and/or applied signs. The Decorated Shed is the essential form of an Architecture as Communication where meaning rather than expression is the quality sought, and where the aesthetic dimension derives from ornamental surface rather than from sculptural articulation.
10. Venturi 1966, p.118.
11. For the Low House and the Casa del Girasole see Venturi 1966, p. 55 and p. 11 respectively.
12. Scully op. cit., p. 12.
13. For a review of this competition see Peter Buchanan 'National Gallery Gamble' *The Architectural Review,* December 1982, pp. 19-25. A full account of the various stages in the process of achieving the final building can be found in Amery 1991.
14. The speech, the keynote of the RIBA's 150th Anniversary gala, was published in HRH The Prince of Wales 'The Hampton Court speech' *RIBA Transactions,* vol. 3, no. 2 (6), 1984, pp. 48-51.
15. The rival projects for this invited competition were published in *Architectural Design,* AD Profile: 63 *The National Gallery,* Vol. 56, no. 1/2, 1986.
16. For the Palazzo Massimo and Cuore Immacolata see Venturi 1966, p. 54 and p. 78 respectively.
17. See Robert Venturi and Denise Scott-Brown, 'Learning from Lutyens', *RIBA Journal,* Vol. 76, August 1969, pp. 353-4.
18. See Gavin Stamp, Leon Krier and John Summerson, Classics Debate, *Architects' Journal,* Vol. 187, no. 11, 16 March 1988, pp. 34-51.
19. My co-author Peter Blundell Jones wrote a critique of the winning project in *Architects' Journal,* 13 May 1987, pp. 22-26. British reviews of the completed building include: David Jenkins 'Capital gains', *Architects' Journal,* 21/28 August 1991, p. 22-33, 36-39; Robert Maxwell 'Both serious and popular: Venturi's Sainsbury Wing', *Architecture Today,* no. 20, July 1991, pp. 30-32, 35-38, 41; and Rowan Moore 'National Gallery', *The Architectural Review* July 1991, pp. 30-36.
20. Venturi 1966, p. 52.

Conclusion

A building that makes a poignant link between the earlier *Modern Architecture Through Case Studies* (Blundell Jones 2002) and this volume is the Barcelona Pavilion by Ludwig Mies van der Rohe. It was built in 1929 but soon demolished, then rose from the ashes like a phoenix to enjoy a second coming in 1986. The perfect reconstruction, adding unexpected colour, suggested how timeless the work of Mies was, particularly as its second arrival seemed to celebrate the end of the eclectic excess known as postmodernism, and the beginning of a new and more determined minimalism across the visual arts. So absolute did it seem as a piece of design that none of the new minimalist houses of the 1990s came near to challenging its supremacy, despite advances in technology, particularly that of glass, which in the original had been made as large and frameless as possible. The old trick of seeming to float on the thinnest of columns still worked, and the building appeared so modern at the turn of the twenty-first century that it served as the set for a Renault car advert, presented as a particularly chic house. For believers in modernism, it comfortably suggested a continuation of the firm course already set in the 1920s, as if the intervening heresies were temporary and could be banished, but all was not quite as it seemed.[1]

For a start there were two buildings, not one. The original pavilion was seen only by a very limited number of people. It gained its reputation through print in black and white photographs. Appearing in almost every book on modern architecture, it made Mies's international reputation. It was supremely photogenic, its lavish materials almost tangible, its sliding planes creating an aura of mystery about how one photograph could lead to another. But just as its paper reputation was being secured, both the host and the guest country of the exhibition succumbed to Fascism, so neither did Germany maintain such an image for exhibition buildings, nor would Spain have supported it. Dismantled and with its components dispersed, the Pavilion slept undisturbed in photographs for fifty years like sleeping beauty, until Hitler had shot himself in his bunker and Franco had died of old age. Sited in Spain's second city, the seat of the left-wing opposition to Franco, its resurrection in 1983-86 accompanied Spain's energetic modernisation, recovery, and reintegration into Europe. It was a homage to Mies by two men, Oriol Bohigas, the city architect, and Ignasi de Sola-Morales, the project architect; but the money would not have been forthcoming without an understanding of the building's historical significance and its potential as a tourist attraction for the festively international Barcelona.[2] It was rebuilt on the original site without any attempt to restore other

1. Ludwig Mies van der Rohe, Barcelona Pavilion, 1929, as rebuilt by Sola-Morales in 1983-86.

elements of the exhibition, so the context was completely changed. The sense of international rivalry had gone, and if the pavilion represents Germany at all, it is not today's Germany but that of the long-vanished Weimar Republic. Its purpose remains display; but today the pavilion displays itself as a cultural icon, along with its Barcelona chairs – the sample of it that is available world-wide. The pavilion has become part of a sophisticated circuit of museums and monuments that are crucial to the tourist economy. In 1929, before reliable flights, let alone the proliferation of cheap ones, such wide-spread and frequent visitation would have been unthinkable. Within the pavilion's general tourist role lies the more specialised one of pilgrimage site for architectural tourists. The building provides a short-lived confirmation for all the senses of what was first learned through print or from the pavilion's beautiful website photographs. Architects and architectural students arrive from across the world to wander and ponder over this impossible ideal for twenty minutes or half an hour, take their own photos to register a personal connection, then depart in search of other curiosities.

Total reconstruction of old buildings in every detail is rare, particularly as in the West so much value is ascribed to the persistence of physical material.[3] But the reconstruction of Mies's pavilion in new materials has actually increased the impression of timelessness by disallowing all signs of age, while improved technologies have secretly secured technically difficult details. Quite what Mies, as self-confessed believer in the *zeitgeist* and the rational use of materials, would have made of this contrivance in denial of change can only be guessed at, but the calm continuity between the two incarnations of his building would surely have fulfilled his stated desire to *'bring a little order into the desperate confusion of our time',* and it is hard to believe that his bid for monumentality was anything but intentional.

Many great works of architecture in the past have fulfilled this role, particularly tombs and temples, not only providing mnemonics for socially important beliefs and rituals, but also helping to sustain the impression that at least something in this fast changing world remains the same. Yet observe how, in the postmodern reading of this modern work given above,[4] the framing, associations, social purpose and angle of view have changed dramatically between the first incarnation and the second, while all the time supporting the illusion that the monument has stayed the same.

Political, economic and social changes

This bid for constancy stood against a background of changes in politics and society more profound and extensive than at any earlier period in history. Having lived through the ravages and uncertainties of the Second World War, the designers and inhabitants of buildings in this book experienced a redrawing of the world map divided by the Iron Curtain. There followed half a century of Cold War between the superpowers, with an uneasy balance between state socialism and free-market capitalism, and although our examples are all situated on one side of that divide, the influence of socialist ideology permeated works by several of the architects, including van Eyck, the Smithsons, Erskine, De Carlo, Rogers and Rossi.

Before 1980, the majority of architects was publicly at least left-leaning, taking for granted the virtues of the welfare state and the need for state-sponsored sharing of social resources. This was often accompanied by a belief that the buildings belonging to such a system should be relatively modest, efficient, and un-rhetorical. The subsequent deterioration of social institutions in the West under the onslaught of market values may account for the comparative individualism of the later examples in the book. Their freedom of expression shows a toleration of difference and an equality of competing positions which is still visible in the diversity of architectural language on offer to the contemporary practitioner.

Economically, there was a slow period of recovery after 1945, but this did allow the implementation of some Utopian projects which had been unrealisable before the war, such as Le Corbusier's Unité d'habitation in Marseilles. In the 1950s and 1960s rapid economic recovery allowed widespread rebuilding and much architectural experiment, but by the late 1960s doubt had set in, as technical failures proliferated and the formulaic nature of orthodox modernism became publicly evident. Doubts about architectural direction were compounded by the energy crisis of 1973 and by the industrial unrest of a period of recession, leaving architects time to think and to regroup. By the time the next economic boom arrived in the 1980s, the stylistic release of postmodernism was in full swing, but the euphoria was again short-lived, as the 1980s ended in recession. Economic boom and bust has meant lack of continuity, and produced marked differences in architectural style and production.

Developing technology

The effect of technological changes on the architecture of the second half of the twentieth century seems at first less marked than in the first, as nothing appears so stark as the style change of the 1920s. But as discussed in the conclusion to Blundell Jones 2002, there was a post-war consolidation of the whole modernist vocabulary and its rationale. Modernist details became technically realisable, and some, like Norman Foster's frameless glazing (Chapter 12) advanced to open new avenues of possibility. Deep plan, flexible, multi-storey buildings became the urban norm, and high land values made them economically compulsory. As hand-work gave way to machine production and transport improved, increasingly well-serviced buildings were assembled out of international components, eroding all necessary connections with place. Meanwhile the city gave way completely to the motor car, which took over its streets, sterilised its squares with parking, and spread its suburbs far and wide. The gradual takeover of car usage for all activities has radically changed the experience of the city, our relationships with buildings, and the nature of the public realm. As if that were not change enough, electronic communication has brought about a further shift in consciousness: a virtual public life shared first through television and then on the internet, which intrudes increasingly into the real world to redefine social relations. Perhaps less obvious than any of the above, but equally insidious for architecture, are changes of bureuacracy and procurement. They have radically affected decisions about how buildings should be organised and should look, removing such matters further from the user as well as undermining the power of the architect.

Shifting paradigms

Against this background of change and development, architecture has passed through two major paradigm shifts (the term 'paradigm shift' was coined by Thomas Kuhn in his *Structure of Scientific Revolutions* to indicate the point in a discipline at which a major restructuring of belief occurs, as for example when Einstein displaced Newton).[5] The first one in the 1920s marked the establishment of modernism, while the other occurred around 1968-73, the centre of the time span covered by this book. The two shifts are complimentary in the sense that the second was a reaction to the first, and while modernism was reductive,

postmodernism was expansive. Following the carnage of the First World War, modernism saw the first wave of social and technological changes as a liberation to be celebrated with Utopian proposals. New materials and mass-production methods, the car, the aeroplane, and science, were to be welcomed with open arms, while old institutions like the monarchy and aristocracy could painlessly be forgotten, their hierarchical expression repressed along with the manners and monuments that bore it. The authors of the Weissenhofsiedlung, who already pursued different ideological paths (Blundell Jones 2002, Ch.1), willingly submitted to the idea of a common front, accepting the formal consistency that made possible the idea of an international style. The cracks were papered over as the new world of appearances and the new psuedo-scientific ideology developed hand in hand until the one was accepted as synonymous with the other. Adoption of the party line was remarkably consistent. If Hannes Meyer marked the extreme with his manifesto *bauen* at the Bauhaus in 1928, which declared confidently that there are twelve and only twelve functions in designing a house,[6] a similar line was taken by much gentler architects. Reports on the teaching of Gunnar Asplund in the 1930s, for example, suggest a stress on technical and functional arguments but little discussion of the attitudes to history and context now considered to be the key to his work.[7] With such a talented figure one might expect the art to run ahead of the ability to describe and analyse it, but he was limited too by conformity to a quasi-scientific world-view that tended to exclude the aesthetic (undefinable), the expressive (personal), and the historical (the styles), as mere irrational superstition.[8] They were not simply jettisoned but ceased to be proper subjects for discussion. A conspiracy of silence arose about them that persisted until about 1970.

This limitation of the discussion had three consequences. First, everything had to be justified in strictly functional and rational terms, whether by the principal in practice speaking to a client or by the student at architectural school presenting at a 'crit'.[9] Second, as a result, a curious gap emerged between what architects said and what they did. A surprising number of instances of this have emerged in this book, but Eiermann's Brussels Pavilion (Chapter 2) will suffice as an example. The constructive rationality claimed was not merely belied by the obvious rhetorical purpose of the building: it was actually contradicted by the constructional headstands required to achieve the all-important impression of purity. The third and most devastating consequence of limiting the discussion was that it was possible for students and assistants to take the discussed part as the whole and to enact it literally, creating a banal form of functionalism or rationalism. This produced the dull and inadequate architecture that gave orthodox modernism a bad name and precipitated its demise. Lip-service was paid to the idea that form should follow function, but in practice form tended to follow the disciplines of construction, allied to a growing obsession with systems and mass-production for which Centre Pompidou (Chapter 14) finally provided the poetic figurehead, poised between the end of the old paradigm and the beginning of the new. The widespread belief in the need to cater for unpredictably changing uses even completetly undermined the idea of responding to specific functions, giving rise to uniform multi-purpose buildings expressive of nothing beyond their own technological logic. Techniques became ubiquitous and international, while repetition was cheap and easy, allowing less work at the drawing board and less trouble for the manufacturer. Buildings placed object-like on open sites left aside considerations of the local, of the surrounding city or country, therefore precluding all sense of place. In defiance of history and precedent, such buildings were also cut off from time and memory. Lucien Kroll aptly calls them 'autistic', and they were the butt of Rolf Keller's savage attack *Bauen als Umweltzerstörung* (Building as Pollution) of 1973, an early but still-pertinent lament about how we are destroying our environment.

Postmodernism strikes

The second paradigm shift of 1968-73 has been called the postmodernist revolution, but the word 'postmodern' defines it only in terms of what was displaced, for even in 2006 we cannot identify a single new tendency that displaces the 'modern', particularly when so many of the effects of modernity are irreversible. There is a symmetry between the two paradigm shifts, however, in the sense that because the first was essentially reductive, a supposed contraction to essentials, the second was necessarily expansive. The defeat of modernist orthodoxy led to an opening up of forbidden territories, a speaking of the unspoken, an end to the conspiracy of silence. Team Ten led the way in the 1950s, with their concern for

the city and history, and their rejection of the zoning strategies that had been the focal point of the Charter of Athens (Chapter 5, Chapter 13). One of their members, Aldo van Eyck (Chapter 3), marked a major shift of attitude when he substituted 'place and occasion' for 'space and time' in defiance of Giedion.[10] Both place and occasion are specific, no longer general and universal, and they carry the implication that there should be many occasions and different places: also implied therefore are layering, memory, history.

History had never really disappeared under the modernist paradigm, as tacit continuities in the works of many leading modernists showed.[11] The kind of interplay between historic buildings and modern additions that had been pioneered by Asplund at the Gothenburg Lawcourts of 1937 (Blundell Jones 2002, Ch. 13) was taken up anew by several architects in this volume. They include Gottfried Böhm (Chapter 4), Carlo Scarpa (Chapter 9), Giancarlo De Carlo (Chapter 13) and Karljosef Schattner (Chapter 17). Each case is highly specific, and all were in their time controversial, but the approach now seems well established, with the general rules that there must be deep historical research, selective editing, and clear contrast. In translating old buildings to new uses there is always loss, but some continuity of memory is maintained, and a creative reinterpretation opens a dialogue between the present and the past. The architect is obliged to engage with the place, and to regard his or her task as adding yet another contribution to the palimpsest, that layering of blurred messages, of one system of order upon another, that constitutes the form of nearly every old town.

Return of historical quotation

The readoption of historical features for new buildings is quite another matter. In the paradigm shift of 1968-73, history regained a more explicit value and a new lease of life. A historical revival waiting in the wings at the modernist defeat led to a burst of anachronism proclaimed as a return to the tried and tested rules of classicism after the 'mistake' of modernism. Monuments to this tendency are Quinlan Terry's Richmond Riverside of 1989, a commercial office redevelopment made to look like a historic townscape around 150 years old, and Poundbury, a suburb of Dorchester actually commissioned by the Prince of Wales, with planning advice from Leon Krier.[12] For architects less obsessed with history than these full revivalists, the modernist taboo on reproducing anything that even looked like the past proved hard to break. So although the postmodern revolution re-legitimised borrowing from 'the styles', the sudden and enthusiastic readoption in the 1970s and 1980s of column orders and arches, of rustication and giant keystones, revealed the ignorance of architects not equipped by their education to play such games, and the novelty soon wore off. The revalidation of history as a source also meant that modern architecture itself became a victim to be pillaged and reinterpreted, and the New York Five made their names in the 1970s by recycling the compositional substance of villas by Le Corbusier, Terragni and others.[13] Few managed to mix antique style elements successfully with modern ones, the great exception being James Stirling with his playful Stuttgart Staatsgalerie (postscript, Chapter 6), whose very success assures immortality in the histories while imprisoning the work in the 1980s. If anachronism was to be avoided, historical borrowing had to be played ironically, as Robert Venturi had predicted with his plea for *Complexity and Contradiction* of 1966, and demonstrated with panache in his and Denise Scott Brown's contribution to London's National Gallery (Chapter 18) which takes that tendency to its logical conclusion.

Return to monumentality

Orthodox modernism had claimed to be anti-monumental,[14] though as we have seen with the example of the Barcelona Pavilion, this was tacitly contradicted. It was the monumentality of antique buildings that launched the late-modernist Louis Kahn on his career as a major architect starting in the 1950s (Blundell Jones 2002, Ch. 16). He managed to evoke a sense of the archetypal partly through the use of elementary geometric forms at large scale, and partly through expressed load-bearing construction. These elemental works seemed timeless perhaps because they were like ruins. Aldo Rossi arrived later on the scene with less interest in materials but an equal fascination for archetypes and for geometric forms as signs of the eternal (Chapter 15). If his projects reminded architects of the importance of the monument, they also showed ways in which the pointed roof and the hole-in-the-wall window could be reintroduced without looking old-fashioned. The vogue Rossi's work enjoyed in the 1980s must rest partly on the extent to which it was transmissable by drawings

and seemed temptingly imitable, and clearly Rossi had touched some nerves: both the archetype and concern for the city. Unfortunately the promised road turned out a cul-de-sac, for Rossi had made the extreme case and there was nothing much more to say. Simple repetition of the simple forms from his work was not enough, and adding elaboration deprived them of their power.

The repressed sins of modernism

Rossi's rediscovery of the archetype offered a radical alternative to the philosophy of 'form follows function': indeed his starting point was the victory of form over function, noting the way that the same form could persist through several uses, as if the uses did not matter. After 1970 functionalism became almost a dirty word, rejected in disciplines like anthropology as symptomatic of the positivist shortcut which precluded deeper interpretation, and castigated in architecture as the primary cause of the orthodox modernist malaise. Under postmodernism it had to be avoided, producing a new conspiracy of silence, this time about the relationship between buildings and use. Many leading architects tried to do without it, rejecting programmatic readings of their and others' work. James Stirling's career shows the reversal, since he produced a strongly functionalist work at Leicester with Gowan, but went on to produce an equally anti-functionalist one at Stuttgart after it (both Chapter 6). Although some commentators have tried retrospectively to save Leicester from the curse of functionalism,[15] there is no doubt about the articulation of the parts of the programme or the sincere attempt to generate a rhetoric expressive of the purpose of the building, an *architecture parlante*. Programmatic readings of buildings can scarcely be avoided once it is accepted that this is not a narrow question of convenience, but a deeper one of meaning and identity. In a world where institutions are reflected in building types, we soon recognise the organisation and its spatial hierarchies, and the conventional identity of domestic spaces is so ingrained that we can read the layouts of each others' houses and obey the social rules on a first visit.[16] Even a building like Centre Pompidou gains a legible hierachy of departments the moment its floors are occupied, despite this spatial identity having been unseen and unintended by the architects. But when architects take the opportunity to reinforce the social order with that of the building, the effect can be compelling. Aldo van Eyck's reflection of the 'family' structure in his orphanage was such an essential act of territorial definition that the building is unthinkable without it.[17]

The postmodern revolution also brought a reaction against the expression of materials and construction. The badly weathered excesses of brutalism, and the banality of orthodox modernist works driven merely by construction, led to rejection of the very principle; yet a work like Lewerentz's St Peter's Church, Klippan, of 1963 (Blundell Jones 2002, Ch. 15) demonstrates the poetic power of rethinking constructional principles. It became the touchstone for a whole series of new buildings around the turn of the millennium.[18] Even the change of a few details can affect whole generations of later buildings, as Foster showed with the glazing at Ipswich (Chapter 12). Equally, the generation of new forms through exploiting new engineering possibilities carries its own aesthetic rewards, as demonstrated by the roofs of the Munich Olympic Complex (Chapter 8). The difficulty of defining pure expressed construction, due to the inevitable process of selection involved, does not invalidate an idea deeply entrenched in architectural history and in that of vernacular construction, where the elaboration produced by craftsmen at play was the main source of rhetoric. The grandchildren of these craftsmen were recently still at work, negotiating their tasks with architects like Scarpa and Schattner (Chapters 9, 17). Architecture can hardly avoid involvement in a debate about its own construction. In contrast, the idea that 'anything goes', combined with the presence of a limitless material vocabulary to be applied at will like wallpaper, has left many postmodernist designers rudderless, their work shallow and whimsical.

City, territory, and place

The modernist compulsion to regard buildings as self-sufficient entitites detached from their context stemmed partly from the complete change in style that they wanted to proclaim, but it also met other demands. The takeover of the motor car has meant a drop in urban density, the domination of highway engineering criteria in replanning of cities, and the wastage of whole city blocks for parking. The widely held belief in the benefits of sunlight and air prompted the choice of open suburban sites, and this also allowed space for modernist master planning, the juxtaposition of a well-placed series of objects in a harmonious composition, as with the Bauhaus complex (Blundell Jones 2002, Ch. 3, see

especially the aerial photograph). The presentation of modernist works through photographs and print even tended to play down the context when the work in question was cleverly integrated, as with Mendelsohn's Schocken Store in Stuttgart (Blundell Jones 2002, Ch. 6). In the case of an architect like Mies, detachment was an article of faith. A carefully limited attitude to the engagement of context both allowed the pursuit of universal types and constrained the extent of the 'problem', allowing a pure and ideal 'solution' to be proposed, unsullied by the dirty reality of the growing city and its constant property battles. Ironically, such total and deliberate detachment has often proved more successful in its naked monumentality than attempts at integration which failed due to the context remaining unfulfilled or being later violated.[19]

From open site to city

Leafing through almost any architectural book or magazine from the 1950s and 1960s, the creation of architectural works as free-standing entities is the overwhelming impression. New British schools, for example, seem mostly to have been built on the edges of towns and villages so that they could enjoy large open spaces for recreation, and green space seems to have been held in high esteem regardless of its actual usefulness.[20] The buildings in the first three chapters of this book are typical of this tendency in different ways. The Eames house (Chapter 1), built on what was then the edge of Los Angeles, enjoyed an idyllic site of natural wildflower meadow with views of the ocean beyond, a 'natural' environment only made possible by commuting with the motor car. Eiermann's Brussels Pavilion (Chapter 2) was set up in a mature park with enough greenery between it and its neighbours to allow autonomy, demonstrating the ideal modernist city as a sequence of beautiful objects set in a continuous garden. Also typical of the time was the choice of an edge of city site for van Eyck's orphanage (Chapter 3), leaving it without real neighbours, marooned between stadium and airport. Only on reaching Chapter 4 is the city re-engaged, with Böhm's attempt to put the heart back into Bensberg by taking on its ancient castle. This new/old contextual theme re-emerged with the works in Chapters 9, 13 and 17. With the Economist Building (Chapter 5) a dense site in central London gains a new building interacting with its context, with the novel idea of giving part of the site back to the public as a small-scale pedestrian network. The contemporary fascination of the Smithsons' project lay, besides its role as a compositional base for the articulated programme, in the public use of the plaza. Adding to the excitement was the positive way it separated vehicles and pedestrians, in contrast with the bland and mechanistic underpasses then proliferating. The Smithsons had been fascinated by the idea of 'streets in the air' since the early 1950s, and their project for the Haupstadt Berlin Competition of 1958 envisioned a two-level city. Repetition of the Economist idea promised to bring this about fragment by fragment within the existing city. Some life might then have accrued to it, but this Team Ten dream remained largely unfulfilled, for it depended excessively on a purely scenographic interpretation of the city.

Life and the modernist city

The greatest success of Centre Pompidou (Chapter 14) when it opened in the 1970s was the evident and vigorous life of the public square next to it, which suddenly fulfilled many architects' dreams about a truly animated city. Creating a large protected area in the middle of a very dense city with plenty of social hinterland, and filling one side of it with a range of cultural goodies, was bound to attract people. But all the same, Piano and Rogers were regarded as having worked some kind of magic. Architects were getting nostalgic about the street life of Venice or the annual enactment of the Palio in Sienna,[21] and it was all too easy to confuse the celebration of tourism and proliferation of souvenir market stalls with the ancient public exchanges of an old city. But Venice would die if the tourists left, while the Palio no longer serves primarily to define the citizen's identity with his or her quarter. The idea that the whole citizenry might assemble in one place to make democratic decisions or to partake in theatrical rituals as occurred in ancient Athens has also long been impossible, even if the memory or idea of such occasions continues to impress us. Even the comforting illusion of the local food market is largely an anachonism in an economy dominated by chain businesses and international production. The question of what the public realm is or could be physically has seemed increasingly urgent as we have witnessed the erosion of its old forms, yet there are no easy answers.

The sins of the autistic object building and the negation of the street were also addressed in the changed architectural atmosphere of the 1970s,

notably by Foster's Willis Faber & Dumas (Chapter 12). But although the building respected the shape of the plot and offered a new kind of urban continuity, it still reflected the possession of a single large company behind its black castle-like facade, and its visual relation with the street asymmetrically presumed a right to mirror the neighbours while precluding the neighbours' right to mirror it. At that stage any sort of engagement with the context was an advance, as was any admission that the pre existing should be taken into account.

Modernist master-plans for cities had tended to assume total unbridled control and a static total organisation, but experience of existing cities suggested the opposite: a complex play of forces constantly in flux, the city as collage,[22] in which new interventions must engage in a dialogue with what is there already. Giancarlo De Carlo (Chapter 13) had recognised this early in taking on the moribund fabric of Urbino in the 1950s, and in his subsequent development of techniques for 'reading the territory'. The smaller scale juxtapositions of Carlo Scarpa (Chapter 9) were equally place-bound, and Karljosef Schattner (Chapter 17) showed how a series of interventions could be knitted in to a historic place, maintaining both its scale and its uniqueness. The buildings by Eisenman (Chapter 16) and Venturi (Chapter 18) are also in different ways place-specific, for both are cued into their sites. The tell-tale tests for such belongingness are whether the building could do equally well elsewhere, and whether the place would do as well without it.

Participation versus global capitalism

Having been a pioneer in reading the territory, it is scarcely surprising that De Carlo also became a pioneer of participation,[23] along with Lucien Kroll and Ralph Erskine (Chapters 10, 11). Participation transfers the responsive attitude from the fabric to the inhabitants; their needs, wishes, and beliefs. It had been presumed by naive functionalists that certain modes of organisation would force people to behave in certain ways, but seldom is architecture coercive. Generally it must work in complicity with its users, who need to understand the role it is suggesting and use it accordingly, both in practice and in bestowing or receiving meaning. When people were able to build for themselves, the feedback between beliefs or practices and built form was more or less automatic, and architecture closely reflected society. But with ever-increasing specialisation, bureaucratisation and architecture's tendency towards autism, people have come to feel alienated by buildings, and even indifferent. The discussion therefore had to be reopened. Erskine's dialogue with the inhabitants at Byker (Chapter 11), despite its limitations, produced both a more humane housing scheme and a greater sense of belonging. Lucien Kroll's controversial Mémé (Chapter 10) went further by providing an alternative and anarchic image which showed up by contrast the narrow and repetitive conformity of the building types then provided by the state. Other participative architects, particularly Peter Hübner in Germany, who has been active in this field since the early 1980s and is still building, have confirmed the extraordinarily liberating effect of allowing people creative involvement in the making of their own buildings. Such architects have also shown how this kind of involvement can generate a permanent sense of commitment which is passed on to later users.[24]

But real participation is rare, and tends to be a local matter relying on face-to-face contact, usually devoid of serious money. The participative process satisfies everyday needs of little interest to the international media, and the messy images that result are the opposite of fashionable. Meanwhile High Architecture, the province of awards, publications and academic discourse, has been taken over increasingly by architecture for architecture's sake. The fall of the Berlin Wall in 1989, the subsequent reunification of Germany, and the collapse of the Soviet Union, mark the end of the period covered by this book, and we can already see these events as the pivot of a geopolitical shift. The disintegration of the Iron Curtain led to the expansion of market values across the European continent, and also to ethnic conflicts in the Balkans, which called the drift towards European integration into question. The Kuwait War of 1991 marked the emergence of conflict about Western influence in the Islamic world. Architecture represents this process of globalisation through the spread of Western models, a process exacerbated by the enormous power of media and information made possible by electronic communication and controlled by the amoral hand of big business, which long ago discovered that it is easier to control the market by manipulating images than by merely supplying what people need. Under the influence of global capitalism, the value of place and cultural identity associated with some of our examples has given way to the hegemony of the signature architect, identified in each case with a particular vocabulary of preferred forms, and commissioned to present a personal cultural cachet in various situations across the globe. Prestige buildings are now 'icons'. They exert their main impact not through experience of use but through mediated images in magazines and on computers, and are therefore likely to be designed more for the sake of producing these images than for the comfort or convenience of users. Since the market relies on built-in obsolescence, the fashion must change regardless of usefulness, rendering last-year's model superfluous. Ideas from High Architecture may trickle down into the realm of the everyday, but they must by definition already be *passé* to provoke the envy that is the engine of the economy. They can therefore hardly present a stable or enduring model. The planet simply cannot sustain endless reconstruction: a more sober course awaits us.

PBJ/EC

Notes

1. See Torrent 1987.

2. See Sola-Morales 1986.

3. The extraordinary exception is the Ise shrine at Kyoto in Japan, which is rebuilt in identical form from new materials every 25 years, with twin sites so that the new one can be finished before the old one is demolished.

4. Postmodernism as a philosophy (not as a style) has meant an acknowledgement of cultural context, of the necessary role of the reader alongside that of the author, of the relativity of cultures and the difficulty of establishing any transcendent values: of the idea that realities are social constructs.

5. Kuhn 1962.

6. Hannes Meyer, '*Building*', reproduced in translation in Conrads 1970, pp. 117-20.

7. This is discussed in Blundell Jones 2006, ch. 8, mainly derived from evidence in Engfors 1990.

8. Asplund had been the main author of the Stockholm Exhibition which launched Funkis (Functionalism) in 1930 and a major contributor to *Acceptera*, the Swedish functionalist manifesto, so he naturally represented the party line.

9. John Sergeant still recalls with pain an occasion in the 1960s when a fellow student at the Bartlett in London presented some work in front of a famous sociologist, describing how sunbeams reflected by the adjacent pond would dance on the ceiling. *'Have you any evidence that this gives pleasure?'* she asked, and the student was crushed.

10. It was an intentional reference to the title of Giedion's most famous book *Space Time and Architecture*.

11. Blundell Jones 2002, passim.

12. For a critique of Richmond Riverside see Peter Blundell Jones 'Richmond Riverside: Sugaring the Pill' in *The Architectural Review* November 1988, pp. 86-90. For Poundbury see *Architects Journal* 3 July 2003.

13. See Arthur Drexler, Colin Rowe, and Kenneth Frampton, *Five Architects: Eisenman, Graves, Gwathmey, Hejduk, Meier*, Witterborn & Co, New York, 1972.

14. A new recognition of monumentality arose in 1960s' Britain with the row over the demolition of the Euston Arch and appearance of Theo Crosby's book *The Necessary Monument*.

15. See Peter Eisenman 'Real and English: the Destruction of the Box' *Oppositions,* October 1974, pp. 5-34.

16. Markus 1993, Jormakka 1995, Blundell Jones 1999, pp.150-62.

17. This followed precedents much older than the Modern Movement. Both the articulation of parts and their hierarchical organisation into a whole are architectural habits familiar from vernacular and indigenous architectures, besides being strongly present in the Gothic and in industrial buildings. The reflection of programme in a building form is therefore of perpetual interest in architecture, and the postmodern reaction against it has meant an unnecessary impoverishment.

18. For example, the thermal baths at Vaals, Switzerland, by Peter Zumthor, and the Wallsall art gallery, UK, by Caruso and St John.

19. We have to admit that this is the case at Berlin's Kulturforum, where Hans Scharoun's master-planning ideas were never fulfilled and have been since much traduced. The Philharmonie still floats uncomfortably, while Mies's adjacent gallery, which declared no neighbourly allegiances, remains indifferent to them when they change. The problem of non-fulfilment affects many projects. Erskine's Byker Wall (Chapter 11) was intended to screen off a motorway that was never built.

20. See Saint 1987.

21. The Palio is an annual horse race held in the central square of Siena, where representatives of the city quarters compete.

22. 'Collage City' was the title of an influential book published in 1978 by Colin Rowe and Fred Koetter.

23. De Carlo's lecture *Architecture's Public* of 1969 is still a great milestone in participation theory as well as providing a swingeing critique of modernist indifference to inhabitants. It was first published in Italian with a poor English translation in the journal *Parametro*, no. 3/4, 1970, but is available in an improved translation in Blundell Jones, Petrescu and Till 2005, pp. 3-22.

24. See Peter Blundell Jones, *Peter Hübner: Architecture as Social Process*, Edition Axel Menges, Stuttgart and London, 2007 forthcoming.

Bibliography

Adjmi, Morris, and **Bertolotto**, Giovanni (eds), *Aldo Rossi, Drawings and Paintings,* Princeton Architectural Press, New York, 1993.

Alberti, Leon Battista, *The Ten Books of Architecture*: the 1755 Leoni Edition, Dover Books, 1986.

Albrecht, Donald, (ed.), *The Work of Charles and Ray Eames: A Legacy of Invention,* Harry N. Abrams, New York 1997.

Amery, Colin, *A Celebration of Art and Architecture,* National Gallery, London, 1991.

Appleyard, Bryan, *Richard Rogers: a Biography,* Faber & Faber, London, 1986.

Aragon, Louis, *Paris Peasant,* Exact Change, Boston, 1994.

Arnell, Peter and **Bickford,** Ted (eds.), *A Center for the Visual Arts: The Ohio State University Competition,* Rizzoli, New York, 1984.

Asplund, Gunnar, **Gahn**, Wolter, **Markelius,** Sven, **Paulsson,** Gregor, **Sundahl,** Eskil and **Åhrén,** Uno, *Acceptera* Tiden, Stockholm, 1931, facsimile reprint, Berlings, Arlöv, 1980.

Augé, Marc. *Non-places: introduction to an anthropology of supermodernity*, Verso, London and New York, 1995.

Bachelard, Gaston, *The Poetics of Space,* Beacon Press, Boston, 1969.

Baird, George and **Jencks,** Charles, *Meaning in Architecture,* London, 1969.

Banham, Peter Reyner, *The New Brutalism,* Architectural Press, London, 1966.

Bayer, Herbert, **Gropius,** Walter and **Gropius,** Ise, *Bauhaus 1919 -1928,* The Museum of Modern Art, New York, 1938.

Bedard, Jean-François (ed.), *Cities of Artificial Excavation: The Work of Peter Eisenman 1978 -1988,* Rizzoli, New York, 1994.

Behnisch & Partners, *Behnisch & Partner Bauten 1952-1992*, exhibition catalogue, Galerie der Stadt Stuttgart, Hatje, Stuttgart, 1992.

Beltramini, Guido, **Forster,** Kurt W, and **Marini,** Paola (eds) *Carlo Scarpa Mostre e Musei 1944-1976,* Case e Paesaggi 1972-1978, Electa, Milan, 2000.

Blundell Jones, Peter, *Hans Scharoun,* Gordon Fraser, London, 1978.

Blundell Jones, Peter, 'Theodor Fischer', *Architects Journal*, 12 April 1989, pp. 38-55, (general article).

Blundell Jones, Peter, *Hans Scharoun,* Phaidon, London, 1995.

Blundell Jones, Peter, *Hugo Häring: the Organic versus the Geometric*, Edition Axel Menges, Stuttgart, 1999.

Blundell Jones, Peter, *Günter Behnisch,* Birkhäuser, London, 2000.

Blundell Jones, Peter, *Modern Architecture through Case Studies,* Architectural Press, Oxford, 2002.

Blundell Jones, Peter, *Gunnar Asplund,* Phaidon, London, 2006.

Blundell Jones, Peter, **Petrescu,** Doina, and **Till,** Jeremy, *Architecture and Participation*, Spon Press, Abingdon, 2005.

Bottoni, Pietro, *Antologia di Edifici Moderni in Milano,* Editoriale Domus, Milan, 1954.

Brownlee, David B. and **De Long**, David G., *Louis I. Kahn: In The Realm of Architecture,* Thames & Hudson, London, 1997.

Brunetti, Federico, *La Torre Velasca,* Alinea, Florence, 1996.

Bucci, Federico and **Mulazzani,** Marco, *Luigi Moretti: Works and Writings,* Princeton Architectural Press, New York, 2002.

Canniffe, Eamonn, *Urban Ethic: Design in the Contemporary City,* Routledge, London and New York, 2006.

Chermayeff, Serge and **Alexander**, Christopher, *Community and Privacy: Toward a New Architecture of Humanism* Doubleday, New York, and Penguin, Harmondsworth, 1963.

Clarke David B. (ed.), *The Cinematic City*, Routledge, London 1997.

Collymore, Peter, *The Architecture of Ralph Erskine,* Academy Editions, London, 1994 (first edition by Architext 1982).

Colomina, Beatriz, *Privacy and Publicity: Modern Architecture as Mass Media,* MIT Press, London and Cambridge, MA, 1994.

Colomina, Beatriz, **Brennan,** Annmarie, and **Kim,** Jeannie (eds), *Cold War Hothouses: Inventing Postwar Culture from Cockpit to Playboy,* Princeton Architectural Press, New York, 2004.

Comte de Lautréamont (Isidore Ducasse), *Les Chants de Maldoror*, 1868-69.

Conrads, Ulrich *Programmes and Manifestoes of Twentieth Century Architecture*, Lund Humphries, London, 1970.

Conrads, Ulrich, **Sack,** Manfred, and **Kühne,** Günther, (eds) *Karljosef Schattner,* Monograph in Reissbrett series no. 2, Schriftenreihe der Bauwelt, Vieweg, Berlin/Braunschweig, 1983.

Costa, Xavier, and **Hartray**, Guido, (eds), *Sert: arquitecto en Nueva York,* Museu d'Art Contemporani de Barcelona /ACTAR, Barcelona, 1997.

Crosby, Theo, *The Necessary Monument,* Studio Vista, London, 1970.

Dal Co, Francesco and **Mazzariol,** Giuseppe, *Carlo Scarpa The Complete Works,* Electa, Milan / Rizzoli, New York, 1985.

Darius, Veronika, *Der Architekt Gottfried Böhm: Bauten der sechziger Jahre,* Beton Verlag, Düsseldorf, 1988.

Davies, Colin *Hopkins: the work of Michael Hopkins and Partners,* Phaidon, London, 1993.

Demetrios, Eames, *An Eames Primer,* Thames & Hudson, London, 2001.

Douglas, Mary, *Purity and Danger,* Routledge & Kegan Paul, London, 1966.

Drexler, Arthur, *Five Architects: Eisenman, Graves, Gwathmey, Hejduk, Meier,* Oxford University Press, New York, 1975.

Durand, Jean-Nicolas-Louis, *Precis des lecons d' architecture donnees a l' Ecole Polytechnique,* 2 vols., Paris, 1802-05.

Dutton, John A., *New American Urbanism: Re-forming the Suburban Metropolis,* Skira, Milan, 2000.

Eiermann, Egon, *Briefe des Architekten 1946-1970* (Letters), Deutsche Verlags-Anstalt, Stuttgart, 1994.

Eisenman, Peter, *House X,* Rizzoli, New York, 1982.

Eisenman, Peter, *Houses of Cards,* Oxford University Press, New York and Oxford, 1987.

Eisenman, Peter, *Giuseppe Terragni: Transformations, Decompositions,* Critiques, Monacelli Press, New York, 2003.

Ellin, Nan, *Postmodern Urbanism,* Architectural Press, New York, 1996.

Empson, William, *Seven Types of Ambiguity* Chatto & Windus, London, 1930.

Engfors, Christina, (ed.), *E. G. Asplund, architect friend and colleague,* Arkitektur Förlag, Stockholm, 1990 (collected interviews with Asplund's assistants, associates and family).

Fierro, Annette, *The Glass State: The Technology of the Spectacle, Paris 1981-1998,* MIT Press, Cambridge MA and London 2003.

Flagge, Ingeborg (ed.), *Helmut Striffler - Licht, Raum, Kunst: eine Ortsbestimmung,* catalogue of an exhibition at the Städtische Kunsthalle Mannheim, Karl Krämer, Stuttgart,1987.

Foot, John, *Milan since the Miracle: City, Culture and Identity,* Berg, Oxford and New York, 2001.

Forster, Kurt W. et al., *Peter Eisenman: Il Giardino dei Passi Perduti / The Garden of Lost Footsteps,* Marsilio, Venice, 2004.

Foster, Hal (ed.), *Postmodern Culture,* Pluto Press, London and Sydney, 1985.

Frampton, Kenneth (ed.), *Aldo Rossi in America, 1976-79,* Institute for Architecture and Urban Studies, New York, 1979.

Frampton, Kenneth, *Modern Architecture: a Critical History,* Thames & Hudson, London, 1985 (1st Edition 1980).

Frampton, Kenneth (ed. John Cava), *Studies in Tectonic Culture: the poetics of construction in nineteenth and twentieth century architecture,* M.I.T. Press, Cambridge, MA, and London, 1995.

Fraser, Douglas, *Village Planning in the Primitive World,* Studio Vista, London, 1968.

Gandelsonas, Mario, *From Structure to Subject: The Formation of an Architectural Language in Peter Eisenman House X,* Rizzoli, New York, 1982.

Garofalo, Francesco and **Veresani,** Luca, *Adalberto Libera,* Princeton Architectural Press, New York, 1992.

Geist, Johann Friedrich, *Arcades, the History of a Building Type,* MIT Press, Cambridge, MA, 1983.

Giedion, Sigfried, *Space Time and Architecture: the Growth of a New Trend* Harvard University Press Cambridge, MA, Fifth Edition 1966.

Girouard, Mark, *Big Jim: the life and work of James Stirling,* Chatto & Windus, London, 1998.

Gowan, James, *James Gowan,* Architectural Monographs no. 3, Academy Editions, London, 1978.

Griaule, Marcel, *Conversations with Ogotemmêli: an introduction to Dogon religious ideas,* Oxford University Press, Oxford, 1965.

Gropius, Walter, *The New Architecture and the Bauhaus,* Faber & Faber, London, 1935.

Hampton, William and **Walkland,** Iris, *Byker Community Development Project 1974-78*, pamphlet published by Newcastle upon Tyne Council for Voluntary Service, 1980.

Harwood, Elain, *England A Guide to Post-War Listed Buildings,* Batsford, London, 2003.

Hatje, Gerd (ed.), *Encyclopaedia of Modern Architecture,* Thames & Hudson, London, 1963.

Hauser, Arnold, *Mannerism: the Crisis of the Renaissance and the Origin of Modern Art,* Routledge & Kegan Paul, London, 1965.

Hertzberger, Herman, 'Huiswerk voor meer herbergzame vorm', *Forum,* no. 3, 1973.

Hertzberger, Herman, *Lessons for Students in Architecture,* 010 Publishers, Rotterdam, 1991.

Holgate, Alan, *The Art of Structural Engineering, the Work of Jörg Schlaich and his Team,* Edition Axel Menges, Stuttgart, 1997.

Huizinga, Johannes, *Homo Ludens: a study of the play-element in culture,* Routledge & Kegan Paul, London, 1949.

Jacobson, Karen, *Zero to Infinity: Arte Povera 1962-1972,* Walker Art Center, Minneapolis, Tate Modern, London, 2001.

Jencks, Charles, *Modern Movements in Architecture,* Penguin, Harmondsworth, 1973.

Jencks, Charles, *The Language of Post-Modern Architecture,* Academy Editions, London, 1977.

Jenkins David (ed.), *On Foster... Foster On...,* Prestel, Munich, London, New York, 2000.

Johnson, Philip and **Wigley,** Mark, *Deconstructivist Architecture,* Museum of Modern Art, New York, 1988.

Jormakka, Kari, *Heimlich Manoeuvres: Ritual in Architectural Form*, Verso, Weimar, 1995.

Kaufmann, Emil, *Three Revolutionary Architects: Boullée, Ledoux and Lequeu,* The American Philosophical Society, Philadelphia, 1952.

Keller, Rolf *Bauen als Umweltzerstörung: Alarmbilder einer Un-Architektur der Gegenwart*, Artemis, Zurich, 1973.

Kipnis, Jeffry and **Leeser,** Thomas (eds.), *Chora L Works: Jacques Derrida and Peter Eisenman,* The Monacelli Press, New York, 1997.

Kirk, Sheila, *Philip Webb: Pioneer of Arts and Crafts Architecture,* Wiley-Academy, London, 2005.

Kirkham, Pat, *Charles and Ray Eames: Designers of the Twentieth Century,* MIT Press, Cambridge, MA, 1998.

Klotz, Heinrich, *Architektur in der Bundesrepublik,* Ullstein, Frankfurt/Berlin/Vienna, 1977.

Konttinen, Sirkka-Liisa, *Byker,* Bloodaxe Books, Newcastle, 1985.

Kroll, Lucien, *The Architecture of Complexity,* Batsford, London, 1986.

Kroll, Lucien, *Lucien Kroll: Buildings and Projects,* Rizzoli, New York, 1987.

Kroll, Lucien, *Tout Est Paysage,* Sens & Tonka, Paris, 2001.

Kuhn, Thomas S., *The Structure of Scientific Revolutions,* Chicago University Press, Chicago, 1962.

Lampugnani, Vittorio Magnago, *Renzo Piano 1987-1994,* Birkhäuser, Basel, Berlin, Boston, 1995.

Lane, Barbara Miller, *Architecture and Politics in Germany 1918-1945,* Harvard University Press, Cambridge, MA, 1968.

Lasdun, Denys, *Architecture in an age of scepticism*, Heinemann, London, 1984 (includes chapters by De Carlo, Erskine, Foster, the Smithsons and van Eyck)

Le Corbusier, *Towards a new architecture,* Architectural Press, London 1927.

Le Corbusier, *The Modulor,* Faber & Faber, London, 1951.

Lefaivre, Liane and **de Roode**, Ingeborg, *Aldo van Eyck: the playgrounds and the city*, NAi Publishers, Rotterdam, 2002.

Lefaivre, Liane and **Tzonis,** Alexander, *Aldo van Eyck: Humanist Rebel, Inbetweening in a Postwar World,* 010 Publishers, Rotterdam, 1999.

Lévi-Strauss, Claude, *The Raw and the Cooked,* Jonathan Cape, London, 1970.

Libeskind, Daniel, *Countersign,* Academy Editions, London, 1991.

Ligtelijn, Vincent (ed.), *Aldo van Eyck Works,* Birkhäuser, Basel/Boston/Berlin, 1999.

Malpass, Peter and **Murie,** Alan, *Housing Policy and Practice*, Macmillan, London, 1987.

Marcuse, Harold, *Legacies of Dachau: the uses and abuses of a concentration camp 1933-2001*, Cambridge University Press, Cambridge, 2001.

Markus, Thomas, *Buildings and Power*, Routledge, London, 1993.

McKean, John, *Leicester University Engineering Building,* in Architecture in Detail series, Phaidon, London, 1994.

McKean, John, *Layered Places* (work of Giancarlo De Carlo), Edition Axel Menges, Stuttgart, 2004.

Moneo, Rafael, *Theoretical Anxiety and Design Strategies in the Work of Eight Contemporary Architects,* MIT Press, Cambridge, MA and London, 2004.

Moneo, Rafael, **Vidler,** Anthony et al., *Wexner Center for the Visual Arts*, The Ohio State University, Rizzoli, New York, 1989.

Murphy, Richard, *Carlo Scarpa and the Castelvecchio,* Butterworth Architecture, London, 1990.

Nerdinger, Winfried, *Theodor Fischer, Architekt und Städtebauer 1862-1938,* Ernst und Sohn, Berlin, 1988.

Neuhart, John, **Neuhart,** Marilyn and **Eames,** Ray, *Eames Design: The Work of the Office of Charles and Ray Eames*, Thames & Hudson, London, 1989.

Newman, Oscar (ed.), *CIAM '59 in Otterlo,* Alec Tiranti, London, 1961.

O' Regan, John (ed.), *Aldo Rossi, Selected Writings and Projects,* Architectural Design, London, Gandon Editions, Dublin, 1983.

Otto, Frei, *Complete Works,* Birkhäuser, Basle, Boston, Berlin, 2005.

Pehnt, Wolfgang, *German Architecture 1960-1970,* Architectural Press, London, 1970.

Pehnt, Wolfgang, *Expressionist Architecture,* Thames & Hudson, London, 1973.

Pehnt, Wolfgang, *Karljosef Schattner: ein Architekt aus Eichstätt,* Hatje, Stuttgart, 1999 (1st Edition 1988).

Pevsner, Nikolaus (revised by Enid Sutcliffe), *The Buildings of England: Suffolk,* Penguin, Harmondsworth, 1974 (2nd Edition).

Pompidou Catalogue, *Georges Pompidou et la Modernité* Editions du Jeu de Paume/Centre Georges Pompidou, Paris, 1999.

Pope, Albert, *Ladders: Architecture at Rice 34,* Princeton Architectural Press, New York, 1996.

Posener, Julius, *Hans Poelzig,* Akademie der Künste, Berlin, 1970.

Posener, Julius, *From Schinkel to the Bauhaus,* AA Paper No. 5, Lund Humphries, London, 1972.

Posener, Julius, *Was Architektur sein kann,* Birkhäser, Basel 1995.

Powers, Alan, *Real Architecture,* catalogue of exhibition held at Building Centre, London, 1988, including work by John Simpson, Robert Adam, Demetri Porphyrios and Quinlan Terry.

Powers, Alan, *Serge Chermayeff, Designer, Architect, Teacher,* RIBA Publications, London, 2001.

Pugin, Augustus Welby Northmore, *The True Principles of Pointed or Christian Architecture,* London, 1853, (various modern facsimiles).

Quantrill, Malcolm, *The Norman Foster Studio: consistency through diversity,* E. & F. N. Spon, London, 1999.

Quinn, Patricia (ed.), *Temple Bar: The Power of an Idea,* Temple Bar Properties, Dublin, 1996.

Raev, Svetlozar, (ed.), *Gottfried Böhm: lectures, buildings, projects,* Karl Krämer Verlag, Stuttgart, 1988.

Risselada, Max and **van den Heuvel,** Dirk, *Team 10: in search of a Utopia of the present,* NAI Publishers, Rotterdam, 2005.

Rogers, Richard et al., *Towards an Urban Renaissance: Final Report of the Urban Task Force,* E & F Spon, London, 1999.

Rossi, Aldo, *The Architecture of the City,* MIT Press, Cambridge, MA, and London, 1982.

Rossi, Aldo, *A Scientific Autobiography,* MIT Press, Cambridge, MA, and London, 1982.

Rossi, Aldo, *I Quaderni di Aldo Rossi 1990-97,* Getty Trust Publications, Los Angeles, 2000.

Rowe, Colin and **Koetter,** Fred, *Collage City,* MIT Press, Cambridge, MA, 1978.

Ruskin, John, *The complete works of John Ruskin,* eds E.T. Cook and A. Wedderburn, 13 vols, London, 1903-12.

Rykwert, Joseph, *The Necessity of Artifice,* Academy Editions, London, 1982.

Sadler, Simon, *The Situationist City,* MIT Press, Cambridge, MA, and London, 1998.

Saint, Andrew, *Towards a social architecture: the role of school-building in post-war England,* Yale University Press, London and New Haven, 1987.

Samasa, Francesco, **Tonicello,** Anna et al., *Giancarlo De Carlo, Percorsi Universita Iuav di Venezia AP archivio progetti,* Il Poligrafo, Padua, 2004, (Italian/English).

Scalbert, Irenée, 'Cerebraal functionalisme: Leicester University Engineering Building', in *Archis* No. 5, 1994, pp. 70-80.

Schirmer, Wulf (ed.), *Egon Eiermann 1904-1970: Bauten und Projekte,* Deutsche Verlags-Anstalt, Stuttgart, 1984.

Schwarz, Rudolf et al., *Rudolf Schwarz,* exhibition catalogue of Akademie der Künste 1963, F.H. Kerle Verlag, Heidelberg, 1963.

Sennett, Richard, *The Fall of Public Man,* Faber & Faber, London 1986.

Sola-Morales, Ignasi de, *Minimal Architecture in Barcelona,* Electa, Milan, 1986.

Smith, Elizabeth A.T. (ed.), *Blueprints for modern living: history and legacy of the case study houses,* MIT Press, London, and Cambridge, MA, 1998.

Starr, S. Frederick, *Melnikov: Solo Architect in a Mass Society,* Princeton University Press, New Jersey, 1978.

Stock, Wolfgang Jean, *European Church Architecture 1950-2000,* Prestel Verlag, Munich, 2002.

Strathaus, Ulrike Jehle-Schulte and **Reichlin,** Bruno, *Parole di pietra - architettura di parole in Il segno della memoria BBPR Monumento ai caduti nei campi nazisti 1945-1995,* Electa, Milan. 1995.

Summerson, John, *Heavenly Mansions and Other Essays on Architecture,* Cresset Press, London, 1949.

Tafuri, Manfredo, *Theories and History of Architecture,* Granada, London, Toronto, Sydney, New York, 1980.

Taylor, Mark C., *Disfiguring Art, Architecture, Religion,* The University of Chicago Press, Chicago and London, 1992.

Torrent, Rosa Maria Subira I., *Mies van der Rohe's German Pavilion in Barcelona 1929-86,* Ajuntament de Barcelona, Barcelona, 1987.

Van Eyck, Aldo, *Projekten 1948-1961 & Projekten 1962-1976,* reprints from *Forum* and other periodicals, Johan van de Beek, Groningen 1981.

Van Eyck, Aldo et al., *Aldo van Eyck Hubertus House,* Stichting Wonen, Amsterdam, 1982, (English/Dutch).

Venturi, Robert, *Complexity and Contradiction in Architecture,* Museum of Modern Art, New York, 1966.

Venturi, Robert and **Scott Brown,** Denise, *Architecture as Signs and Systems for a Mannerist Time,* The Belknap Press of Harvard University Press, Cambridge, MA, and London, 2004.

Venturi, Robert, **Scott Brown,** Denise and **Izenour,** Steven, *Learning from Las Vegas,* MIT Press, Cambridge, MA,1972.

Wilson, Sarah, *Paris: Capital of the Arts 1960-1968,* Royal Academy, London, 2002.

Wilson, Colin St John, *Architectural Reflections,* Butterworth, London, 1992.

Wilson, Colin St John, *The Other Tradition of Modern Architecture: The Uncompleted Project,* Academy Editions London, 1995.

Wittkower, Rudolf. *Architectural principles in the age of humanism,* London 1949, 1952.

Wittkower, Rudolf, *Gothic versus Classic: architectural projects in seventeenth century Italy,* Thames and Hudson, London 1974.

Zucchi, Benedict, *Giancarlo De Carlo,* Butterworth, Oxford, 1992.

Zutshi, Mavis *Speaking for myself: a report on the Byker redevelopment,* published by Newcastle Council for Voluntary Service, April 1978.

Sources of Illustrations

Chapter 1 (Eames)
1, 8, 10: © Tim Street-Porter/Esto. All rights reserved.
2: Hermann Miller.
3, 6: Architectural Forum.
4: Conde Nast.
5, 7, 12: Library of Congress.
9, 11: RIBA Professional Services Limited.

Chapter 2 (Eiermann)
1-7, 9, 12, 13, 17, 19-21: Südwestdeutsches Archiv für Architektur und Ingenieurbau an der Universität Karlsruhe, Nachlass Egon Eiermann. (Photographers: 1, 5, 12, 13: Eberhard Troeger, Hamburg; 3: Arthur Koester, Berlin; 4: E.M.
Heddenhausen, Berlin; 6: Franz Lazijun, Stuttgart; 9: Rudolf Eimke; 17: Heidersberger, Braunschweig; 19: Alexander Studio, Wheaton, Maryland.)
8, 16: The Architectural Review, August 1958.
10: The Architects' Journal, 29 May 1958.
11, 14, 15, 18: Schirmer 1988 (photos Georg Pollick, Düsseldorf).
22: Peter Blundell Jones.

Chapter 3 (van Eyck)
1: Gemeentearchief Amsterdam.
2, 3, 6, 7, 9-14: A. en H. van Eyck Architektenbureau.
4, 5, 8, 15, 18: Peter Blundell Jones.
16: Ligtelijn 1999.
17: Griaule 1966.

Chapter 4 (Böhm)
1, 4, 6, 10, 20: Darius 1988.
2, 18: Pehnt 1973.
3, 5, 7, 11-17, 19, 21-24: Peter Blundell Jones.
8, 9: Pehnt 1970.
25: Raev 1988.

Chapter 5 (Smithsons)
1: Michael Carapetian .
2, 4, 11, 14, 18: Peter Blundell Jones.
3: Risselada and van den Heuvel 2005.
5, 7-9, 15,16: Smithson Archive.
6, 12, 13: Eamonn Canniffe.
10: Deutsches Architektur Museum, Frankfurt.
17: Peter Lathey, University of Sheffield.

Chapter 6 (Stirling and Gowan)
1: Architect and Building News, 7 January 1959 (slightly edited: the drawing is now at the Canadian Centre for Architecture).

2, 9-11: James Gowan (his 35mm slides taken at the building's completion).
3-8, 12, 20, 21: James Gowan (line drawings of Leicester as originally prepared for publication).
14, 15, 19, 22: James Gowan (Stirling and Gowan drawings now at the Canadian Centre for Architecture). Published with the permission of the Canadian Centre for Architecture/Centre Canadien d'Architecture, Montréal.
13, 18, 23, 25, 28-30: James Gowan (own drawings still in his possession).
13, 15, 27, 34-43: Peter Blundell Jones.
14: David Wild.
26, 31, 32, 33: Published with the permission of the Canadian Centre for Architecture/Centre Canadien d'Architecture, Montréal.

Chapter 7 (Striffler)
1, 2, 4, 6, 10, 17, 18, 20-23: Robert Häusser.
3, 5, 7, 9, 12-15, 19: Helmut Striffler.
8, 10, 11: Peter Blundell Jones.

Chapter 8 (Behnisch)
1, 2, 3, 6: Behnisch & Partners.
4, 5, 7-18: Christian Kandzia of Behnisch & Partners.
19-23: Peter Blundell Jones.

Chapter 9 (Scarpa)
1, 7: Direzione Generale per l'architettura e l'arte contemporanee Rome.
2, 4, 9-14, 16-20: Peter Blundell Jones.
3, 8, 15: Eamonn Canniffe.
5: Comune di Verona.
6: George Ranalli (drawings edited).

Chapter 10 (Kroll)
1-7, 16-18, 21-23, 27: Peter Blundell Jones.
4, 8-12, 14, 15, 19, 20, 24-26: Lucien Kroll.

Chapter 11 (Erskine)
1, 11-14, 17, 19-22: Peter Blundell Jones.
2: The Swedish Museum of Architecture, Stockholm, photo Ralph Erskine.
3, 4, 18: The Swedish Museum of Architecture, Stockholm, photo Anna Gerdén.
5, 6, 7: Newman 1961.
8: Newcastle Libraries and Information Service.
9, 15, 16, 18, 23, 24: The Architects' Journal 14 April 1976.
10: Architectural Design, Erskine special issue 1977.

Chapter 12 (Foster)
1, 4-10, 12-15, 18-21: Peter Blundell Jones.
2: Eamonn Canniffe.
3, 11, 16, 17: Foster and Partners.

Chapter 13 (De Carlo)
1, 2, 3, 5, 6, 15-20, 22-27: Peter Blundell Jones.
4, 7-14, 21: Giancarlo De Carlo.

Chapter 14 (Piano & Rogers)
1, 7-12, 16-17, 19, 21: Peter Blundell Jones.
2, 3, 6, 20: Richard Rogers Partnership.
4: Peter Cook.
5: Cedric Price Archive.
11: Martin Charles.
13-15: The Architectural Review, May 1977 (drawings edited).
22. Eamonn Canniffe.

Chapter 15 (Rossi)
1, 4-5: Peter Blundell Jones.
2-3, 8, 10-15, 17: Eamonn Canniffe.
6-7, 9, 16, 18-19: Direzione Generale per l'architettura e l'arte contemporanee Rome.

Chapter 16 (Eisenman)
1, 4-6, 11-14: © Jeff Goldberg/Esto. All rights reserved.
2-3, 7-10, 15-16: Eisenman Architects.
17: Eamonn Canniffe.
18: Peter Blundell Jones.

Chapter 17 (Schattner)
1, 2, 10-14: Diocesan Building Office, Eichstätt (site drawing 2 modified to identify buildings by colours).
3-9, 15-21: Peter Blundell Jones.

Chapter 18 (Venturi)
1-4, 6-19: Venturi, Scott Brown and Associates.
5. Ahrends, Burton & Koralek.

Conclusion
1: Peter Blundell Jones.

While every attempt has been made to trace the source and copyright of images used, the circumstances surrounding some of the older images are obscure. The authors and publishers apologise for any copyright unknowingly infringed, and invite owners to identify themselves so that appropriate acknowledgement can be made in subsequent editions.

Index